DEAD
CENTER

How Political Polarization Divided America

and What We Can Do About It

FORMER CONGRESSMAN

JASON ALTMIRE

SUNBURY PRESS

Mechanicsburg, PA USA

Published by Sunbury Press, Inc.
Mechanicsburg, Pennsylvania

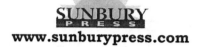

www.sunburypress.com

For information about special discounts for bulk purchases, please contact Sunbury Press Orders Dept. at (855) 338-8359 or orders@sunburypress.com.

To request one of our authors for speaking engagements or book signings, please contact Sunbury Press Publicity Dept. at publicity@sunburypress.com.

ISBN: 978-1-62006-754-3 (Hard cover)
ISBN: 978-1-62006-777-2 (Trade paperback)
ISBN: 978-1-62006-755-0 (Mobipocket)

Library of Congress Control Number: 2017950245

FIRST SUNBURY PRESS EDITION: July 2017

Product of the United States of America
0 1 1 2 3 5 8 13 21 34 55

Set in Bookman Old Style
Designed by Crystal Devine
Cover by Derek Murphy, CreativIndie
Edited by Janice Rhayem

Continue the Enlightenment!

CONTENTS

——·•·——

INTRODUCTION

———— •◆• ————

ON THE MORNING OF SUNDAY, JUNE 12, 2016, AMERICANS woke up to the horrific news that a deranged gunman had opened fire in a crowded Orlando nightclub, killing forty-nine people and wounding sixty-eight others. Not long ago, such an attack would have had a unifying effect on the country, bringing together Americans of all backgrounds in a shared sense of grief. But not this time—at least not within the political world.

The many unique facets of the shooting—the gay-friendly venue, the New York City-born Muslim shooter, the easily acquired arsenal of weapons—provided fodder for partisans looking for a reason to point fingers. Politicians and activists wasted no time in spinning the story for their political advantage. Democratic officials repeatedly referred to the "mass shooting,"[1] while Republicans insisted it was an act of "radical Islamic terrorism."[2] Talking heads on cable news programs debated whether the problem had been caused by easy access to guns or a weak foreign policy. When it became apparent the victims had been targeted because of their sexual orientation, some Democrats criticized Republican officials for having the alleged "hypocrisy" to offer support to the LGBT community following the attack.[3]

It was not long before the rhetoric degenerated into personal attacks. Senator John McCain said that President Obama was "directly responsible" for the massacre, citing the domino effect that McCain believed occurred after Obama withdrew American troops from Iraq.[4] Republican presidential candidate Donald Trump made similar accusations and called for Obama to resign from office.[5]

Democrats kicked their political operation into high gear, criticizing Republicans for their infrequent use of the term "hate crime," and for their opposition to gun control measures.[6] Those hoping for unity among the political class were sorely disappointed. Unfortunately, the chatter in blogs and social media was even worse.

In Twitter and Facebook posts beginning the day of the attack, hundreds of partisans hurled insults back and forth, casting blame and making every manner of inappropriate comment. Some focused their attention on the party affiliation of the shooter, while others listed by name specific public officials who they claimed were responsible based upon their position on issues ranging from gun control to immigration to gay rights. Bloggers wrote mean-spirited posts about every aspect of the crime. The morning of the attack, the lieutenant governor of Texas posted a religious-themed tweet—thought by some to be a reference to the victims—about those with immoral values reaping what they sow.[7] The tweet was deleted after a public outcry.

Bill Nelson, who lives in Orlando and is one of Florida's two US senators, opened his Orlando office on the Sunday of the attack. The office was immediately flooded with phone calls. At first, calls were almost entirely from people from around the country who wanted to help. But by the following day, Nelson estimated that 95% of the approximately 600 calls that came in were harshly negative and politically motivated. Both sides called to blame the other, often using language that Nelson called "hateful." This is the polarized state of American politics today.[8]

The tragedy also inspired a different, more positive, side of America. While political activists blamed each other and positioned for political advantage, millions of everyday Americans rose to the occasion. These Americans came together not because of politics but because they knew people were hurting, lives had been lost, a community had been shattered.

Hundreds of people lined the streets in Central Florida, waiting for hours to give blood. Thousands attended memorial vigils, not just in Orlando but around the country. Millions of Americans, touched by the awful killing spree, did what they could to help. They donated money, sent notes of support, and organized relief efforts. Relief funds would be established, combining to raise and distribute more than $40 million to Pulse survivors and victims' families.[9] For all the pessimism that pervades our polarized political process, this is the America that gives us hope.

The reaction to Orlando provides insight into the divided state of our country. A level of polarization and distrust exists in Washington that has not been seen in more than a century. A Congress paralyzed by gridlock. A nation where partisan extremists on both sides dominate the electoral process. A campaign system where money talks and centrist voices are silenced. A political structure that is broken and threatens the preeminence of our nation. An American people stuck in the middle.

As with the divided response to Orlando, Americans see a similar disconnect in Washington. The partisan activists have the loudest voice but are not a majority of the country. Not even close. Most Americans just live their lives and don't think about politics on a daily basis. When they do, they want our representatives in Washington to get along, to compromise, and to get things done. Unfortunately, the people who serve in Congress are becoming more divided, more detached, and less accountable to those everyday Americans. The political extremes discourage bipartisan agreement and punish the compromisers. It is a vicious cycle that has marginalized reasonable voices while empowering those with the most extreme views.

This book explores the root causes of political polarization by examining the combined impact of the social and psychological characteristics that dissuade rational behavior, in tandem with the flaws in our political process that incentivize the election of partisan ideologues. The story is told from the perspective of a political moderate who served three terms in Congress during a time of tremendous political change and increasing polarization—a congressman who was rated as the most centrist member of the entire House of Representatives. Drawing upon that experience and the related scientific research, he offers several proposed solutions to the polarization that has paralyzed Washington.

This book is written in the belief that America can do better. There are realistic cures for what ails our political system, and by understanding the problems and the process, we are better able to make the necessary changes to set our political process back on course. Until then, mainstream Americans, trapped between the two political extremes, will continue to grow even more disenchanted with a government that fails to hear their voice.

CHAPTER 1

PORTRAIT OF A PARTISAN

———•◆•———

Whose Lapdog?

A CROWD GATHERED TO TAKE IN THE SPECTACLE THAT was about to occur. The front entrance to a suburban grocery store was freshly decorated with balloons and signs directing visitors to the small information table outside. There was a chill in the air on this cloudy spring day so typical of Western Pennsylvania. I arrived that morning just before the scheduled 10:00 a.m. start time, greeting the attendees as I made my way to the sidewalk in front of the store. As I began another "Congress on Your Corner" event, I thanked the people who had taken the time to attend, then provided brief opening remarks before taking questions from the two dozen people who had come to talk to their congressman. Within seconds of my arrival, something happened that used to frustrate me, but by now—after only four months in office—came as no surprise. Standing no more than ten feet away, one of the attendees raised a small, handheld video camera and focused it directly upon me. I was used to this because it happened in every public meeting I held. A party activist was recording my words in the hopes of capturing me saying something that could later be used in an incendiary social media post or thirty-second campaign ad.

Then another attendee turned on a second video camera and pointed it towards me. Based on their reactions to what I was saying and the questions that came later, I soon realized they were not working together, as I had originally assumed. In fact, one was a Republican and one was a Democrat. Both sides were trying to capture video evidence of my disloyalty to their cause. As a centrist who prided myself on working with both sides, I took this as a compliment. If both extremes were unhappy with me, I must be doing something right.

The town where the public meeting was taking place—Allison Park, Pennsylvania—was right in the heart of the sprawling six-county district I represented. Because it was located in the geographic center of the district—between working-class Rust Belt river towns and affluent suburban communities—Allison Park was a perfect bellwether of public opinion across the political spectrum. But as usual, those in the middle of the political spectrum chose to stay home, thinking about things other than politics. The people who showed up that day represented the two political extremes, which made for an interesting conversation but didn't shed much light on where mainstream voters stood on the issues.

The first question came from a Democrat who said he had supported my first campaign but was now disappointed that I wasn't taking a more aggressive approach in impeaching President Bush and pulling the troops out of Iraq. He spoke quietly in a scolding tone, saying, "It seems like you are acting like a Republican . . ."

A woman standing a few feet away interrupted him with a loud shrieking sound, expressing utter disbelief: "What? What are you talking about? Everyone knows he's just a lapdog for Nancy Pelosi!" The two then turned towards each other and began a heated argument, each proclaiming my politics to be outside the mainstream of the district and the country. I stepped back, folded my arms in front of me, and leaned against a nearby post.

Such is the life of a centrist in Congress.

The Unrepresented Center

MOST PEOPLE DO NOT THINK ABOUT POLITICS ON A DAILY basis. Instead, they think about things that are more immediately important to them, like what time tonight's activity starts for their kids, who their favorite sports team is going to select in the upcoming draft, or what next week's work schedule looks like. Few people give a second thought to what their congressman is doing in Washington.

In my experience, I find that those who think about politics on a daily basis—those who wake up every day wondering what Congress is doing—are the people most likely to inhabit the political fringe. Many have an unhealthy obsession with politics. They are also the people who work on campaigns, contribute to candidates, and talk to friends and social media followers about politics. They make up the vast majority of people who attend town hall meetings or call a congressman's office to register their opinion. Importantly, they are not the majority of Americans.[1] But these partisans are unquestionably the people who decide elections and drive politics to the extremes. Unfortunately, the voices of those on the ideological extremes are magnified due to the lack of engagement of those in the center.

Today, political campaigns use the unprecedented technological power of precision data to pinpoint and mobilize their most likely supporters rather than to identify and persuade centrist and swing voters. The result, according to NBC's Chuck Todd, is "today's crisis of governing, with the halls of Congress populated by lawmakers who feel beholden not to all their constituents, but only to their supporters."[2]

Americans who desire compromise and consensus are now largely unrepresented in Washington. Writing about the common misconception that ideologically polarized Americans make up the majority of the country's population, political scientist Morris Fiorina says it is a mistake "to assume that what is true for a fraction of Americans who are politically active also holds true for the great preponderance of us. Normal Americans are not very well informed about politics and public affairs . . . do not hold many of their views strongly, and are not ideological."[3]

Nevertheless, in recent years there has been a steady increase in the number of people who self-identify as liberal or conservative,[4] indicating a shift in the country toward the extremes. The strength of Senators Ted Cruz and Bernie Sanders in the 2016 presidential primaries was indicative of the fact that the far right and far left voting blocks are becoming stronger and will continue to play an increasingly important role in elections for the foreseeable future.

Fiorina and many other researchers have confirmed what has become increasingly obvious to political candidates of both parties: the political class holds more extreme views and participates more actively in the political process. For example, delegates to the national presidential conventions have been shown to have views that are more extreme than those of a majority of their own party's voters.[5] Nevertheless, the activists remain a minority within their own parties. This helps explain why ideological partisans are so vastly overrepresented in the political arena,[6] while the center is barely represented at all.

It may not be precisely accurate to state unequivocally that most of America is politically moderate, but it is true that most Americans are substantially more moderate than their representatives in Congress and that they prefer political compromise to confrontation.[7] Some have argued that Congress is polarized because the country as a whole is equally polarized, but this is simply not the case.

In 2014, the non-partisan Pew Research Center published the results of its largest ever political survey, released as part of its landmark study of political polarization in America. The results showed that the overall share of Americans who express consistently conservative or consistently liberal views is 21%. The intensity of the views of these partisans is so extreme that many distrust the other side so much that they believe the opposing party "threatens the nation's well-being." However, the Pew survey clearly shows that these views are out of step with mainstream America.

In addressing the partisan views of the 21% of Americans on the political fringe, Pew says: "These sentiments are not shared by all—or even most—Americans. The majority do not have uniformly conservative or liberal views . . . and more believe their representatives should meet halfway to resolve contentious disputes . . ."[8]

In contrast to the compromise-supporting centrists, large majorities of both liberal and conservative partisans define their ideal legislative outcome simply as one in which their side wins.[9] The Pew survey confirms these intense partisans do indeed have a greater impact on the political process than do those in the ideological center.

Liberals and conservatives share a passion for politics. When asked about the topics about which they are most interested, partisans listed politics at the top of the list, while those in the center listed it in the middle of the pack. A large majority of those on the extremes closely follow government and public affairs, while the overall population follows those topics much less closely.[10] Similarly, partisans are much more likely to engage in political activities, making them the most sought after base of support for candidates running for office. Strong partisans represent a heavily disproportionate share of the more politically engaged segment of the population, resulting in increased polarization and limiting the ability of members of Congress from different parties to work together.[11] According to the Pew survey, "the most politically polarized are more actively involved in politics, amplifying the voices that are the least willing to see the parties meet each other halfway."[12]

The Pew survey confirms not only my own personal experience, but also the findings of countless political scientists.[13] Perhaps the most convincing research comes from the American National Election Studies (ANES), a massive collaborative of public opinion research conducted by the University of Michigan and Stanford University. Data for ANES has been collected before and after nearly every national election since 1948. Referencing the 2012 survey results showing that large portions of Americans place themselves in the midpoint of a seven-point scale of partisan ideology, researchers Marc Hetherington and Thomas Rudolph concluded: "If polarization means that most Americans are staunch liberals or conservatives, like the people who represent them in Congress, the answer is a resounding no."[14]

In his seminal work on the subject of polarization, *The Second Civil War: How Extreme Partisanship Has Paralyzed America*, political commentator Ron Brownstein also uses ANES data to support his conclusion that everyday Americans are not as deeply divided as Congress. According to Brownstein, the number of "deeply committed ideologues (in the general public) . . . probably isn't much larger today than at earlier points in our history."[15] Although the problem has surely gotten worse in the decade since Brownstein wrote those words, the point still rings true.

Political candidates succeed by winning the support of those who show up at the polls. Increasingly, those who show up at the polls are disproportionately polarized. "When partisans become more likely to vote and moderates less likely to vote, the voting public becomes more partisan even though individuals' partisanship did not change," according to political scientist Markus Prior.

The relative lack of political activism among moderates skews the electorate further towards the extremes. This drives primary elections in the direction of ideologically oriented candidates, but does not change the fact that most Americans want their members of Congress to work together rather than engage in partisan warfare.

Unlike members of Congress, most Americans are not reflexively partisan. Prior says, "On most issues, Americans take moderate positions and their disagreement has not intensified noticeably in recent decades. In fact, the most thorough examination of attitudes about social issues finds convergence (that is, 'depolarization') on many issues."[16] Unfortunately, as I learned firsthand, these moderates are not the people who drive the political discourse and determine the outcome of elections.

Low turnout among moderates pushes candidates away from the center, limiting the choices of voters in the general election. Centrist voters, Fiorina notes, "can choose only among the candidates who appear on the ballot," adding that there is "little evidence that Americans' ideological or policy positions are more polarized . . . although their choices often seem to be."[17]

Stanford professor Adam Bonica has written about what he calls the "incongruence between the ideological extremity of elected politicians and the relative centrism of the electorate they were elected to represent." Bonica blames "a system that gives voters the final say in general elections, but much less control over the set of candidates that appear on their ballot."[18]

Emory University professor Alan Abramowitz has a different opinion. He argues that the nation as a whole is polarized and the percentage of the electorate that is centrist is quite small.[19] Likewise, two of the preeminent scholars on the subject, Thomas Mann and Norman Ornstein, have written about what they call "the myth that there is a broad middle of independent, open-minded voters," claiming that "genuine swing voters . . . make up only 5% of the electorate."[20]

In my experience representing a politically diverse district, I believe this is an inaccurate view. Just because people are registered Democrat or Republican and usually vote that way does not mean they support unyielding partisanship. I remain convinced that most people—a majority of Americans, regardless of party affiliation—want a Congress willing to work across the aisle to find compromise on important issues.

Brownstein calls this group "soft partisans."[21] They are not the people causing the polarization. Yes, there are still large portions of the electorate that are bitterly partisan. That's the point of this book and is discussed in detail throughout. But the reason there is so much partisanship in Washington is not because the general public is polarized; it is because we have a system designed to elect and protect partisans. This results in a divided Congress that is much more polarized than the nation as a whole, and it is why Congress has chronically low public approval ratings. This disconnect between public opinion and the actions of Congress frustrates many centrist and less politically engaged citizens.[22] That is the fundamental problem we have to solve.

These days, bipartisan agreement is difficult to find in Washington. Nevertheless, studies have repeatedly shown that "most Americans consider themselves to be near the center of the ideological spectrum,"[23] and that members of Congress "take positions that are considerably more extreme than those of their constituents."[24]

Political columnists Jonathan Rauch, Joe Klein, and Robert Kuttner, among many others, have each argued persuasively that Americans on the whole are not deeply divided.[25] Professors Hetherington and Rudolph say there is "plenty of evidence" that shows members of Congress "are more ideologically motivated" than their constituents.[26] Other political scientists agree that most "Americans support bipartisanship, compromise and consensus, and all but the strongest partisans respond negatively to violations of these norms."[27] Studies have shown that we are not "a nation of moderates that dislike each other, but rather, an increasingly moderate core with extreme wings," and that "partisanship in the Congress . . . exceeds partisanship in the electorate as a whole."[28] The same often holds true at the state legislative level.[29]

Unfortunately, neither side takes responsibility and each blames the other as the cause of the polarization. Scholars Keith Poole and Howard Rosenthal sum it up: "In a world of polarized parties and moderate voters, each party will attempt to portray the other as the real extremists."[30]

Fiorina's research has shown that the animosity partisans show towards one another dissipates dramatically among those with more moderate views. "Most Americans are like the unfortunate citizens of some third-world countries who try to stay out of the crossfire while left-wing guerrillas and right-wing death squads shoot at each other."[31] This is a perfect analogy for what it is like to be a centrist in the halls of Congress.

The Very First Time

ORGANIZED LABOR HAS LOST CONSIDERABLE INFLUENCE since its heyday in the mid-twentieth century. Today, approximately 11% of wage and salary workers in the United States are members of unions, down from more than 30% in the mid-1950s.[32] Although private sector union membership has declined precipitously, organized labor is still a political force in the Democratic Party in some areas of the country. This is particularly true in Pennsylvania, where leadership in organized labor carries with it a type of influence that would be unimaginable in most other states.

The history and influence of organized labor throughout the Pittsburgh region is unmistakable. At political events across Western Pennsylvania, union leaders are introduced to the crowd as distinguished guests. The region is also home to several historic landmarks meaningful to the union movement—sites that in some cases are viewed by union activists as almost sacred ground. Two such landmarks are located along the Monongahela River in Homestead, Pennsylvania.

During the infamous 1892 "Battle of Homestead," the Bost Building served as the headquarters of the iron and steel workers union—the most powerful trade union in the country at the time. The building was also home to many of the newspaper correspondents who had traveled to Homestead to report on the imminent confrontation between the striking union workers and the Pinkerton security agents that had been hired by Andrew Carnegie to restore order at his steel company's Homestead Works.

Traveling along the river by barge, the three hundred Pinkerton guards arrived at the nearby Pump House on July 6 and initiated a violent encounter that ended when the Pinkertons surrendered to the union after a bloody battle that left ten dead and dozens wounded. The union's victory would be short-lived, as Pennsylvania's governor sent in eight thousand state militiamen to restore order. The strike was soon broken, and the workers returned to their jobs released from their union commitments.[33] Today, the Bost Building and Pump House are restored historic landmarks.

Soon after moving back to Pittsburgh at the age of thirty, I attended an event at the restored Pump House site hosted by the United Steelworkers of America.[34] The key attraction of the event was a display of photographs depicting scenes from the Battle of Homestead. One of the most prominent guests was John DeFazio, a statewide leader of the Steelworkers union and an influential member of the Democratic Party in Pennsylvania. In time, DeFazio would come to epitomize my relationship with the unions throughout my political career. Occurring seven years before I first won political office, the event at the Pump House would prove to be the first of many occasions that I would meet John DeFazio for the very first time.

Following in his father's footsteps, DeFazio began working in the steel mills at the age of eighteen. He spent his evenings working out at a local YMCA, picking up a little judo and karate along the way.[35] It wasn't long before he was introduced to the world of studio wrestling. DeFazio won fame in the 1960s and 70s as a studio wrestler on local Pittsburgh television, where he and many other "wrestlers" would ham it up in scripted bouts for the small but passionate in-studio audience.[36] The show became popular during its regular Saturday evening time slot[37] and played a role in the nationwide growth of professional wresting under the leadership of businessman and consummate showman Vince McMahon.[38]

Known as Jumpin' Johnny, DeFazio became wildly popular himself—so much so that he refused to take on a fictional persona or wear a costume as many of his peers were doing at the time.[39] Although he was primarily a local talent and never achieved national stardom,[40] DeFazio was recognized as a minor champion, winning tag team and junior heavyweight title belts at various points in his career.[41] He retired from the sport in 1985 after competing in nearly five hundred matches.[42]

During his time in wrestling, DeFazio continued his work in the steel mills, quickly rising up through the ranks to become president of his local union at the age of twenty-nine.[43] No doubt helped by his celebrity, he became a leader with the United Steelworkers of America. He was heavily involved in the bitter labor disputes that engulfed the steel industry in Pittsburgh during the early 1980s, eventually leading to the shuttering of area steel mills and the loss of hundreds of thousands of jobs.[44]

Nevertheless, his influence within the union continued to grow. As the years went by he also became a leader in the Democratic Party, joining his brother, Pete, who in 1997 was elected to the high-profile position of sheriff of Allegheny County. For years, the brothers were a fraternal power couple, ubiquitous at Western Pennsylvania political events and actively involved in Democratic Party king making.

In 1999, John DeFazio announced his candidacy for a seat on the Allegheny County Council with a press release in which he referred to himself as a labor leader and former professional athlete.[45] He was elected and has served in the seat ever since, eventually becoming council president.

Pete DeFazio was not so lucky. He resigned his sheriff's position in September 2006, insisting that his resignation had nothing to do with the ongoing investigation into his alleged campaign finance irregularities. The investigation had dragged on for five years and was led by Mary Beth Buchanan, the ambitious local US Attorney with whom I would later become quite familiar. Two months after his resignation, former Sheriff DeFazio was convicted of coercing his deputies to contribute to his political campaigns.[46] Although Pete thereafter disappeared from public view, John DeFazio was unscathed and continued to be a prominent player in Pennsylvania's labor and political circles.

I attended the event at the Pump House site along with a sparse group from organized labor and a handful of locals and history buffs. It was the first time I had met most of the union leaders, many of whom would in time become key actors in my own political drama. The tone of the meeting was somber, even though the events that were being described occurred more than a century before. The physical setting certainly lent itself to such remembrances. With the help of the histories being presented, one could almost see the Pinkerton guards coming down the river toward us as the speakers added details of the battle that had occurred on that very site.

During the reception that followed, I casually walked around introducing myself and asking attendees about their connection to the event. I didn't know much about DeFazio at the time, but it was clear from the reverence with which others treated him that he was one of the leaders. As our paths crossed, I opened with a line that would for years be my standard conversation starter with DeFazio: "Hi, I'm Jason Altmire. . . ." We chatted for a while about the infamous history of the site and the growth and decline of the American steel industry. All in all, I enjoyed the event, learned a little bit of local history, and went home thinking it had been worth my time to attend.

As the years went by, I attended hundreds of community events across Western Pennsylvania. My job at the University of Pittsburgh Medical Center (UPMC) was primarily external—both community and government affairs, as well as charitable giving—which provided me the opportunity to meet people across a variety of social circles.

It doesn't take long to realize that the crowd is predictable based upon what type of event you are attending. Charity fundraisers and galas involve the same high-society couples and corporate elites that you saw at last week's black-tie affair. On Monday mornings, week after week, those same corporate donors and serial philanthropists rushed to check the morning paper to see whose photograph would appear in the society page summary of the weekend's charity calendar. Surprise! It is the same people who were in last week's photos. And the week before that. This gets old in a hurry, but it makes it easy to quickly get to know people around town.

Political events in Western Pennsylvania operate in much the same way, allowing the political elite to showcase their own cast of characters. Perpetual candidates, glad-handing politicians, overzealous party activists, entitled local committee members, union leaders, and developers looking for government contracts—all rotating around from town to town, gathering at this week's fish fry, next week's spaghetti dinner, and the occasional golf outing or skeet shoot. Like the philanthropic round-robin tour, travels along the political circuit can get monotonous. At both types of events, it is impossible not to get to know the regular attendees. This gave me the opportunity, over and over again, to meet Jumpin' Johnny DeFazio for the very first time.

Attending dozens of these events as time went by, I would inevitably encounter the regulars who seemed to be at every political event. Among them was John DeFazio, although he never seemed to remember me. Each time we crossed paths, I could tell he didn't recall the previous times we had met, so I would reintroduce myself. "Hi, I'm Jason Altmire. . . ."

DeFazio would eventually figure out who I was, but long before I became a political candidate myself, this situation was a source of levity for me. Whenever I saw DeFazio across the room, the slowly building guitar riff that opens the rock group Foreigner's iconic 1977 hit "Feels Like the First Time" played endlessly in my head, followed by the repeating lyrics: "*It feels like the first time/Feels like the very first time.*"

The seven years I shuttled between the different types of events—charity galas, political fundraisers, nonprofit board meetings, and community gatherings—were a valuable learning experience that helped me better understand people and politics. The two most important lessons were: 1) People generally stick with their own kind and don't attend all the different types of events; and 2) The attendees at political events, both Republican and Democrat, were much more partisan and extreme in their views than everybody else I encountered outside of politics. They were more steadfast in their beliefs and much more likely to look at partisans on the other side as the enemy.

I took both lessons to heart. Or perhaps more accurately, took them to Hart. (You'll understand later). Ironically, while both lessons were keys to the early success of my centrist political career, they also led to my eventual defeat, providing further evidence of just how difficult it is for moderates to remain in political office.

Sorting

AMERICA'S RUST BELT REGION PROVIDES EXCELLENT EX-amples of the phenomenon about which Bill Bishop writes in his best-selling book *The Big Sort*. Bishop describes the geographical sorting that has occurred in the country, segregating Americans based upon not just their political views but entire ways of life. It may be self-evident that those who show up in tuxedos and gowns at posh hotel ball rooms to attend events benefiting the city opera are quite different from those who attend spaghetti dinners at the local American Legion banquet hall to support a low-level political candidate. But the segregation extends well beyond the events people attend.

"As people seek out the social settings they prefer—as they choose the group that makes them feel most comfortable—the nation grows more politically segregated—and the benefit that ought to come with having a variety of opinions is lost to the righteousness that is the special entitlement of homogeneous groups," Bishop poignantly writes.[47] This sorting has had disastrous consequences for America's politics.

As Ron Brownstein has described, the partisan sorting of the population has been driven by the fallout of the fierce political battles of the 1960s and 70s, when Southern Democrats left the party in droves. The partisan realignment was driven by a series of divisive issues, from civil rights to Vietnam to busing to *Roe v. Wade* to taxes to crime. According to Brownstein, "The result of all these upheavals was to trigger the great sorting out in American politics."[48]

In many parts of the country, there has been a growing alignment between ideology and partisanship. The population has sorted itself into political parties based much more on conservative or liberal ideology than had been the case in the past. Brownstein correctly argues that Americans themselves did not become more partisan, but they sorted themselves into more distinct geographies, leading to more antagonistic political parties.

In 2016, during one of the closest presidential elections in American history, more than 60% of voters cast ballots in counties that gave either Hillary Clinton or Donald Trump at least a twenty-point margin of victory. Nearly one in five Americans currently lives in a county where one of the candidates won by a margin of at least fifty points![49] Of the fifty counties with the nation's highest voter turnout, only two—Pinellas and Duval in Florida—had results that were relatively even.[50]

Unlike those in the Deep South and other parts of the country, conservative Democrats in blue-collar Western Pennsylvania, for the most part, have not switched parties following this upheaval; they remain Democrats but have increasingly voted Republican. The combination of these factors, leading to the sorting of communities across America, has become quite evident in the post-industrial Midwest.

I saw this philosophical and geographic segregation as I traveled around Western Pennsylvania in the years before I decided to run for Congress. The wealthy suburbs extending around Pittsburgh have a completely different feel and vibe than the blue-collar river towns extending to the Ohio and West Virginia boarders. Their politics are different. Their community priorities are different. The educational opportunities available in their public schools are decidedly different. It is not only about household income, but the choices people make about where to live, whether to go to church, and which community activities to support.

Residents of these disparate communities share passionate but differing beliefs about both past and future and look skeptically at those who don't share their same political outlook. These neighborhoods have become "pockets of like-minded citizens that have become so ideologically inbred that we don't know, can't understand, and can barely conceive of 'those people' who live just a few miles away," as Bishop says about similar sorting across America.[51] In traveling through these Western Pennsylvania towns it becomes obvious that, although these neighborhoods are geographically close, their citizens simply don't understand one another. Bishop describes it perfectly, referring to this sorting as having created "balkanized communities whose inhabitants find other Americans to be culturally incomprehensible . . ."[52]

In the years to come, I would get to know and work with people throughout the entire region—people encompassing both sides of this philosophical divide. In time, I would decide to attempt a political campaign based upon a message designed to appeal to both sides, to bring them together in a way that few had tried and even less had succeeded. As I worked toward that moment, I continued to travel around the region—serving on boards and attending events—in a way that exposed me to sorted communities closely resembling those about which Bishop was writing when he lamented, "Mixed company moderates; like-minded company polarizes. Heterogeneous communities restrain group excess; homogeneous communities march toward the extremes."[53]

I found that most people in these communities thought about politics only infrequently. But those who did think about politics lived and breathed it. They were the activists—those who put up yard signs, organized rallies, and showed up in force at town hall meetings. In this particular congressional district, they represented two distinct groups.

On the left were the partisan Democrats, including wealthy liberals, labor leaders, and a small handful of rank-and-file union members who showed up at every political gathering. They were passionate and unyielding, but much further left-of-center than mainstream voters in the district.

On the other side were the far-right partisan ideologues who would soon latch onto the burgeoning Tea Party movement. Unlike the left-wing Democrats, the conservative Republicans recognized that their views were out of step with most of the district, but they considered it to be their mission to force their views upon everybody else.

Those were the two activist groups that stalked candidates and were ubiquitous at political events. Those were the people I saw most often during my time as a candidate and three terms in Congress.

However, the majority of the residents of the district were moderates. Depending on which side of the district you were on, these moderates were pro-business Republicans concerned about taxes and runaway entitlements, or blue-collar Democrats who were socially conservative and economically liberal. The two groups were very different, but both trended toward the political center. And like the rest of America, they were geographically sorted, living in clusters throughout the region. These were the people I saw at non-political events, like school functions, sporting events, and dinner out at restaurants. These were the normal folks—the centrists—who were turned off by the political process and therefore vote less frequently in primaries.

Bishop could have been describing exactly the type of partisan activists I encountered in the district when he wrote: "Like-minded groups create a kind of self-propelled, self-reinforcing loop." In promoting among themselves a series of circular one-sided arguments to justify their views, members of these groups drive each other further to the extremes. "Group members send signals bolstering their existing beliefs as they vie to stand out as the most Republican or most Democrat in the group."[54] Social psychologist Robert Baron says that in these groups, "it's hard to be a moderate Republican or a moderate Democrat," because others in the group will criticize you for straying too far away from partisan orthodoxy.[55]

James Madison and Alexander Hamilton understood the dangers of geographic sorting and homogeneous groups. In *The Federalist Papers*, they wrote extensively about the moderating influence of diverse opinions and fresh ideas, and the dangers of "factions" cut off from opposing points of view.[56] They knew different opinions and conflicting ideas were healthy for democracy and an antidote to extremism. Their words still ring true, as our nation's political system has broken down due to the extremism of factions.

Nearly 230 years later, author David Blankenhorn perfectly summed up the segregating effects of polarization. The "growing residential and geographical segregation are almost certainly socially harmful, in part because they produce social echo chambers in which people increasingly rarely befriend or even personally encounter someone who disagrees with their political views, and in large part because ideological segregation is the proven ally of ideological certitude and extremism."[57]

Hart Berner

THE DAY AFTER THE 2004 ELECTIONS, I REVIEWED THE results in the congressional district in which I lived, where incumbent Congresswoman Melissa Hart had once again been reelected in a landslide. Only forty-two, she had already served fourteen years in public office and was energetic, popular, and politically savvy. She was universally considered to be a rising star in the Republican Party, having just co-chaired the Platform Committee at the 2004 Republican National Convention. There was every reason to believe she was politically invincible.

Hart portrayed herself around the district as a moderate, but in Washington her voting record was quite conservative. Pennsylvania's 4th Congressional District included 146 towns equally split between the upscale suburban communities north of Pittsburgh and the post-industrial river towns near the Ohio and West Virginia borders. Hart had learned that the key to success in the Republican areas of the district was to project strong conservatism, but she had also learned to appease blue-collar Democrats by conveying a more centrist message. The problem was her record on Capitol Hill didn't match her rhetoric at home. I believed the district would be better represented by a moderate who would work with both sides.

For the next several months following the 2004 election, I discretely explored the possibility of running for Hart's congressional seat. I studied issues and Hart's voting record. I spent countless hours analyzing prior election results, going as far as to calculate the potential to convert Hart voters in each of the district's 538 voting precincts.

Hart was well-liked, especially among conservative Republicans. Democratic activists wanted a liberal alternative who would aggressively challenge what they perceived to be the excesses of President Bush, even though such a candidate stood no chance of winning in a district that had just supported Bush by a nine-point margin and reelected Hart by twenty-eight points. Those in the political center—the majority of the district—believed that Hart was unbeatable and challenging her was a fool's errand. Some centrists found her reflexive partisanship distasteful and were frustrated at their inability to do anything about it. They believed the hard-working congresswoman was the better alternative to an out-of-touch liberal candidate who would be unable to win the district.

One of the people I talked to during this period was Georgia Berner, a sixty-three-year-old millionaire businesswoman. Georgia was a liberal Democrat who was also considering a race against Hart. Viewing me as a potential rival, she organized our meeting to her advantage, pulling every power play in the book. She called me to her office in New Castle, where I was told to wait in the company conference room. I was seated across from a wall of plaques, awards, and photographs documenting her career. After keeping me waiting some twenty minutes, Georgia finally entered the room. We then began an hour-long discussion of the politics of the district.

It was clear she was going to run for the seat, as she had already hired a pollster and team of political consultants. She vehemently disagreed with me that the district was mostly centrist, and in fact she said the district and the country were fundamentally left-of-center but had been hoodwinked by President Bush and Karl Rove, whom she believed had used fear mongering to get Democrats to vote against their own self-interest. Georgia scoffed at the notion of successfully waging a centrist campaign, insisting instead that the only way to beat Hart was by offering a liberal alternative. The meeting was cordial and ended with a mutual recognition that we were likely to be seeing a lot more of each other over the next year leading up to the Democratic primary.

Although almost nobody thought I could make the race for Hart's seat competitive, I believed more than ever that Washington needed an infusion of thoughtful centrists. The hyper-partisanship on Capitol Hill was anathema to everyday Americans. The popularity of Congress was in steep decline and I knew my centrist message would resonate with voters who had up to that point been presented only options from the partisan extremes.

The personal risk for me was enormous. Having never run for office before, I would have to spend the next seventeen months campaigning for a congressional seat viewed by the political pundits as safely in the hands of the incumbent. Despite my optimism, I realized the possibility of failure greatly outweighed the chances of success. Nevertheless, I could sense a growing unease among people in the district about the direction of the country and the consequences of congressional dysfunction. I shared that unease, so I left my job on June 30, 2005, to begin my campaign.

Primarily Partisan

THE INCREASE IN POLITICAL POLARIZATION IN AMERICA and especially in Congress is due to many factors. The nation's changing demographics, the geographic sorting of Americans, an increasingly confrontational media and Internet, district gerrymandering, and the outsized role of money in campaigns are all part of the problem. Each plays a major role in distorting our political system and coarsening the dialogue in ways that have undermined the integrity of the entire process. Each directly contributes to the toxic polarization that has infected Washington. Together, these issues conspire to create one overlying problem—the fact that extreme partisans dominate our electoral system.

The many causes of polarization negatively impact the process political parties use to select their nominees for the general election. This applies not only to campaigns for Congress, but at every level of government. Even in swing districts, primary elections often act as a funnel of toxicity, allowing out-of-the-mainstream candidates to advance to the general election, leaving the electorate to choose between candidates representing the two extremes. Guess what happens in this all-too-familiar scenario? An extreme candidate wins and centrists continue to be unrepresented.

Partisan activists have a disproportionate impact on primary elections because politically moderate Americans tend to be less interested in politics and therefore vote in much lower numbers. "Primary races tend to be dominated by highly motivated extremists . . . ," says journalist Jonathan Rauch. This leaves "moderates and broader, less well-organized constituencies underrepresented."[58] Rauch correctly highlights Delaware's 2010 US Senate primary, where the highly respected moderate congressman Mike Castle was defeated in the Republican primary by a zany, Tea Party-backed political neophyte named Christine O'Donnell.

Mike Castle was a thoughtful pragmatist, genuinely interested in working with both sides to advance sensible legislation. His reputation for compromise drew the ire of the extreme wing of his party, fueling O'Donnell's challenge. When only one-sixth of Delaware's registered Republicans bothered to vote in the primary, the highly motivated partisan activists had the advantage they needed to put O'Donnell over the top. In the general election, O'Donnell proceeded to run a comically inept campaign, handing the Democrats a Senate seat almost everyone agrees would easily have been won by Castle, a popular former governor. Commenting on the increasing prevalence of this type of outcome in congressional primaries, a 2014 *Brookings Institution* report said: "The universe of those who actually cast primary ballots is small and hyper-partisan, and rewards candidates who hew to ideological orthodoxy."[59]

Indeed, low-turnout primaries strongly favor the more ideological candidates. This is particularly true in closed primaries, which have been proven to produce more extreme nominees than open primaries, where independent voters are also able to participate. Taken together, the low turnout among moderates and the built-in advantage for partisan activists make the voting block that shows up at the polls more ideologically homogeneous, resulting in more extreme general election candidates.[60]

Only about a dozen states still have completely closed primaries. About a dozen others have completely open primaries, permitting any registered voter to participate regardless of party affiliation. The remaining states have systems that fall somewhere in between, often leaving it to political parties to determine eligibility of independent and unaffiliated voters to participate in the primary.[61]

Movement toward greater access for all voters to participate in primaries would be a step in the right direction in reducing polarization in Congress. In addition to skewing the results toward the extremes, closed primaries disenfranchise increasingly large portions of the electorate. In Florida, voters registered as "No Party Affiliation" represent one-quarter of the state's thirteen million registered voters and are growing at a rate nearly double the registration rate of the state's Republicans and Democrats combined.[62]

Primary voters in states with open primaries more closely mirror the views of the more centrist general electorate, while primary voters in states with closed primaries are more ideologically polarized. As a result, candidates nominated in open primaries tend to be ideologically similar to the more centrist general electorate, as compared to successful candidates in closed primaries, who tailor their message to appeal to partisan voters.[63]

Low voter turnout adds fuel to the fire. Political scientists have observed that "because primaries are low-turnout affairs dominated by the most ideologically committed voters in the electorate, would-be representatives have both personal and electoral incentives to be extreme."[64]

Even in general elections, the United States has one of the lowest rates of voter turnout in the developed world. In presidential-year general elections, only about 55% of America's voting-age population shows up to vote. In 2016, Donald Trump was elected president despite winning only 27% of eligible voters.[65] The problem is even worse in non-presidential years. In 2014, the most recent midterm election, only 17% turned out—the lowest level in 72 years.[66]

The highest primary turnout ever recorded in a presidential election is 30.4% in 2008, when both Democrats and Republicans had contested campaigns that dragged on until late in the race. Similarly, the 2016 presidential primaries drew 28.5% of the vote.[67] But even in those historic elections, where saturation media coverage dominated the airwaves for months, more than two-thirds of voting-age Americans stayed home in the primaries. This allowed Donald Trump and fringe candidates like Senators Bernie Sanders and Ted Cruz to over-perform expectations by appealing to the most extreme elements of their activist base.

As I would eventually come to find out, low turnout primaries are the most powerful weapon in the arsenal of the political extremes.

CHAPTER 2

BETTING ON BIAS

——— •◦• ———

Fireworks Capital of America

NO CITY BETTER EPITOMIZES THE POLITICAL TRANSFOR-
mation and boom and bust history of the Rust Belt than New
Castle, Pennsylvania. It's story is emblematic of hundreds of
post-industrial towns across the Midwest—the region that
turned the tide of the 2016 election.

Located near the Ohio boarder along the Shenango River,
New Castle was once one of the leading manufacturing cen-
ters in the United States. Fifty miles northwest of Pittsburgh
and eighteen miles east of Youngstown, Ohio, New Castle was
an early industrial railroad hub. The city's population tripled
between 1890 and 1910, making New Castle one of America's
fastest growing cities.[1] This growth was fueled primarily by an
influx of European immigrants, particularly from Italy.[2]

Soon after the turn of the twentieth century, three young
Polish immigrant brothers first visited New Castle as part of
their fledgling motion picture traveling road show. Having already tried and abandoned a variety of only moderately successful business ventures—including shoe repair, a bowling
alley, a butcher shop, a grocery store, and a bicycle shop—the
brothers now decided to try their luck in the new and exciting
world of movies.[3]

After a stint traveling around Ohio and Pennsylvania with a used movie projector and make-shift screen—showing the twelve-minute silent film *The Great Train Robbery* at carnivals and other public gatherings—the brothers decided to take a risk and open up their own nickelodeon movie theater in New Castle.[4]

The brothers, Sam, Albert, and Harry Warner, chose New Castle because of its population growth, lack of other entertainment options, and the fact that their previous movie showings had done well there. They pooled their savings and purchased a small three-story building, which they equipped with a sturdy stand to support the hand-crank projector placed across the room from a white painted wall. The Cascade Movie Palace first opened its doors to the public on February 2, 1907.[5] Although nobody knew the significance at the time, the Cascade was the first movie theater in what would become the Warner Bros. empire.

The brothers soon opened a second movie theater in New Castle, this time with ninety-nine chairs borrowed from a local funeral home. Although a seemingly unorthodox number of seats, it was precisely calculated. If the theater sat one hundred or more, it would have required compliance with costly local safety regulations, which the increasingly business savvy brothers wanted to avoid. However, this strategy also came with some risk, because if there happened to be a funeral on the night of a movie, unfortunately for the Warner brothers, the show in that case did not go on.[6]

The Warner brothers eventually left New Castle and moved their business operations to New York and then to Hollywood, where they founded what would become Warner Bros. Studio.[7]

During the early decades of the twentieth century, New Castle was home to profitable limestone quarries and mills of nearly every type imaginable, most notably paper, steel, and tin.[8] There was an automobile construction plant, a bronze blushing plant, and a fine-china business—Shenango China—that would become so successful that it was the source of the White House china collections of Presidents Dwight Eisenhower and Lyndon Johnson.[9] When its population hit is peak of nearly fifty thousand in 1950,[10] New Castle truly had it all.

Just outside of town there is an Amish community that was first settled in 1847.[11] The approximately three thousand residents are Old Order Amish, the most conservative of the Amish groups.[12] Old Order Amish are known for their plain dress and prohibition of conveniences such as cars, electricity, and modern technology.[13] They speak with a thick, halting accent inherited as part of their Pennsylvania Dutch ancestry. The easily recognizable Amish horse and buggy is often seen along the roadways outside of New Castle, sharing the right of way with cars passing through from the modern world.

Few outsiders ever get to know members of the Amish community in a personal way. Photographs are strictly prohibited, and church officials, led by the governing bishop, dictate the terms of the Amish community's way of life. Although their interaction with the outside world is limited, the Amish pay attention to current events and have high participation rates in one of the most important activities of American society—voting. They usually vote uniformly as recommended by the bishop. As I would later come to find out, mostly they vote Republican.

While the Amish community continues to live by the same traditions that have governed followers for hundreds of years, neighboring New Castle has changed dramatically. After reaching its peak just after World War II, New Castle has experienced decades of steady decline. Like countless Rust Belt towns across the Northeast and Midwest, New Castle today is a shell of its former self. The local economy continues to struggle, and the population has decreased steadily for the past half century. Shenango China stopped production in 1991,[14] and much of New Castle's manufacturing base is gone, leaving the once-bustling downtown eerily quiet. The urban core has been hollowed out, but the strong character of the town remains. The people are hardworking and proud of the legacy they still hope to revive. Although most of New Castle's economic engines are long gone, the fireworks industry is booming.

Zambelli and Pyrotecnico, two of the nation's five largest fireworks companies, both call New Castle home. Fireworks is a billion-dollar industry, and these two companies together produce five thousand fireworks shows a year and have combined to set world records and win international awards for their elaborate displays.[15] They have provided the fireworks for some of the nation's largest events—think Disney, Super Bowls, etc.—as well as July 4th and New Year's Eve shows across America. Although they are business competitors, each company takes turns working the city's biggest event, the annual fireworks festival, which draws tens of thousands of visitors.[16] The industry has become so important to the city that New Castle in 2006 trademarked its longstanding nickname, Fireworks Capital of America.[17]

New Castle was once also a hub for organized crime. Rumors of a mafia presence in New Castle have persisted during the decades in which the city has been in decline, and investigations and prosecutions of organized crime figures continued in the area well into the 1990s and early 2000s.[18]

Perhaps unsurprisingly given New Castle's own history, the county's long-time Democratic Party chairman, Pete Vessella, had a colorful story and a shady past. By 2005, Vessella, then seventy-one, had been Chairman of the Lawrence County Democratic Party for most of the past thirty-three years,[19] reaching a level of notoriety—some might say infamy—that few local party officials achieve.

For as long as anyone could remember, he had conducted his political and personal business in the grimy Hudson Lunch diner in downtown New Castle. Candidates and elected officials of all levels would pay homage to Pete, sitting at the lunch table with him and his dwindling band of backslapping acolytes, each of whom were by then also in their seventies.

Pete was often aloof and condescending, but he was feared by any candidate who had hopes of performing well on the Lawrence County ballot. Everyone knew he usually had the ability to carry the county for any candidate he supported—by any means necessary and no questions asked. Crossing him usually meant writing off the county, so candidates paid him the respect of a political godfather.

During his meetings at the Hudson Lunch, Pete was fond of recalling his youthful successes for anyone who would listen. Understandably, he often edited from his fond recollections the memories of what occurred during what can charitably be called a rough patch in his life.

In the mid-1970s, Vessella and a business partner conspired to defraud a Pennsylvania power company with which his coal company did business.[20] Indicted on dozens of counts including conspiracy, racketeering, and mail fraud, Vessella eventually negotiated a plea bargain and was sentenced to five years in prison.[21] At about the same time Vessella was carrying out his coal swindle, a fire at a hotel he owned in New Castle killed four people.[22] Two of the fire doors were reportedly blocked open, and the hotel had no fire escapes, sprinklers, smoke detectors, or fire alarms.[23] After the local magistrate disqualified herself from the legal proceedings due to a family connection with Vessella, a hearing was held and criminal charges were quickly dismissed.[24] This led critics to question why key witnesses, such as the state police fire marshal who had personally investigated the fire, had not been called to testify.[25] Nevertheless, Vessella had escaped conviction, although in subsequent years he settled lawsuits with the families of the victims in terms reaching hundreds of thousands of dollars.[26]

Now What?

ONE OF THE HIGHEST-SELLING DVDS OF ALL-TIME IS THE animated film *Finding Nemo*, which features an oddball cast of aquatic characters, mostly exotic fish, who find themselves trapped in a fish tank in an Australian dentist's office. The fish orchestrated a plot to escape by damaging the tank's filtration system, thereby forcing the dentist to drain and clean the tank. He removed the fish and placed them individually in sealed, water-filled plastic bags, right next to an open window. Still in their bags, the fish wiggle their way out the window, across the busy street, and into a nearby harbor. As the others float in the harbor, the last fish finally falls into the water, completing their mission. Or so they thought. As the other fish cheer, one of them looks at the group—each still in their tightly-sealed bags—and quickly recognizes the problem. He asks, "Now what?"

I was asking myself that same question as I began my first campaign on July 1, 2005. I spent a couple of weeks thinking through my next steps, which included completing the burdensome documents required to establish a campaign and fundraising committee, as well as my personal financial disclosure forms. Mundane tasks that I had not thought about before suddenly occurred to me, such as what colors to make my campaign logo and where to open the campaign post office box. The answer to that last question was easy. One of the 146 towns in the district was named Freedom, Pennsylvania. Even though Freedom's small community post office had less than 300 boxes, I convinced the local postmaster to name one of them PO Box 1776, which went well with the Freedom mailing address. After that was accomplished, it was time to get down to the real business of starting the campaign.

I made some phone calls and did a few interviews to find potential campaign staff. Few credible politicos were interested in a fledgling campaign that may or may not get off the ground, especially one led by a novice candidate with an unproven ability to raise the money necessary to pay staff.

The first person to whom I offered a job—after a lengthy interview in which I discussed in detail my campaign strategy— decided to instead go work for Georgia Berner, my primary opponent. Another person I interviewed agreed to be my campaign manager, but he quickly revealed himself to be a bust. I fired him, making me zero for two in staff hires. I was not off to a great start, but then I caught my first break.

While attending a political picnic late in the summer, I encountered Pete Vessella, the ex-con chairman of the Democratic Committee based in New Castle. I had known Pete for years, having crossed paths with him at various events around the region. I updated him about my campaign and asked for his support. He demurred, saying we should meet another time. He pulled from his jacket a business card, handed it to me, and said, "Here, put this in your pocket and look at it later." Thinking nothing of it, I did just that. That night, when I pulled out the card, I saw it was Georgia Berner's campaign business card. I laughed in frustration but knew that was just how Pete rolled.

Sitting next to Pete that day was a young woman from New Castle named Christina Stacey. Christina was attending the fundraiser along with a group of other members of Vessella's Democratic Committee. She looked as though she would rather be anywhere else but there and openly rolled her eyes at Vessella's shtick. As I walked away, she said she'd like to talk to me about my campaign. Vessella looked incredulous, but I took her number and called the next day. After meeting for coffee at one of New Castle's premier meeting spots—the downtown Dunkin' Donuts—we agreed that she would join my campaign, soon becoming campaign manager. As loyal and dedicated as they come, Christina and I would spend the next year and a half traveling across the district. She became indispensable, even as we eventually brought on more staff when enough money started to come in, which took months.

Pelosi Strengthens Her Grip

THERE IS A CLEAR COROLLARY BETWEEN THE ACTIONS of Congress today and what occurred the last time Republicans controlled Washington and public opinion began to turn against them. A look back at how Democrats handled that situation—and the success of their strategy—is instructive, especially given the fact that House Minority Leader Nancy Pelosi has said that she plans to employ the same tactics leading up to the 2018 midterm elections.[27]

During my first campaign, as I traveled across the district, I consistently made the case for moderation and the need to add more centrist voices to Congress; but on Capitol Hill, Pelosi was "strengthening her grip"[28] and working overtime to divide Congress into two warring factions.

Ron Brownstein provides one of the best descriptions of what Pelosi was doing on Capitol Hill in 2005 and 2006, at exactly the same time I and many other centrist Democratic candidates were running races against partisanship in Washington. Pelosi "discouraged Democrats from cosponsoring bills with Republicans" or negotiating on bills moving through committee. She argued that "a minority's goal should not be to tweak the other party's legislation but to develop a clear record of contrast that could be used to unseat the majority in the next election." In a move that would later prove embarrassing, she even refused to allow Democrats to participate in the investigation into the Bush administration's response to Hurricane Katrina. These tactics helped Pelosi secure the Speaker's gavel, but they also infuriated Republicans and heightened the level of confrontation in Congress.[29] Although I did not know it at the time, this would foreshadow my relationship with Pelosi and her partisan leadership team during my three terms in the House.

While Pelosi was engaging in hand-to-hand combat with Republicans on Capitol Hill, liberal activists were inexplicably focusing their fury on wayward Democrats, whom they loosely defined as those willing to work with Republicans. When President Bush proposed private investment accounts as part of his plan to restructure Social Security, Democrats pounced on the opportunity he had served up on a silver platter. Although defensible from a policy and budgetary perspective, any attempt to overhaul Social Security—the deadly "third rail" of politics—was guaranteed to be politically controversial, especially among the senior citizen population that votes in the highest numbers of any age demographic.

Pelosi refused to negotiate with Bush or even offer an alternative plan, believing the more politically advantageous play was to use the issue as a wedge and repeatedly hammer Bush and Republican incumbents running for reelection. Melissa Hart was one of the strongest supporters of Bush's Social Security plan, going so far as to bring Vice President Dick Cheney into the district to host a town hall meeting on the topic.

Meanwhile, external groups such as MoveOn.org threatened to support primary opponents against incumbent Democrats who had the audacity to consider compromise with Republicans. Liberal interest groups even went so far as to run television ads in the North Florida district of Democratic Congressman Allen Boyd, who represented a conservative district that had supported President Bush by an eight-point margin only months before. Liberal blogs kept an online tally sheet of Democrats who dared to *say* anything positive about Bush's plan.[30] These and similar acts of aggression against centrist Democrats played out all the way through my campaign.

Going Postal

THROUGHOUT THIS BOOK, I REFERENCE SOCIAL EXPERIments carried out to test human thought and behavior. Early in my campaign, I unknowingly conducted an experiment that was more instructive than I could have ever imagined.

Needing to raise money to get my campaign off the ground, I sent a fundraising letter to my entire holiday card list, which at the time numbered about two thousand people. For years, I had added people to the list as I met them, usually through business or family circles. The mailing list was, for all intents and purposes, a list of everyone I knew. My letter explained why I was running and why I thought I could win, followed by a request for a contribution. The results were surprising.

People I thought were sure things failed to contribute. Some of them sent an encouraging note in lieu of money, but others didn't respond at all. Conversely, contributions arrived from some of the people I considered to be a lost cause, even though I almost didn't bother to send them a letter to avoid wasting a stamp. Distant relatives I barely knew sent checks, as did colleagues I only tangentially worked with in past jobs. Close cousins and uncles of limited financial means sent more than they should have, while others on more secure financial footing did nothing. Some friends sent large contributions, while others sat on their hands. It turned out to be completely unpredictable.

In retrospect, some of my biggest campaign supporters came from that initial mailing. A neighbor I knew only in passing contributed the maximum allowable amount and would do so again in all my subsequent campaigns, even though he was a lifelong Republican. He told me it was because he appreciated my centrist message and that I planned to work with both sides. Dr. Tom Braun, dean of the dental school at the University of Pittsburgh, was among the first to respond, sending five hundred dollars despite the fact that we had met only once. Without being asked, he would continue to send contributions regularly over the course of my entire career in Congress. There are countless stories just like those, as well as many others with contrastingly negative results. The moral of the story is, if you really want to find out who your true friends are, send a letter asking them to contribute to a campaign nobody thinks you can win.

Cognitive Bias

IN INTERACTING WITH POLITICAL PARTISANS, IT DIDN'T take me long to figure out that it is difficult to win a debate with someone if that person does not agree with you to begin with. I also came to realize that different people can come to different conclusions when presented with the exact same facts. Even worse, partisans often stick to their argument even when presented with strong evidence that their point of view is misguided.[31] Research has shown that partisans will often dig in after being shown evidence contradicting their views, becoming even more certain that they are right. The contrary evidence actually reinforces their misperceptions.[32]

To understand the psychological motivation behind the arguments partisans make, one must first recognize that humans are inherently biased. Studies have repeatedly shown that when processing information, people look for evidence to support their preconceived notions while ignoring evidence to the contrary. Scientists have proven this "motivated reasoning" allows people to minimize inconvenient facts in order to reach a preferred conclusion.[33] As professor of social psychology Peter Ditto has said, "What's clear from decades of social psychological research is that people's emotions get involved in their reasoning, their motivations, their intuitions. Those shape and bias the way we process information."[34]

Hetherington and Rudolph have studied the way motivated reasoning affects partisan thinking. Their research has shown that partisans evaluate the same set of circumstances differently based upon whether or not the evidence casts their party in a positive or negative light. Partisans will be swayed by weak arguments offered by their own party's leaders but reject much stronger arguments emanating from the opposing party's leaders. As the authors write in their book *Why Washington Won't Work*, "people tend to see things the way they are predisposed to see them, regardless of whether their perceptions are fully grounded in reality," adding that "partisans act as biased information processors by selectively focusing on information that favors their political allies or disfavors their political adversaries."[35]

Both Democrats and Republicans will adjust the way they perceive information about their home state's economic circumstances based solely upon the party affiliation of the governor. Likewise, people will allow their partisanship to supersede factual information about the nation's economy if those facts benefit the opposing party. In polls taken in times of post-recession economic growth, both Democrats and Republicans answered factual questions about whether the economy had recently improved based entirely upon which party controlled the White House.[36]

When President George W. Bush was in office, Democrats tended to deny economic growth even though it was measurable as fact. The reverse was true during Barack Obama's presidency. Similarly, Democrats and Republicans flipped their views about whether presidents had the power to affect gas prices after Obama succeeded Bush in the White House.[37] "Partisans increasingly base government evaluations . . . on the performance criteria that are most favorable to their preferred party and least favorable to their non-preferred party," according to Hetherington and Rudolph. In other words, partisans focus their attention upon supporting their own side rather than honestly considering all available information.[38]

During the last week of October 2016, voters in the crucial swing state of Wisconsin were asked whether the national economy had gotten better or worse "over the past year." By a margin of twenty-eight points, Republicans overwhelmingly believed the economy had gotten worse. Then something unexpected happened—Donald Trump was elected to replace Barack Obama in the White House. Four months later, in March of 2017, Wisconsin voters were asked the exact same question. This time, GOP voters by a margin of fifty-four points believed the economy had gotten better. Democrats who were polled experienced a similar conversion, but in reverse. As noted by the *Milwaukee Journal Sentinel*, the change in control of the White House "did more than change the expectation of Republicans and Democrats about the economy's *future* performance, it altered their assessments of the economy's *actual* performance."[39]

As Congress has become more polarized, much has been written by academics and political commentators about the role played by the cognitive biases that drive the decisions and opinions of political activists. David Blankenhorn of the Institute for American Values calls polarization an "intellectual deficiency that for practical purposes is akin to a handicap. Polarized thinking is almost always distorted thinking."[40]

Confirmation bias is the tendency of humans to interpret new evidence in ways that confirm what they already believe to be true. The term was coined by English psychologist Peter Wason, who conducted a series of experiments that showed people often made decisions based upon their preconceptions rather than a genuine desire to discover the truth.[41]

Wason's most famous study was his 1960 report on the so-called "2-4-6 problem." Wason showed participants a series of three numbers and told them the series conformed to a rule. In order to discover the rule, participants could only create their own set of three numbers and ask the experimenter if those numbers also conformed to the rule. When respondents were confident they knew the rule, they informed the experimenter of their guess. As described by Jonathan Haidt in his 2012 best-seller *The Righteous Mind*:

—

SUPPOSE A SUBJECT first sees 2-4-6. The subject then generates a triplet in response: "4-6-8?"

"Yes," says the experimenter.

"How about 120-122-124?"

"Yes."

It seemed obvious to most people that the rule was consecutive even numbers. But the experimenter told them this was wrong, so they tested out other rules: "3-5-7?"

"Yes."

What about "35-37-39?"

"Yes."

"OK, so the rule must be any series of numbers that rises by two?"

"No."

People had little trouble generating new hypotheses about the rule, sometimes quite complex ones. But what they hardly ever did was to test their hypothesis by offering triplets that *did not conform to their hypothesis*. For example, proposing 2-4-5 (yes) and 2-4-3 (no) would have helped people zero in on the actual rule: any series of ascending numbers.[42]

—

As the Wason study demonstrated, people's unwillingness to consider that they might be wrong can prevent them from finding the right answer. This type of motivated reasoning is common among partisans. It clouds their judgement and makes it more difficult for them to see validity in the viewpoint of the other side. It even disrupts their ability to solve simple numerical problems. Decades after the Wason study, another experiment would confirm these results while offering a more sobering conclusion about the impact of cognitive bias on the decision-making ability of political ideologues.

In 2013, a research team led by Yale University law professor Dan Kahan published results of a study on how political ideology impacts people's ability to accept conclusions that go against their own beliefs. In the study, Kahan and his team tested the hypothesis that "citizens of all levels of science comprehension generally form positions with the best available evidence . . . those who enjoy higher than average capacities for science comprehension use those capacities to make even better science-informed decisions." In other words, people will use available evidence to inform their decisions, and the most well-informed people will make the most well-reasoned decisions. Unfortunately for Kahan—and for America—his study proved quite the opposite was true when the topic at hand was politics.[43]

Using a sample of more than one thousand American adults who had been surveyed and categorized based upon their math skills and political views, Kahan's team devised four versions of a mathematical problem. The first two versions involved a fictitious skin-rash treatment. Subjects were told to evaluate the effectiveness of the rash treatment based upon the results of two study groups, one of which was given the skin-rash treatment and one of which was not. Experimenters provided the study participants with information about how effective the skin cream was over a two-week period, based upon how many patients in each group got better and how many got worse. Subjects were asked to interpret the results to determine whether those who applied the skin cream had better results than those who did not.

The problem was designed to be more difficult than it first appeared. Solving it required a second step of deduction beyond just choosing the higher number in each group. In order to correctly interpret the data, subjects would have to not only determine the number of subjects experiencing positive outcomes, but they would also have to compare the ratio of success for those who did and did not apply the skin cream. Respondents had to resist the temptation to intuit the answer based upon their first impression and instead take the time to complete the second step of the problem—interpreting the ratios.

The second version of the study was identical to the first, with one exception. Rather than evaluating the effectiveness of skin cream, respondents were asked to evaluate the data to determine the effectiveness of gun control measures. Subjects were told a "city government was trying to decide whether to pass a law banning private citizens from carrying concealed handguns in public." Like the skin cream problem, results were broken down into two groups—those cities that had recently enacted bans on concealed weapons and those that had no such bans. Identical to the skin cream problem, information was then provided about the number of cities that had experienced an increase or decrease in crime under both circumstances. To get their partisan juices flowing, respondents were told their answers would help government officials determine whether gun control laws decrease crime by lowering the number of people carrying guns, or increase crime by making it harder for law-abiding citizens to defend themselves. Although both the skin cream and the gun control problems were designed in identical fashion and used the same data, the results were wildly different depending on whether or not the political context was used.

The number of respondents who correctly answered the skin cream problem corresponded to their relative math skills and remained consistent across the entire group, regardless of their political affiliation. The same did not hold true for the gun control problem. In determining the effectiveness of the gun control measures, both liberals and conservatives showed extreme levels of bias in their decision making. Liberals were much more likely to answer correctly when the fictitious data showed a decrease in crime in cities that had imposed gun control laws, while conservatives were more likely to answer correctly when the data showed an increase in crime in those same cities. But if the same data supported a conclusion that went against the political beliefs of the partisans, the respondents fared poorly. If the data contradicted their biases, they simply could not bring themselves to answer correctly, even though the evidence was right there in front of them.

To the surprise of the Kahan research team, the higher an individual's proficiency in math, the worse they did on the politically motivated gun control problem compared to the skin cream problem. The researchers had hypothesized that those with high-proficiency math skills would be able to more easily see the correct conclusion, even if the results went against their personal beliefs. But the respondents' partisanship proved to be a blind spot. Those with high-level math skills experienced an even more magnified political polarization. The partisans who possessed greater mathematical ability than their peer respondents should have been able to make proper use of the quantitative information presented in a manner that generated a correct answer. Instead, they were selective in their answers, choosing the one that corresponded to their political beliefs.[44] Science writer Chris Mooney may have said it best in the headline of his commentary about the study: "Science Confirms: Politics Wrecks Your Ability to Do Math."[45]

These results should be unsurprising for anyone who has served in elected office. The findings are consistent with the countless conversations I have had with political activists over the years. In most cases, once they have made up their minds, there is very little you can do to persuade them, even if most available evidence runs contrary to their point of view. "People tend to be a lot more skeptical of information they don't want to believe than information they want to believe," Professor Ditto told the *Washington Post*.[46]

The consequences of the Yale study cannot be overstated. The unwillingness of people to support conclusions that run counter to their pre-existing beliefs plays a major role in driving political polarization. The activists who participate in campaigns and elections—and the members of Congress who rely on their support—are increasingly unwilling to agree on even the most basic facts surrounding an issue. They see only what they want to see, interpreting the facts as they would like them to be rather than as they are. But that's only the beginning.

Once partisans make up their minds, they expend little mental energy evaluating facts that may support an alternative viewpoint. Instead, they compile evidence that conforms to their own views while disregarding evidence to the contrary, giving them supreme confidence that their opinion is correct.

In *The Righteous Mind*, social psychologist Tom Gilovich explained to author Jonathan Haidt that even one tiny shred of evidence, no matter how dubious, is enough to convince people that their political opinion is correct. Likewise, exposure to a single reason to doubt a contrary claim is enough to disregard it in its entirety. The person can stop thinking, they've been proven right.[47]

Worse yet, people often don't remember counter arguments to their opinions even if they are exposed to them. Political scientist Charles Taber has explained that when presented with contradictory information, partisans may invoke a subconscious defense mechanism that alters the memories and associations formed in the brain, blocking the new information and reminding them of their own beliefs.[48]

In *The Big Sort*, professor Diana Carlin described the tendency of partisans to watch political debates only to reinforce their own opinions, dismissing anything the opposing candidate says. This is far from a new trend. Studies over the course of decades have proven that partisans ignore concrete facts presented in opposition to their beliefs but will uncritically accept bad information if it supports their position.[49]

Political scientist Brendan Nyhan is one of the leading authorities on this phenomenon. In one study, Nyhan and a colleague provided participants with mock news stories containing undeniably false claims about various public policy issues. Afterwards, participants were given correct information, proving conclusively that the previous claims were outright falsehoods. Nyhan found that extreme partisans on both sides were unlikely to change their positions, with many claiming to be even more certain of their views after learning the contradictory facts.[50]

In a later study, Nyhan used both text and graphs to show partisans the results of politically controversial policy decisions, such as President Obama's economic interventions and President Bush's troop surge in Iraq. An alarming number of partisans rejected the information being presented to them, even after they saw factual data disproving their opinion.[51] It should therefore be unsurprising that a large number of Trump voters who were shown side-by-side aerial photographs of the crowd turnout at the 2009 Obama Inaugural and the 2017 Trump Inaugural said there were more people at Trump's, which drew an estimated 250,000 people. This despite the fact that the estimated 1.5 million people who attended Obama's first Inaugural covered an undeniably larger portion of the landscape compared to the other picture.[52]

Partisans rarely let facts get in the way of their opinions. A study by James Kuklinski of the University of Illinois asked respondents questions about social welfare programs. Although a majority expressed confidence that their answers were correct, a paltry 3% of respondents got more than half the questions right. Perhaps predictably, those who knew the least about the subject expressed the highest degree of confidence in their "knowledge." A 2007 experiment by researchers from George Washington University and the University of California at Berkeley provided accurate information to previously misinformed respondents about immigrants in the United States.

Even after being told the facts, many study participants still did not change their views.[53]

Political partisans are the least likely to change their minds because they are also the most confident in their opinions. The more passionate people are, the more biased they are likely to be. And often the more misinformed. Research by psychologist Jeremy Frimer has shown that partisans will go to great lengths to avoid learning about alternative points of view even if that information is made available to them. This "motivated ignorance" results in a situation that has become all too familiar in political discourse today—partisans exhibit supreme confidence in their own opinions even though they are entirely unfamiliar with the facts supporting the viewpoints of those with whom they disagree.[54]

Professor Ditto found no distinction in the way liberals and conservatives are affected by cognitive bias in selecting evidence. "Both sides show a clear bias," he concluded. "They're more likely to accept the same information as valid if it supports their views than if it doesn't, and the magnitude of that effect is exactly the same" regardless of party affiliation.[55] Ditto knows what he is talking about, having led a team of seven political scientists on a comprehensive 2017 research project analyzing the results of forty-one different experimental studies of partisan bias involving more than twelve thousand participants. Liberals and conservatives "showed nearly identical levels of bias across studies."[56]

In his article "The Science of Why We Don't Believe Science," Chris Mooney highlights a litany of other studies that show similar results, proving the near impossibility of getting partisans to change their minds or think openly about policy issues. When shown fake research studies about the effectiveness of the death penalty as a deterrent, advocates on each side strongly sided with the study that coincided with their own position on the issue, even though neither of the fake studies was more compelling than the other. Whatever the issue—gay rights, gun control, affirmative action—partisans have proven to be unable to exercise unbiased judgement when evaluating evidence.[57]

Worse yet, as Mooney discovered, partisans use their biases to cast doubt upon the qualifications of scientific experts who put forth facts that contrast with the partisan's own beliefs.

Partisans do not trust those who hold differing views, regardless of academic credentials.[58]

One experiment studied the effect of this bias using highly polarizing issues such as climate change, nuclear energy, and gun control. Subjects were asked to evaluate the merits of a fictitious book about one of the controversial subjects, using the resume of the author as a guide. The resumes highlighted the scientific qualifications and pertinent academic credentials of the author, who was portrayed as having a PhD from an elite university and being a member of the National Academy of Sciences. Subjects were then shown an excerpt from the book. The excerpt made clear which side of the issue the scientist advocated. Even though the credentials of all the authors were essentially the same, respondents only accepted the opinions of the authors that agreed with their own position. They rejected not just the conclusion but the personal credibility of the scientist if those conclusions were in opposition to their own point of view.[59]

This lack of trust casts serious doubt on the efforts of Facebook and others in the media to limit the impact of the fake news epidemic that dominated the 2016 election cycle. It also makes it almost impossible for partisans to build consensus and work towards compromise.

Joseph Hopper has likened this lack of trust to the process of divorce. As trust is lost, anger grows, and the perceptions of the relationship change and become more extreme. A feeling of shared responsibility is replaced by projections of blame almost entirely upon the other spouse. Often, separating spouses refuse to acknowledge any redeeming qualities of the marriage, instead thinking, "it was never a good relationship, it was wrong from the beginning." The bitterness of separating spouses is replicated in the political polarization driving the animosity in Washington. The two sides are now so far apart it is almost impossible to imagine a time when there was ever bipartisan cooperation.[60]

The Gambler

OUR POLITICAL SYSTEM HAS SUFFERED AS A RESULT of these human cognitive biases. They have led to a coarsening of our civil discourse, bad outcomes at the ballot box, extreme polarization on Capitol Hill, and complete dysfunction in the American political system. Although advocates of good government may be frustrated at the bad decisions people make as a result of cognitive bias, there is one group of people who are exceedingly happy that these biases exist—professional gamblers. Just as some politicians have achieved success pandering to the lowest instinct of human bias, professional gamblers capitalize on these same flaws. They make comfortable livings betting against the bad decisions of others.

I unknowingly stumbled into the intersection of these two worlds—gambling and politics—when I first met Bill Benter in the fall of 2005. Bill, then forty-nine, was a somewhat mysterious Pittsburgh businessman who was known to have made a fortune in gambling but was turning his attention to politics and philanthropy. Over the years, Benter's gambling exploits had become legendary. His career has been profiled around the globe, and he has been called the world's most successful sports bettor—a moniker that carries with it some high expectations to be sure.[61]

Bill Benter is a mathematical genius who can calculate numbers and equations with the same ease with which Claude Monet manipulated paints and brushes. After reading Edward Thorp's famous guide to card counting, *Beat the Dealer,* Benter realized that, in his own words, "anyone who read this book and learned the strategy could walk into any casino and be playing with a positive edge against the casino."[62] The book changed Benter's life. As he describes it, "That's how I got into the game, I was caught up in this. I read the book and quit what I was doing, which was attending university, and moved to Las Vegas and became a professional gambler. It worked."[63]

The mere existence of Las Vegas serves as living proof of the axiom that a fool and his money are soon parted. Every one of the enormous casino hotels in Sin City was built thanks to the bad decisions of amateur gamblers, often hindered by their ignorance and bias. But Bill Benter was no fool. He rode an incredible wave of success at the blackjack table, racking up wins and collecting chips up and down the Las Vegas strip. Along the way, he met the eccentric but increasingly successful Australian actuary-turned-card-counter Alan Woods, who would also become one of the world's most successful and well-known gamblers. Together Benter and Woods experienced extraordinary success, which inevitably led to both of them being banned from nearly every casino in Las Vegas.[64]

Benter and Woods could not have been more different. Benter is quiet and unassuming, impeccably dressed, and methodical and relentlessly calculating in his approach. Woods, who died in 2008 at age sixty-two, was brash and flamboyant, dressed down casual in appearance, and known for outrageous parties and recklessness with his money.[65] It was Benter's love of mathematics and calculation—and the use of computer technology programmed to beat the odds—that led the pair to their next venture.

Benter had always been fascinated by the use of computer technology to give an upper hand to savvy gamblers. The card counting techniques taught in the book *Beat the Dealer* were derived from computer models—the first time computer-driven statistical analysis had been used to study gambling. Benter decided to create a program of his own that would exponentially increase his winnings. During his time in Las Vegas, Benter experimented with various computer programs he designed for this purpose, such as one that calculated the speed of the ball on a spinning roulette wheel in an attempt to predict which quadrant of the wheel the ball would land.[66] As he continued winning at the blackjack table, he kept searching for the perfect way to use mathematics and statistical analysis to fully capitalize on his knack for numbers and computer programming. He found it in horse racing.[67]

Up to that point, most people believed the results of horse racing were too unpredictable for bettors to use data and statistical analysis to consistently win at the track. But Benter knew better. "That's a misconception that certain events that are thought to be random or hard to predict, such as horse racing, is in fact one of the most predictable phenomenon that there is in the sporting world. The results of a horse race can be predicted with more accuracy and a greater ability to discern winners from losers than in almost any other sport," he said in an interview years later.[68]

Bankrolled partly by Woods, Benter continued work on a computer program that would, in time, make them both hundreds of millions of dollars. The idea was to collect data on the past performance of horses and create a computer program based upon a variety of weighted factors, such as time between races, record of the jockey, and success of the horse in all types of conditions and scenarios. Benter's program weighted the results based upon every conceivable factor, such as whether the horse has previously finished second in a field of eight or fourth in a field of fourteen. The computer program could even tell when the race tracks had been slightly reconfigured or sloped based upon the way horses performed on them.[69]

Hong Kong was the perfect place to implement the program because the same one thousand or so horses run in the same racing circuit multiple times per year, making it easy to accumulate valuable data about how they perform against each other. Importantly, the governing body of horse racing in Hong Kong, the Hong Kong Jockey Club, is reported to be scrupulously honest in its oversight of racing, eliminating the possibility of race-fixing that would obviously undermine the statistical validity of Benter's program.[70]

A key component of the program was finding the best way to cast bets so as not to draw the attention of other bettors or unprofitably distort the odds for the horses with the best chance to win. In calling Benter the most successful sports bettor in the world, *Wired* magazine highlighted his computer betting model and his ability to disguise his bets to avoid negatively impacting the odds.[71]

Due to kinks in the program, a limited number of calculation variables, and lack of historical data on the horses, it took Benter and Woods five years to turn a profit. Having expended much of his gambling savings, Benter returned to Las Vegas in an unsuccessful search for additional investors. Even his closest gambling buddies rejected his offer of 70% of the profits—largely due to the fact that, after years of trying, the program had yet to turn a profit.[72]

They finally had their first winning season in 1987. It was about that time that the business partnership of Benter and Woods would break up in a bitter dispute over money and control of the decisions made at that track. After their contentious split, Benter went off on his own and perfected the program. The breakup led to incredible stories of betrayal and *Mission Impossible*-style self-destructing computer programs designed to sabotage the data.[73] Nevertheless, both men became wealthy beyond their wildest dreams.

Later in life, Woods admitted that a driving force in his own gambling success had been his rivalry with Benter, although he admitted that Bill had been more successful after they ended their partnership.[74] Also much later, in a rare bit of self-promotion, Benter in a 2004 speech to The Third Congress of Chinese Mathematicians displayed a graph showing his profits in the years since he invented the computer program. The graph's slope is so improbably steep that Benter says he had to use a logarithmic mathematical process to compress the chart and prevent the profit slope from carrying off the page.[75]

Why was Benter so successful at gambling and sports betting when so many others had failed? Most of the answer of course lies in Benter's almost superhuman math skills and willingness to persevere through the streaks of bad luck that every gambler encounters. But part of the answer can also be attributed to the role that cognitive bias plays in the way the other gamblers—most notably the losers—cast their bets. The money Benter won through mathematical calculation came from bettors who made bad decisions based upon factors other than probability and statistics, often factors driven by personal bias. This is particularly true when betting on sports, perhaps the only pastime that evokes more passion and bias in people than politics.

People allow their biases to lead them into bad decisions—decisions for which Benter literally made them pay. In discussing this dynamic, Benter compares himself to a professional golfer playing among amateurs. What does he say when asked where his winnings came from? "If we do make money, the money has to come from somewhere. Well, yes, the general public loses to a somewhat higher ratio," he says with a smile.[76]

A connection between cognitive bias and profiting on horse racing can be found in the term *overlay*. In horse racing, an overlay exists when the betting public makes a mistake in judging the competing horses in a race and fails to recognize the potential success of one particular horse. Operating on a pari-mutuel system, the betting odds at most horse racing tracks are based solely on public opinion, which is often completely out of touch with reality. The amount of money being bet on the race determines the odds for each participating horse. Horses that are expected to win will have the lowest potential payout. Long-shot horses not expected to do well will have comparatively less money bet on them, which therefore provides better odds and a higher potential payout if that horse does happen to win.[77] A key to Benter's success is finding the large overlays—the horses that his program shows have a strong chance to win but still have high odds because the public has not been betting on those horses in proportion to their statistical chance to win. Large overlays provided Benter the window of opportunity he needed to maximize profits.[78]

Fortunately for Benter, large overlays are common because mistakes in the betting public are common. He created the perfect system to take advantage of these mistakes. As one magazine profile put it, "people are idiots and there is usually one [large overlay] per race."[79] *Wired* magazine put it more discretely: "Someone with the right research capabilities can easily find the public's miscalculations and exploit them for great financial gain."[80]

While most people bet based upon biased factors such as the name of the horse, color of the jockey's uniform, or tip from a friend, Benter's computer program is designed specifically to take advantage of these mistakes to earn enormous profits. Benter made a fortune betting against public opinion. It is the same lesson learned by today's politicians, media commentators, and political activists who advance their own interests by taking advantage of the public's ignorance and bias.

CHAPTER 3

CENTER STAGE

———·•·———

The First Step

DURING THE FIRST FEW MONTHS OF MY CAMPAIGN, I FO-
cused on raising money and meeting people across the six-county district. I attended every imaginable type of event, including
community picnics, pancake breakfasts, parades, senior citizen
bingos, factory employee shift changes, and high school football
games, just to name a few.

In every setting throughout that first campaign, I emphasized my intention to be bipartisan and work across the aisle. I
frequently used a line about how I wouldn't need to look to my
party leadership to decide how to vote because I would always
put the district first. This received a rousing response at some
community events, but it quickly became apparent that the
partisan Democrats who attended the political rallies weren't so
thrilled with that concept. Many of them told me they preferred
the approach advocated by my primary opponent, Georgia Berner, who took a more partisan and confrontational tone. I argued that hers was a losing strategy in the conservative-leaning
district. For months leading up to the primary, Georgia and I
continued this contrast, especially in our many debates and
joint appearances.

Early on, I met a young Pittsburgh lawyer named Charles
Lamberton, who would become a key member of my campaign's

inner circle. Charles was a partisan Democrat but also a pragmatist. He knew the political demographics of the district
required a centrist candidate in order to have any chance of
defeating the popular incumbent. Charles contributed money,
gave me balanced advice, and allowed me and Christina, my
campaign manager, to use an available phone in his office for
fundraising calls whenever we were in the neighborhood. It is
people like Charles that are the unsung heroes of any successful underdog campaign.

At first, raising money was slow going. After the initial re-
ceipts of my mailing to everybody I knew, the money dried up. I
then had to reach out by phone to those on the list who hadn't
yet contributed. Once those calls ran their course, I had to turn
my attention to people I had never met and ask them for money.
This is unquestionably the worst part of running for office. Nobody likes to ask for money, especially from strangers. But in
order to accumulate the resources necessary to sustain a professional campaign and get my message out to voters, I had to
do it. I spent countless hours calling people who didn't know
me and didn't think I could win. Few took the time to return
my calls and even fewer contributed. Many said to get back to
them after the primary. Then I caught the biggest break of my
campaign. Bill Benter had agreed to meet with me.

We met for lunch at the historic Duquesne Club, the premier
social club in Pittsburgh. Founded in 1873, the Duquesne Club
for decades was the place to see and be seen among the Steel
City's industrial elite. Today, it remains a frequent venue for
high-level meetings, receptions, and political events. Decorated
with expensive artwork and elegant furniture, the club still has
the look and feel of the Gilded Age.

As tuxedoed waiters circled the restaurant, Benter quickly
brought me down to Earth. He told me he had done some research on my campaign and determined it was not winnable.
Hart had won her past two reelections with 64% of the vote, and
I was a political unknown. In fact, he thought it was unlikely I
would even make it out of the primary. Luckily for me, at the
time I didn't fully realize Benter's aptitude for numbers. If I had,
I would have been quite discouraged by his pessimism.

I explained to him that I knew the district well, having attended hundreds of social, charitable, and political events there
during the years I worked for UPMC, as well as the early days

of my campaign. I was confident that a centrist candidate could appeal to voters in the district, and that the political winds were already starting to stir discontent with President Bush and Pennsylvania's ultra-conservative senator, Rick Santorum. By strategically reminding voters of the similarity of Hart's record to Bush's and Santorum's—while promoting my own message of bipartisan moderation—I said there was about "a one-in-three chance of success," using language I knew Benter would appreciate.

He wanted to know my position on the issue about which he was most passionate—peace in the Middle East. Obviously, this is a question with no easy answers, and I began to stumble in my response. He politely cut me off and explained his support for a two-state solution to the Israeli-Palestinian conflict, as well as his views on what he perceived to be Bush's misguided policies in Iraq. He went into a level of detail I didn't expect, talking about visits he had made to the region, contacts with high-level officials, and friends with whom he was working to achieve his objectives. He wanted to know if I was open-minded on the issue and if I had heard from AIPAC, the powerful pro-Israel lobby, which has a completely different viewpoint than Benter's. I said I hadn't heard from AIPAC and that I would keep an open mind. As he signed the tab, Benter said he would think about our discussion and what he might do to help my campaign. Although I hadn't completely sealed the deal, I knew I had made progress.

Throughout the winter and into the spring, I continued attending events and trying to raise money. Berner did a good job of throwing red meat to the liberals but she lacked depth on the issues, which gave me my opening. The lines were clearly drawn—Berner was attracting the support of liberals and people around her home base in New Castle, while my support came from more pragmatic Democrats who sought a candidate with the best chance to beat Congresswoman Hart in the general election.

Among the groups in the latter category were the blue-collar trade unions. I earned the financial and grassroots support of John DeFazio's Steelworkers union, as well as the "building trades" unions, such as the Steamfitters, Electrical Workers, and Plumbers. Although the law only permits unions to contribute up to five thousand dollars through their Political Action

Committees (PACs), in a race where neither Berner nor I were raising much money, those PAC checks made a huge difference.

Members of the blue-collar unions were generally more socially conservative than members of the service-industry unions to whom Berner's liberal message resonated. The service unions were also skeptical of me due to my previous work for UPMC, which strongly opposed attempts to unionize nurses in its hospitals.

Given my professional background, the topic of health care reform came up frequently in the campaign. In a lengthy conversation with DeFazio and other union leaders, we discussed our shared goal of lowering the cost of health care. I took note of the fact that they failed to see the irony of advocating for lower costs while fiercely protecting the lavish and costly health plans unions had fought so hard to achieve.

Leading up to the May primary, I raised just over $200,000—not enough to do any media advertising or other campaign messaging, but enough to run a viable campaign. Bill Benter proved to be extremely helpful, personally contributing to my campaign and hosting a successful fundraiser at his home. The rest of the money came as a result of my many months of fundraising calls and meetings, as well as the PAC checks from the blue-collar unions.

Because neither Berner nor I had done any advertising before the primary, the race came down mostly to geography and hard work. Berner overwhelmingly carried New Castle and the surrounding region, while I carried my home area in the more highly populated northern suburbs of Pittsburgh. My ten-point victory was due to the regional vote advantage and the perception among Democrats that I was the better candidate to take on the powerful incumbent congresswoman. Now it was on to the general election in the fall.

Power of the Internet

THE GROWTH OF THE INTERNET NEWS INDUSTRY—especially political blogs and social media—has exacerbated the problem of polarization by giving an expanded platform to partisans, allowing them to further segregate themselves and their news sources. Equally important, the Internet has allowed partisan political organizations to raise funds in ways that were previously impossible, thereby giving them the ability to support fringe candidates who might otherwise have been unable to sustain a viable campaign.

Social media allows rank-and-file members of Congress to leapfrog their leadership and the seniority system to raise their stature by quickly attracting huge national followings. From the start of their careers in the Senate, Ted Cruz and Elizabeth Warren effectively used social media to raise their visibility and promote their distinctly non-centrist messages far beyond what would have previously been possible. In the 2016 presidential election, Senator Bernie Sanders used the Internet and social media to build and solidify his base of far-left supporters, raising millions of dollars through small donations from around the country. President Trump has famously used Twitter to energize his followers and drive media coverage during and after his campaign.[1]

Partisans now rely almost exclusively on social media as their primary method of organizing like-minded activists to disrupt a congressional town hall or gather for a protest march. The rise of the Tea Party, Occupy, and Black Lives Matter movements were all largely driven by social media, as were the 2011 Arab Spring demonstrations across the Middle East. Nevertheless, mainstream news outlets are still behind the times to some degree, often underestimating the intensity of emotion that drives the protests that have become commonplace in today's global political environment.

In the days leading up to the massive Women's March protests following President Trump's Inaugural, network television news programs gave the march only cursory coverage, while newspapers outside of Washington largely ignored it altogether. But the march is the best example yet of the power of the Internet and social media in organizing political protests. According to the *Washington Post*, the march began as a single Facebook post the day after the 2016 election, when Hawaiian retiree Teresa Shook posted a seemingly innocuous note to her online friends. She suggested they create an event page to organize a women's rally in Washington coinciding with Trump's Inaugural. Within twenty-four hours, more than ten thousand people had already responded.[2] University of Virginia journalism professor Marcus Messner says the success of the march proves that "organizers don't need media coverage anymore to reach large audiences and turn out large crowds for protests when people are passionate about issues and connect via social media."[3]

Taking a page from the playbook of their polar opposite Tea Party rivals, liberals have perfected the use of social media to draw attention to their cause by organizing protest rallies and disrupting public events hosted by Republican members of Congress. Progressive groups like *Resistance Near Me* and *Town Hall Project* use Twitter and Facebook to let their followers know the location of nearby public meetings by highlighting upcoming events on an interactive national map.[4] Entertainment celebrities such as *Star Trek* icon George Takei, comedian Patton Oswalt, and actress Alyssa Milano, among others, use social media to fan the flames by circulating those maps to their millions of followers.[5] As a result, Republican town halls across the country have devolved into theatrical farce, as angry protesters descend by the hundreds—and sometimes thousands—with the sole purpose of heckling, shouting down, and embarrassing the hosting member of Congress, who in many cases is not even the elected representative of the most vocal protesters in attendance. Needless to say, the use of social media to organize such protests has only intensified the polarization that plagues our national political process.

The first presidential candidate to effectively harness the power of the Internet was former Vermont Governor Howard Dean, who in the 2004 Democratic presidential primary went from longshot to frontrunner seemingly overnight. With a populist message targeted to partisan Democrats angry with the unwillingness of other candidates to fight for a liberal agenda, Dean was able to build an unmatched national network of grassroots activists. His ability to raise funds from small donors and to virtually connect his like-minded supporters became a model for future candidates.

The infrastructure for Dean's method was put in place over the preceding few years through the growth of the liberal grassroots organization MoveOn, which sustained itself by using email to raise funds and awareness for candidates and causes important to liberals. The website and organization that would become known as MoveOn.org energized the disaffected Democrats who resented the resistance of the party establishment to aggressively confront Bush's war policies.[6] As Ron Brownstein has astutely pointed out, "Maintaining the leadership of such a turbulent constituency required MoveOn to constantly position itself at the forward edge of Democratic opposition to Bush and the GOP."[7] Centrist Democrats had no websites or mass email capabilities to carry a more moderate message to voters. The Democratic voice that was heard came loud and clear from the far left.

While Republican-leaning news aggregation websites like the Drudge Report supplemented talk radio as a way to galvanize right-wing partisans, liberal bloggers used the Internet to connect with each other and expand their influence. Eventually becoming known as the "netroots" movement, the liberal blogosphere—led by websites such as Daily Kos—catapulted their far-left message into the mainstream of political discourse. But unlike their Republican counterparts, liberal Democrats used the Internet to target voters, strengthen campaigns, and raise enormous sums of money for candidates by soliciting previously untapped small donors throughout the country. Although Dean was unsuccessful in 2004, future candidates would learn from his strategy of using the Internet to activate liberal partisans. This would prove devastating to Republicans in 2006, by which time MoveOn.org had amassed a mailing list of more than three million people.[8]

Beating the Odds

BY SUMMER OF 2006, MY GENERAL ELECTION CAMPAIGN was in full swing. I had spent every second of every day for more than a year completely absorbed in the campaign, but few others seemed to be paying attention. And those who were paying attention still didn't believe I could win.

In June, I released the results of my first internal poll, which showed me trailing Hart by thirteen points. As I expected, local media and political blogs reported the story in not-so-glowing terms, suggesting I was hopelessly behind. I had accomplished what I wanted to do—get people talking about my campaign. The poll showed that, although I was losing, Hart's support was soft, and my campaign could expose that weakness if I had the necessary financial resources. The poll results were not lost on Democratic Congressional Campaign Committee chairman Rahm Emanuel, or on Howard Dean, then the high-profile chairman of the Democratic National Committee. Both called to let me know they noticed the results and to encourage me to keep working hard.

Meanwhile, at about the same time my poll came out, several hundred political bloggers were gathering in Las Vegas for a convention of netroots activists. The event was widely covered in liberal blogs and attracted many big-name Democratic officials. The convention struck a confrontational tone, but not in the way one might expect. According to Brownstein, "the names that provoked the loudest catcalls . . . were not Bush or any of his Republican allies, but Democrats who the crowd thought cooperated too much with the GOP."[9] I did not attend the conference, but I took note of the anti-compromise rhetoric that was reported to have been espoused by the liberal activists. It concerned me that the type of Democrat they were booing—compromising consensus builders committed to working with both sides—was exactly the type of member of Congress I planned to be. It was a harbinger of things to come.

Shortly thereafter, the DNC called with some exciting news—Howard Dean wanted to come to the district to personally campaign with me. Dean had set in motion a plan to have dozens of prominent Democratic elected officials fan out across the country to campaign with congressional candidates on July 29, which was one hundred days before the election. He particularly focused his attention on races that were considered longshots—those in conservative-leaning districts where Republicans had an advantage and Democrats had to run centrist campaigns to have any chance of success. This strategy caught the attention of the netroots activists, who viewed the plan as a waste of resources that could otherwise be going to "real Democrats" who wouldn't try to appeal to Republicans. Despite the criticism, Dean went through with his plan, which proved to be extraordinarily successful.

Dean and I joined several campaign volunteers to go door-to-door in the Republican stronghold of Murrysville, an upper-class suburb of Pittsburgh. For the first time, my campaign was in the media spotlight. The press coverage legitimized my campaign, a positive that far outweighed my private concern that being seen and photographed with the liberal firebrand Dean could hurt me with the centrist voters to whom I needed to appeal in order to win in November. Although I doubt we swayed very many voters in conservative Murrysville, the visit made a huge difference for my campaign, which from that point forward was viewed both locally and nationally as a competitive race that was ripe for an upset.

The race tightened going into the fall, as other Democratic officials visited the district to appear with me and headline fundraisers. Among these were Senator John Kerry and comedian Al Franken, a netroots favorite who would later become a senator. The Franken event was a raucous affair hosted at Bill Benter's enormous Pittsburgh loft condominium.

As drinks flowed generously for the guests, Franken brought the house down with his hilarious, politically inspired routine. He stayed well past the scheduled ending time, taking pictures and mingling with the hundred or so guests who had paid to attend. I was thankful for his having taken the time to fly across the country to be there, especially when I later learned that he had suffered throughout the day with a severe migraine headache.

In late October, a poll was released by the conservative *Pittsburgh Tribune-Review* newspaper, which ran the results above the front page fold.[10] The race was virtually tied as I was polling within the margin of error against Congresswoman Hart. Later that day, I received a call from Rahm Emanuel, with whom I had not spoken in months. He wanted to make one point perfectly clear—I now had a realistic chance to win, but in order to do so I would have to be much more aggressive in my fundraising.

"Let me ask you a question," he began, dismissing with the pleasantries and getting straight to the point. "Why have you never asked me for money?" I flubbed my response, murmuring something about not wanting to bother him. Using the type of colorful language for which he was known, Rahm said in no uncertain terms that my hesitation was a weakness and that I would lose a now-winnable race if I didn't raise the necessary resources to compete. Then there was silence. Not knowing what else to say, I began to wrap up the call. Rahm had one more question:

"Do you have something you want to ask me?"

"Um, can you contribute to my campaign?" I hesitatingly answered.

"How much?" he pressed.

Pulling out of the air a number that seemed like a lot to me, I said, "One thousand?"

Rahm exploded, using multiple expletives to remind me that he was legally able to contribute a total of seven thousand to my campaign—two thousand from his own reelection account and five thousand from his leadership PAC—and that I shouldn't be shy about asking for it. He reiterated that I had to be more aggressive or I would blow the opportunity I had worked so hard to create. Then he hung up. I did not hear from him again until he called to congratulate me on the night of the election. But the message had been received loud and clear. From that point forward, I spent even more time on the phone "dialing for dollars."

As the election drew closer, the money chase picked up. In order to have any chance to be competitive, I would have to wage a strong and expensive advertising campaign. With only a month to go, neither Hart nor I had run any television ads, largely because I didn't have enough money and she still didn't take the race seriously. Having only raised enough money to pay for one week of television, I planned to wait until the final week of the campaign to begin my commercials. But with polling showing her lead evaporating, Hart went on the air with a saturation-level ad buy four weeks before the election. My team knew we had to counter with our own ad or else I would fall too far behind to have any realistic chance to catch up. So I gambled.

My first television ad aired with three weeks remaining. I was betting that the ad would create enough buzz to raise the profile of my race and help me raise enough money to stay on the air through the election. My fundraising picked up slightly, but only enough to afford one more week. I was facing the very real prospect of having to "go dark"—discontinue my ad buy— for the entire week before the election. With Hart's ubiquitous ads running all over the airwaves, this would have spelled certain defeat. Then help arrived from an unexpected source.

With less than two weeks to go, Senator Barack Obama sent a national fundraising email asking Democrats across the country to contribute to my campaign. Twenty-four hours later, the email had raised $150,000, almost entirely in small-dollar contributions. Now I knew I would have the resources to stay on the air through the finish line.

The campaign became a focal point of the national fight for control of the House of Representatives. Outside money poured in on both sides, and the airwaves were flooded with negative ads from independent groups. A turning point in that last week may have been the intervention of an outside group called Vote-Vets, which represented Iraq War veterans opposed to the policies of President Bush and his allies in Congress. The ad featured a young Iraq War veteran sitting at a table talking about how disappointed he was that Congresswoman Hart had voted to cut funding for veterans. As the camera pulled back to reveal him seated in a wheelchair, he delivered his devastating tagline: "That might make sense from where she sits in Congress, but not from where I'm sitting."

It was an incredibly powerful ad that appealed to voters across the district. In accordance with federal campaign law, the ad had not been coordinated with my campaign, and I was as surprised as anybody when it aired. I knew as soon as I saw it that it might be just enough to make the difference in a neck-and-neck race. I was starting to feel confident that I would win, but Bill Benter wasn't so sure.

In the final week leading up to the election, Bill gave me daily updates on his personal calculations of my chances of success. I didn't know what exactly he was including in his calculations, but he alluded to a combination of polling results, prior and expected turnout, and precinct-by-precinct historical performance. Every day, the update was the same: it is going to be very close but Hart is going to win. On the day before the election, he told me it was too bad there wasn't one more week left in the campaign because, with the momentum on my side, I probably could have caught Hart and won the race.

On election night, I gathered with my staff in our campaign office. Local television stations reported on the returns, which showed the race deadlocked for most of the night. Bill Benter was there, spending his time staring at numbers on a computer screen while the rest of us fielded phone calls and nervously paced around the office and pizza shop next door.

Less than two hours after the polls closed, with the race still too close to call, it looked like we were heading for a long night. Amid the continuing buzz of excitement, Benter unexpectedly turned off his computer. He then methodically took off his glasses, sat back, crossed his arms, and calmly said, "That's it, you won." The room fell silent as everyone stared back at Bill.

I asked him what he meant, because all indications were that the race was still very much up for grabs.

"By my calculations, there are approximately nine thousand votes yet to be counted."

"And?" I nervously replied.

"And you're up by ten thousand votes."

"What does that mean?" I asked.

"It means you're going to Washington."

The room broke into cheers. Two more hours went by before the news organizations officially called the race, which I won by ten thousand votes.

Freshman Class

ACROSS THE COUNTRY, DEMOCRATS PICKED UP THIRTY seats, winning control of the House and giving the speaker's gavel to Nancy Pelosi. Many of the seats that flipped were won by centrist Democrats in districts that usually tilted Republican in congressional elections. Nineteen of those seats, including the one I had just won, had been carried by Bush in the presidential election just two years earlier. Many pundits optimistically believed the newly elected centrists might be able to bridge the partisan divide, bringing moderation and bipartisan compromise to Congress.

Time magazine ran a cover story about the election results titled "Why the Center is the New Place to Be."[11] E. J. Dionne[12] and Chuck Todd[13] each credited the Democratic victory to a "revenge" of independent and centrist voters seeking a more compromising tone in Washington. Journalists around the country agreed, highlighted by Mort Kondracke's suggestion that leaders of both parties "heed voters' call for moderation."[14]

Ignoring this consensus, the liberal left wasted no time in discouraging compromise. "First, let's disabuse ourselves of the bipartisanship idea," wrote a prominent left-wing blogger the morning after the election.[15]

Despite claims to the contrary from Democratic activists, the 2006 wave that swept across the country was not a result of Democratic voters rising up to take the country in an aggressively liberal direction. As Ron Brownstein has noted, "it was overwhelming support from moderates and independents rather than increased turnout among liberals or Democrats that powered the 2006 Democratic victories."[16] Gallop exit polling showed that, compared to recent elections where Republicans had prevailed, this time Democrats saw slight increases in their share of the vote across the board in multiple demographics. Writing about the Gallop results, Bill Bishop accurately said: "There wasn't a surge of votes from any one group, no realignment or stunning desertion. There was just one general—perhaps even momentary—change among a small percentage of the public."[17]

There was one important exception—a whopping eighteen-point Democratic advantage among independent voters.[18] In a midterm election where sixty-six races, including mine, were close enough for small swings of voter preference to have made the difference, that huge advantage among independents played the decisive role in Democrats winning control of the House. In words that would prove prophetic, Brownstein wrote that Democrats needed to govern "with the awareness that the swing voters who had created their majority could revoke it if they veered too far out of the mainstream."[19]

I was one of fifty-three newly elected members of Congress—forty Democrats and thirteen Republicans. It was a class of would-be reformers, hoping to bring to Washington a new spirit of cooperation. Writing about the new freshman class, Brownstein noted that "dozens of Democrats (and for that matter many Republicans) ran directly against the partisan polarization in Washington, stressed their independence, and promised to serve as bridge builders between the parties . . ."[20]

The week after the election, the new freshman class gathered for the first time at the Capitol Hill orientation for newly elected House members. In addition to meeting each other for the first time, we attended seminars about the legislative process and office procedures. Reporters were everywhere, trying to interview the rookie members in the hopes of capturing an interesting quote. It didn't take long.

"How to hire a chief of staff, how to hire other staff, how to stay out of jail," Michele Bachmann, the new representative-elect from Minnesota, told the *New York Times* as she described what she had learned during the orientation. "The usual things that congressmen need to know."[21]

The eccentric Bachmann was not the only member of our freshman class who would soon become well-known. Perhaps as a result of the historic nature of the House election, the class of 2006 had an unusual number of high-profile members,[22] including:

- KEITH ELLISON from Minnesota. The first Muslim to serve in Congress, Keith would be sworn into office using a Koran that had been owned by Thomas Jefferson.

- MARY FALLIN from Oklahoma. A conservative Republican, Mary would later become a popular governor of Oklahoma.

- GABBY GIFFORDS from Arizona. Fluent in Spanish, the former Fulbright scholar was elected to Congress at age thirty-five after being the youngest women ever elected to the Arizona Senate. A conservative Democrat with many friends on both sides of the aisle, Gabby's career would be tragically cut short when she was shot in the head at a public event in her Tucson district.

- KIRSTEN GILLIBRAND from New York. Elected in 2006 as a conservative Democrat representing the Hudson Valley, Kirsten won reelection in 2008 before being appointed to the Senate to replace Hillary Clinton, who vacated the seat to become Secretary of State.

- JOHN HALL from New York. The singer/songwriter is best known for founding the 1970s rock group *Orleans* and writing their hit songs "Still The One" and "Dance with Me."

- KEVIN MCCARTHY from California. A whip-smart, hard-charging Republican who oozed ambition, he surprised no one when he quickly rose up through the ranks to become House majority leader in only his fourth term in office.

- Former NFL quarterback HEATH SHULER. Elected to Congress from his home state of North Carolina, Heath was a runner-up for the Heisman Trophy and a first-round draft pick of the Washington Redskins. A conservative Democrat who would become chairman of the Blue Dog Coalition, Heath ran against Nancy Pelosi for Democratic leader following the 2010 Republican takeover of the House.

Dressed in a sparkling silver and black-checkered suit, Pelosi hosted a dinner in honor of the newest members of the Democratic Caucus. Circular tables of ten were arranged under the lights in the ornate Statuary Hall, just off the House floor in the Capitol. When I joined my freshmen colleagues in searching for our table assignments, I found to my surprise that I was to be seated right next to Pelosi and her husband Paul. During the dinner, we shared stories of our families and chatted about Pennsylvania politics and the conservative nature of my district. Pelosi then led the incoming freshmen on a walk-through of the House floor, taking pictures with each of us at the speaker's podium. There was a shared sense of unity and excitement at what was to come.

Two weeks later, Harvard's Institute of Politics (IOP) hosted its biennial program for newly elected members of Congress.[23] After every congressional election since 1972, Harvard's IOP has invited all incoming members to attend a multi-day, bipartisan conference featuring issue experts from the highest levels of government, academia, and business. The goal is to provide new members with intensive policy briefings on the major domestic and foreign policy issues of the day.[24] Although the program is highly respected, Republicans sometimes encourage their new members to skip the event due to concerns about its allegedly left-of-center bias.[25] Most years, the roster of attendees represents a solid bipartisan cross-section of the incoming class. In 2006, only one Republican attended—Vern Buchanan, a thoughtful and inquisitive Florida businessman with whom I would have many bipartisan policy discussions in the years to come.

On the first full day of the program, *Vanity Fair* corralled the newly elected members for a photoshoot for the magazine's upcoming spread titled "Blue is the New Red."[26] At lunch, Comedy Central personality Stephen Colbert, speaking in full satirical character, delivered a semi-funny, tongue-in-cheek speech that was more akin to a comedy routine than a keynote address. Whether Republican charges of political bias were real or imagined, the subsequent issue discussions were entirely bipartisan and much more serious.

The intensive material presented in the seminars reminded me of late-night cram sessions before a final exam. Issue experts would sit at the head of the table, leading in-depth discussions about major pending issues. The sessions were highly interactive, with members asking questions that frequently turned into lengthy policy discussions involving the entire group. The session on environmental policy featured three illustrious speakers, each of whom agreed that climate change is real and much of it is caused by human activity. As the conversation turned to the much more difficult discussion of potential solutions, Buchanan raised his hand.

"Wait, wait, wait. Hold on now, just a minute," he said, cutting off one of the speakers. "I thought this was supposed to be bipartisan. Where's the other side?" The IOP's associate director, David King, rushed to the front of the room. "Well, you see, Congressman, we tried to find somebody on the other side. The problem is, with this issue there is no other side." Buchanan silently shook his head as the program continued, although he would throughout his career establish a thoughtfully moderate position on climate change.

Stephen Colbert invited me to New York to tape a segment for his popular *Colbert Report* program. The segment would be part of his ongoing *Better Know a District* series, which featured satirical one-on-one interviews with members of Congress under the guise of talking about the districts they represented. During the new members' orientation in Washington, Rahm Emanuel strongly discouraged the rookies from going on Colbert's show due to the large number of members who had embarrassingly flopped on previous episodes. Colbert relished the opportunity to make politicians squirm, using politically inappropriate lines of questioning to put them in hilariously awkward positions. Over Rahm's objections, I decided to accept Colbert's offer and appear on the show.

In mid-December, we taped the segment in a hotel meeting room decorated to look like a congressional office. We chatted informally before the taping, and I presented him with a sweatshirt I had purchased in my district at Oakmont Country Club, site of the upcoming U.S. Open golf championship. Because the episode was scheduled to air weeks later, we talked during the interview as if I had already been sworn in.

There was one camera on me and one on him the entire time, filming every move we made. We talked for more than an hour, lightheartedly bantering back and forth. As the interview drew to a close, one of his assistants handed him a yellow legal pad with a long list of handwritten questions. He told me not to answer them, because he was just repeating some questions to make sure the camera angle was right. The camera zoomed in on him as he asked a series of questions I had never heard before. They were completely different from what we had talked about during the hour-long interview. I asked him if he was sure he didn't want me to answer. He smiled mischievously and said, "Don't worry, you already did."

As it turned out, the final segment that aired in January featured a mixture of questions, answers, and reaction shots from throughout our interview, all spliced together as though we had actually talked for only five minutes. It was very well done, and it turned out fine.

Channeling Partisanship

IN THE DAYS BEFORE AMERICANS HAD HUNDREDS OF CA-ble television options, people disinterested in politics were more likely to vote than those who are equally disinterested today. Why? Because today there are so many more entertainment options for individuals who want to avoid politics, whereas until the early 1980s, people generally had only a handful of channels from which to choose. Every night at the same time, the three major networks would broadcast the evening news. With no other options, viewers had to sit through the news or get up off the couch and turn off the television. Likewise, in earlier periods of the twentieth century, attendees at movie theaters became more politically aware because they had to sit through the newsreel feature before the movie began.[27]

Before cable television and the Internet, those who were not interested in government and current events gained unintentional exposure to it through the news, and were therefore more likely to vote. Now, with hundreds of channels from which to choose, television viewers uninterested in politics watch entertainment programming instead.[28] They used to sit through Walter Cronkite, because news was their only option, but now they change the channel to keep up with the latest escapes of the Kardashian sisters. I believe this helps explain in part why Donald Trump was able to attract early attention in the 2016 Republican primary from voters who normally only vote in general elections. Those sporadic voters were familiar with him and attracted to his persona as a reality television star, giving them reason to follow his race more closely and be motivated to go to the polls to support him.

The ability to avoid political news has had a detrimental impact on the voting participation of moderates, which in turn has led to increased polarization among voters, and by extension, the candidates from which they are able to choose.

In his landmark research on the topic, professor Markus Prior found: "For many of these less politically interested viewers, exposure to a few newscasts each week made the difference between voting and not voting. As the media environment changed, they could find content more to their liking than news. As a result, they stayed home on Election Day."[29] Simply put, "Exposure to political information increases the likelihood that an individual will go to the polls . . ."[30] This holds true in every part of the country.

Cincinnati, Denver, and Seattle each experienced decreased voter turnout and political engagement in areas served by their daily newspapers after those papers folded. Likewise, voter turnout is much higher in congressional districts where local media has covered the race than it is in districts where relatively less media coverage was provided.[31]

Ironically, increased media choice in the Information Age has actually increased the share of politically uninformed people.[32] Prior observes: "Even though Americans may consume more news, more Americans also tune out the news altogether." He adds, "although cable has fostered a core of 'news junkies' who immerse themselves in [television news], a more significant effect has been to contribute to a steep decline in the overall size of the news audience."[33]

Rather than using the hundreds of available television channels and their infinite choices of Internet content as a way to seek knowledge and learn about issues, many people instead use those resources as a way to avoid politics. As a result, those who seek political news and information have been found to be twice as likely to vote as people who prefer general entertainment content instead.[34]

"Technology simply facilitates participation of the more partisan news-seekers and abstention of the less partisan entertainment seekers," according to Prior, who astutely adds that "increasing the share of people who avoid news completely is not an indication of reduced political interest" among the overall electorate. It simply means those who are disinterested today are better able to avoid exposure to political news than when there were no other television options except the evening news. Greater choice in media options "leads to an increasing turnout gap between news junkies and entertainment fans." Those who choose entertainment news over political news are predominantly politically moderate, but their likelihood of voting decreases as their media choices increase. This impacts the way candidates position themselves for election and further polarizes those already in office.[35]

According to political scientists Larry Bartels and Wendy Rahn, failure to go to the polls often "results from a lack of knowledge of what government is doing and where parties and candidates stand, not from a knowledgeable rejection of government or parties . . . Exposure to political information is likely to increase peoples' political interest." This directly impacts polarization, because past exposure to broadcast news "motivated less educated citizens to go to the polls, but, being less partisan, they cast their votes based not on partisanship but on nonpartisan criteria . . ." When these less interested voters dropped off, the remaining pool of voters became proportionately more polarized.[36]

Multiple opinion surveys have shown voters' media preference to be directly related to increased voter polarization, particularly in low-turnout House elections. Prior writes that the "people who do not vote because increased media choice allows them to follow their preference for entertainment are among the least partisan members of the electorate."[37] To make matters worse, "news-seekers become more partisan after increased media choice allows them to watch more news. In fact, previous research suggests that more information makes people's views more partisan . . ."[38] It is no wonder Congress is more polarized than the nation as a whole when those who show up to vote are the most partisan citizens our nation has to offer.

Compounding the problem, the politically interested news seekers are selecting the sources of media that most closely align with their preconceived opinions and are filtering out programs that offer contrary points of view. Most Americans don't watch partisan cable television shows to begin with, but those who do are already ideologically committed. Their minds are made up and exposure to politically slanted messaging only reinforces their existing opinion.[39] If you know a person's position on key political issues, you can often safely guess their sources of informaiton.[40]

Discouraging Treason

WITH WASHINGTON ABUZZ ABOUT DEMOCRATS' NEW-found ability to win conservative-leaning seats that had for years eluded them, the 110th Congress convened amid optimism that the new centrist members might be the key to breaking through the gridlock and polarization that infected Congress. Unfortunately, that optimism proved to be short-lived. Although the success of centrist candidates had been the key to Democrats retaking control of Congress, ideologically driven advocacy groups wasted no time in setting the tone for the confrontation that was to come.

In the opening days of the new Congress, before incoming centrist members had a chance to catch their collective breath, activists from the liberal blogosphere joined forces with organized labor to create a new political action committee designed to make the newest Democratic members think twice before straying too far afield of party orthodoxy.

Called "Working For Us," the new Super PAC warned against moderation and compromise, vowing to promote and fund credible primary challenges against centrist Democrats "who vote to undermine the progressive economic agenda."[41] The announcement also included a "Top Offenders List"[42] of more senior Democratic incumbents deemed to be too willing to bargain with Republicans. As one who garnered substantial support from organized labor in my Western Pennsylvania district, the message could not have been more clear: "Either you toe the party line, or we'll find somebody else who will." Not quite the "Welcome to Washington" message I might have expected from my own party in my first few weeks on the job.

Political commentator Chris Cillizza wrote at the time that "Working For Us is modeled explicitly on the Club for Growth, an independent organization that over the last several election cycles has transformed itself into an electoral force by endorsing fiscally conservative candidates in contested primaries and then pouring hundreds of thousands of dollars into districts to help those candidates win."[43]

In the years since its 2007 start, Working For Us has never come close to achieving for Democrats the same power and influence that Club for Growth has sustained for Republicans. Working For Us has, however, fulfilled its promise of funding primary challenges against moderate Democrats across the country, including its high-profile but unsuccessful attempt to defeat Congressman Chris Van Hollen in Maryland's 2016 Democratic Senate primary. This despite the fact that Van Hollen would never be confused with a conservative, having loyally served in Nancy Pelosi's leadership team in the House.

Are the two parties better off for the existence of ideological groups like Club for Growth and Working For Us? Let's look at the facts:

When Working For Us was founded, Democrats had just regained the majority in Congress, thanks to the presence of dozens of newly minted freshmen members whose centrist messaging resonated with the moderate voters who had long ago abandoned the party. Democrats had realistic hopes for controlling the chamber for years to come. Instead, due in large part to uncompromising rhetoric and a party-line agenda that was perceived by moderate voters to be out-of-step with mainstream America, Democrats within two election cycles had lost almost all of the swing seats that had given them the majority in the first place. The most crucial losses came in the 2010 electoral tsunami, when Republicans gained control not only of Congress, but also governorships and state legislatures across the country—just in time for states to draw the new federal and state district boundaries as part of decennial redistricting. The few surviving centrists were then targeted for defeat by extreme elements within their own party, effectively killing the last remaining opportunity to bridge the partisan divide in Congress.

The results for the Republican Party are mixed. Club for Growth-backed lawmakers played a major role in Republicans' 2010 takeover of the House, but they also helped to create an environment so toxic that the House became all but unmanageable. The divide in the party has become so pronounced that when Speaker Paul Ryan speaks about "working with both sides," he is just as likely to be talking about working with both sides of his own party as he is about working with Democrats. The open hostility toward compromise and negotiation, which has fractured the national Republican Party, was emboldened by groups like Club for Growth and has further widened the ideological division between the two parties.

Republicans solidified their power in 2016, but the Club for Growth played little role in President Trump's victory, having openly opposed his candidacy for most of the campaign. However, after a relatively unsuccessful primary season, Club for Growth supported several members of Congress who survived close calls in the general election, giving the organization continued influence within the party.

The presence of these types of groups—whose sole purpose is to discourage bipartisan compromise—incentivizes candidates to eschew moderation and move further toward the extremes. The fact that Working For Us appeared on the scene at the precise moment Speaker Pelosi was initiating her new centrist members goes a long way towards explaining the pressures faced by the incoming class of moderates and the events that would lead to their eventual demise. All of this has combined to dissuade compromise and contribute to the polarization we see in Congress today.

Unfortunately, the problem continues to get worse. In February 2017, liberals associated with the failed presidential primary campaign of Senator Bernie Sanders launched a new PAC targeting centrist Democrats for primaries. Menacingly named "WeWillReplaceYou.org,"[44] the group somehow misses the irony that their affiliated social media hashtag #AllofUs seems comically inconsistent with their stated goal of purging from the party those the group deems to be ideologically impure. The first order of business for the group was to organize primary challenges against Democratic senators who opposed using the filibuster to prevent President Trump's Supreme Court nominee, now-Justice Neil Gorsuch, from receiving a confirmation vote on the floor of the Senate.

Partisan activists on both sides look at compromise as something akin to treason, a crime worthy of political death in the form of a primary challenge to the offending "DINO" or "RINO"— Democrat or Republican "In Name Only." Jonathan Rauch captures it perfectly when he writes, "even when Republicans and Democrats do find something to work together on, the threat of an extremist primary challenge funded by a flood of outside money makes them think twice—or not at all. Opportunities to make bipartisan legislative compromise slip away."[45]

Even members of Congress with rock solid partisan credentials can fall victim to a primary challenge from the extreme if they are portrayed as even having considered compromise. Rauch references what has become perhaps the most infamous example:

> WALLED SAFELY INSIDE their gerrymandered districts, incumbents are insulated from general election challengers that might pull them toward the political center, but they are perpetually vulnerable to primary challengers from extremists who pull them toward the fringes. Everyone worries about being the next Eric Cantor, the Republican House majority leader who, in a shocking upset, lost to an unknown Tea Partier in his 2014 primary.[46]

A 2016 University of North Carolina (UNC) research experiment showed just how deeply ingrained opposition to compromise can become. The study found the importance of a particular issue, or its personal relevance to the activist, has little to no impact on the activist's opposition to compromise. "If the other side is for it, then I'm against it," goes the familiar refrain. Add to the mix a moral conviction—a feeling of certainty that they are right—then you can forget it; the partisan is unpersuadable.

The UNC experiment was carried out using people with various levels of partisan commitment. To frame the study, scientists chose the issue of Social Security because necessary reforms are politically difficult and attitudes among partisans are therefore often irrational. Study participants were sorted by their level of partisanship—moderate to extreme. They were asked about their own views on Social Security, then presented with information about two fictional congressional candidates who held views identical to the participant. The only difference between the two candidates was that one of them was "negotiable" on various Social Security reform options, while the other opposed compromise. As expected, support for the candidate willing to compromise was inversely related to the participant's level of partisanship.[47]

Taking it a step further, study participants were offered money as a test of their partisan commitment. They could select the amount, but offsetting funds would be donated to an organization to which the respondent would be philosophically

opposed, such as the Tea Party Patriots in the case of an extreme liberal. If the participant chose no money, the organization would also get no money, but if the participant took the
maximum amount—four dollars—the organization would get
five dollars. If the participant chose a middle option—three dollars—the organization would get the same amount. The middle
choice was the least popular option. Refusing any money was
the most popular choice among both liberals and conservatives,
apparently willing to forgo their own financial gain to prevent
their political opponents from benefiting.[48]

A 2016 Pew Research Center survey found that the most
partisan Americans overwhelmingly defined compromise as
an agreement where their own side gets more. The trend was
slightly higher among Democrats, but large majorities of partisans from both parties were guilty of expecting the opposing
side to give up more than their own if an agreement was to be
reached. On the other hand, among those who are less ideologically driven, the results were the exact opposite. Majorities of
the most moderate Americans believed that compromise meant
the other side should get at least as much or more than their
own side.[49] For those concerned about Congress's inability to
work together, it's not hard to see where the problem lies.

CHAPTER 4

FINANCING THE GAVEL

———·◆·———

Special Orders

IN 1978, AN OBSCURE HISTORY PROFESSOR AT TINY WEST Georgia College won election to the US House of Representatives on his third try.[1] Right from the start of his career in Congress, Newt Gingrich was recognized as a rising star with a lethal combination of visionary intelligence, ruthless determination, and blinding ambition. It didn't take long for him to make his mark.

He began his term the same year C-SPAN began its gavel-to-gavel broadcasts of every House session. Gingrich set out on a long-term strategy to dislodge Democrats from control of Congress for the first time since 1955. He assembled a band of like-minded true believers who adopted a confrontational style designed to provoke Democrats into overreaching retaliation. It worked like a charm. Things came to a head six years later as legendary House Speaker Tip O'Neill finally gave Gingrich the spotlight he so desperately craved.[2]

The House has a tradition of "Special Orders" speeches, which are usually delivered after the close of regular House business. Special Orders speeches allow members of Congress the opportunity to reserve time to speak for up to an hour on any subject they wish. House rules dictated that the C-SPAN cameras remained fixed on the speaker without panning across the chamber, which was inevitably empty for the late-night sessions.

Gingrich, who was often joined in the speeches by other conservative colleagues, took full advantage of this rule, using his time to harshly criticize the Democratic-controlled Congress as corrupt, while carefully avoiding violating House rules against personal attacks against individual members. He would flamboyantly turn and motion to what the television audience believed were other members in attendance, pointing as though he was confronting people sitting right in front of him. This infuriated Speaker O'Neill, who had grown to detest Gingrich and his tactics.[3]

Gingrich's late-night performances developed a small but loyal cult following. Rush Limbaugh, then a young local radio broadcaster, later claimed to have been a regular viewer.[4] In an attempt to embarrass Gingrich and his followers, O'Neill ordered the C-SPAN cameras to pan across the chamber, exposing the fact that Gingrich had been standing in front of empty seats. Undeterred, Gingrich continued his antics until tensions boiled over. An exasperated O'Neill finally spoke out against Gingrich, but in his anger used language that violated House rules against directly impugning another member. The subsequent parliamentary ruling led to a rebuke against the speaker and a celebration among Gingrich's colleagues. The incident received widespread media attention, dramatically raising Gingrich's profile and paving the way for his rise into House leadership.[5]

In the years ahead, Gingrich grew more powerful and escalated his war to delegitimize Congress. Democrats played right into his hands by modifying House rules to tighten their grip on the majority, further marginalizing the minority Republicans.[6] He used ethics charges as a weapon, leading to the eventual resignation of Speaker Jim Wright following an investigation Gingrich initiated. When a bipartisan banking scandal engulfed the House, public opinion against congressional excess had finally reached a tipping point.[7]

Gingrich spent the first two years of Bill Clinton's presidency rallying his troops in a successful effort to demonize and delegitimize the president, including killing his signature health care reform plan. After the Republican landslide in the 1994 midterm elections, Gingrich finally achieved his goal of winning the Speaker's gavel. His subsequent overreach is well documented. After two government shutdowns, the impeachment of the president and some scandals of his own, Gingrich stepped down after four years as speaker.

The Caucus

THE NEXT TIME A TRANSITION OF POWER OCCURRED IN the House was in 2007, when Nancy Pelosi won the gavel following the thirty-seat Democratic gain. Even before being sworn in as new members of the House, the Democratic freshman were asked to clear their calendars every Wednesday when Congress was in session for a recurring 9:00 a.m. group meeting with Speaker Pelosi in the conference room of her Capitol office suite. She rarely missed the meetings, which would continue on schedule for all four years of her speakership.

Pelosi used the meetings to talk about the upcoming congressional agenda and current political issues. She always allowed attendees to ask questions and voice concerns. She seemed legitimately interested in hearing about what was happening in each of our constituencies, always paying particularly close attention to the concerns of members from swing districts, where moderate constituents could easily become dissatisfied with a Congress they perceived to be veering too far to the left. She was fond of pointing out that "your title is 'representative' for a reason," meaning we should always be comfortable representing our districts, even if it occasionally meant voting against her priorities. She frequently claimed that "nothing is more important" to her than our reelections. The centrists were, after all, the reason Democrats were in the majority in the first place.

Sometimes her meetings featured an interesting guest, such as a committee chairman with whom the group would discuss and provide input on pending legislation. Sometimes there was a *really* interesting guest, like the time Pelosi brought superstar musician Bono into a meeting to lead an hour-long discussion about poverty in Africa. I was impressed by Bono's depth and genuine passion for the issue to which he has devoted countless hours of his time and millions of dollars of his own money. He was well informed about the various policy options and spoke in bipartisan terms, going out of his way to commend President Bush for his commitment to stemming the AIDS epidemic in

Africa. Seeming to speak directly to those of us at the table who represented conservative-leaning districts, he said he recognized that foreign aid might not be politically popular, but he believed it was the right thing to do. He made a compelling case, and his presence at the meeting helped raise awareness about an issue that is often missing from America's political dialogue.

It wasn't long before the freshman Democrats formed their own dedicated speaking group, taking advantage of the same Special Orders rules that had fueled Gingrich's rise. At first, I and other centrist freshmen attended regularly and joined the group in speaking about whatever issues Congress was currently debating. The freshman Special Orders group then scheduled recurring planning meetings to take place in Pelosi's office suite just prior to our Wednesday morning meetings with the Speaker. Predictably, this arrangement quickly morphed into just another distribution channel to promote the Democratic talking points. When it became clear that some of those talking points would not play well in moderate districts, centrist participation dwindled.

The weekly meetings of the entire Democratic Caucus had a similar evolution during Pelosi's two terms as speaker. At first, there was great enthusiasm for the new centrists and a recognition that they had come from districts that Democrats had not been able to win in recent election cycles. After Pelosi and her leadership team would open the caucus meetings with a pep talk and updates on pending legislation and other political matters, members would rise to ask questions or speak about issues of importance to them.

Even with the infusion of new centrists, the caucus was still overwhelmingly liberal. After the initial honeymoon period wore off, noticeable tension existed among the group as groans and eye rolls would occur when the centrists encouraged a more moderate course. The fissure would grow as time went by, especially when a new class of centrist Democrats came in after the 2008 election cycle. Particularly frustrating to the liberals was the fact that many of them had contributed money from their campaigns to help the centrists win their seats, only to see those same members advocate against liberal causes.

Until most of the centrists were either defeated or just stopped speaking at the meetings, speeches at the caucus gatherings followed a familiar script. A few moderate members rose to talk about how the issue of the day was not well received in their districts, often relaying anecdotes about personal interactions with outraged constituents. Then, a long line of liberal members elected to safe seats would preach about the righteousness of their cause and quote from select national polls that supported their position. From the perspective of their safely drawn districts, these members couldn't understand how anyone in the caucus might have a different point of view.

To her credit, Pelosi did a masterful job of juggling the varied interests as she managed the meetings. She knew she needed the votes of at least some of the centrists to pass her preferred legislation, and she worked hard to cultivate and appease them. But after major Democratic losses in 2010 and 2014, the Democrats regained and solidified their minority status. By that point, the centrists were gone, and speakers at the caucus meetings would be left to preach solely to the choir.

After Democrats under-performed yet again in the 2016 elections, some House Democrats expressed dissatisfaction with Pelosi and the direction of the Democratic Party. She easily survived a challenge to her leadership, even as Democrats continue to debate how best to respond to their most-recent electoral drubbing.

Call Time

IT TOOK EXACTLY ONE WEEK AFTER BEING SWORN IN FOR centrist Democrats to have their attention directed toward fundraising for the next election. On the evening of January 11, 2007, the Democratic leadership convened a meeting of freshman Democrats who were thought to be vulnerable in the 2008 general election. Other members of the caucus were invited as well, in part to show support, but also to encourage their continued financial commitment to the freshmen who were responsible for Democrats being in the majority.

Members were still filing through the well-stocked dinner buffet line as House leaders began their presentation, walking the freshmen through a slide show outlining the difficult task ahead—raising enough money to scare away any credible Republicans who might be considering a race. Information was presented about the astronomical cost of running a successful reelection campaign in a nationally targeted district.

"Campaigns are won in the off-year," emphasized outgoing DCCC chairman Rahm Emanuel, speaking about the need to build a substantial campaign war chest in order to show strength and discourage potential challengers. (I had already heeded his advice, having scheduled my first Washington fundraiser for the next morning).

The overriding message of the first of what would be many similar meetings was that fundraising should always be top of mind. Slack off, and you will dig yourself into a hole. Another unsubtle point was that the DCCC would only help members who helped themselves. Don't count on the DCCC coming in to bail you out if you haven't raised enough money on your own to run a viable race. We were told not to become complacent with our success in winning the first time during a historic wave election. Although it was possible to run a poor race and be swept into office on a wave of public discontent, the degree of difficulty is magnified once you take office. We were told there was simply no margin for error the second time around, when we would all have voting records to defend.

The discussion reminded me of an amusing but poignant conversation I had with Democratic Congressman John Barrow, whom I first met two months earlier during my congressional orientation. Barrow represented a strongly Republican district in the heart of deep red Georgia. First elected in 2004—a rough year for Democrats nationally—Barrow liked to joke that he "won swing districts before it was cool to win swing districts"—a reminder that there were a few centrists within the Democratic Caucus before the arrival of the much-heralded Class of 2006, whose election was helped considerably by a category five hurricane-force tail wind.

Barrow came across as somewhat eccentric, but that was by design. A successful trial attorney, Barrow cultivated the "small-town country lawyer" persona, which he played to perfection. His white hair, Southern drawl, and subtly sarcastic wit came right out of central casting. In his hard-fought reelection battle in a newly drawn rural Georgia district, his opponent made an issue of Barrow's degree from Harvard Law School and his use of big words like "assimilate." Barrow responded by closing his next campaign advertisement with: "I approve of this message, and I approve of them Dawgs, too," referencing his undergraduate degree from the University of Georgia.[8]

During a break in the orientation, Barrow approached me to introduce himself. He put his arm around my shoulders and spoke about the widely held perception that many members of the incoming freshmen class were flukes. "Son, throughout history, there's been a lot of people who got elected to this House by accident," he said quietly as he glanced around the room. "But there ain't nobody—nobody—who ever got *reelected* by accident." Although he delivered it softly, I heard his message loud and clear.

It is a misconception that all members of Congress spend inordinate amounts of time fundraising. Some do, but many do not. Congressional leaders will travel all over the country raising money, and some safe seat members dedicate substantial time to raising money for their party. But for the most part, rank-and-file House members do not wake up each day thinking about fundraising to sustain their own campaigns. Because the majority of House members occupy safe seats where a viable election challenge is unlikely, the amount of money necessary to win reelection is much less compared to a member representing a targeted swing seat. For the approximately 20% of House members who represent those swing seats, fundraising is not just an unwelcome distraction but an unavoidable fact of everyday life. These members are all but guaranteed to have a well-financed general election challenge, so they spend much more of their time raising money. Simply put, representing a swing district is more expensive than a safe seat. It's another key factor in understanding what it is like to be a centrist on Capitol Hill.

A quick look at the daily schedule for any House member from a competitive district will reveal large blocks of time dedicated to "call time," the euphemistic name for the "dialing for dollars" fundraising that almost all swing seat House members have to do to have any chance to be reelected. Freshman senators, for their part, are told to spend at least *four hours a day* on fundraising.[9]

This is how it works: For hours at a time, members will call through pre-sorted lists of potential donors, some of whom the member has never met. Calls go to both wealthy individuals and to directors of Political Action Committees. I preferred PAC calls because the people on the other end of the line are used to receiving fundraising calls. It's their job and they do it all day long. It's all part of the game. Calling individuals seemed more intrusive to me, and it was much more unpleasant. Over time, the member ends up calling the same people over and over again. Individuals who have given multiple times remain on the call list, even though they thought they had done their part after contributing the first time. Asking people for money is never fun. The monotonous routine is degrading and extremely frustrating.

Cell phones have made the process more mobile, but many members still do their daily fundraising calls from the office buildings of each party's national headquarters. Throughout each and every day Congress is in session, members can be seen going in and out of their respective party's office building. If floor votes occur during call time, the member leaves the call sheets at the desk, walks the few blocks over the Capitol, then returns to call time after the votes.

Most weeks, members will also host one or more fundraising events benefiting their campaigns. The PAC calls are made in the hope that one of the PAC's lobbyists will bring a check to an upcoming event. Breakfast events are popular because they do not run the risk of conflicting with votes, but lunch and dinner fundraisers, as well as happy-hour receptions, are equally common. Committee hearings, floor votes, and other business of the House are scheduled specifically to give members time to attend morning and evening fundraising events. Often, members will stop by their colleagues' events to lend support and greet the roomful of paid guests. Back home in the district, fundraisers are almost always hosted by local campaign supporters and are sometimes headlined by a prominent national political figure to help increase attention for the event.

Like many members, I always tried to increase interest by hosting fundraisers in unique venues. Concerts and sporting events were particularly popular, and over the years I held fundraisers at professional sports and NCAA tournament basketball games in Washington and in Pittsburgh. The atmosphere at those events is always more relaxed, making the fundraising aspect more tolerable.

Many members will host signature events that become popular annual getaways for Washington's lobbying elite, such as a weekend in South Beach, ski vacations in Colorado, or suite tickets for the Grammys. Representing Western Pennsylvania, my options for exciting destination events were more limited, but I did the best I could to find ways to make the fundraisers fun. In addition to sporting events, I held an annual summer golf outing and an early spring skeet shoot. I once held a fundraiser at the Washington office of one of the major gaming technology companies, inviting guests to try out the newest virtual reality and video games. Although some of these events were fun, the day-to-day drudgery of fundraising calls is easily one of the least appealing parts of the job for any member of Congress.

Fundraising has become so important that it is commonplace for it to be covered in the media.[10] Every quarter, when campaigns are required to release their fundraising results, journalists and pundits speculate on the "winners and losers," judging the strength and viability of candidates based upon their most-recent fundraising numbers. Media stories on campaign fundraising resemble sports reports, with comparisons of the cash-on-hand position of candidates, along with highlights of notable contributors. With the onslaught of independent outside groups, the playing field has expanded to the degree that rarely a day goes by without one or more of the daily political journals mentioning campaign finance activities.

Attempts to limit the influence of money in American politics are nothing new, dating back more than a century to the Tillman Act, which banned direct campaign contributions from corporations. Without fail, every attempt to close one window into which money flows results in the opening of another.

The US Supreme Court first ruled on campaign finance in 1921. In subsequent decades, the court would make at least two dozen more campaign finance rulings, some of which contradicted previous opinions. Direct contributions from unions were banned under the 1947 Taft-Hartley labor relations bill, which resulted in the formation of the first PAC. In order to get around the ban on direct contributions, the AFL-CIO created an independent PAC to which union members could contribute. That money would then be distributed to campaigns through the PAC. In the late 1980s, after several legal, legislative, and regulatory challenges and modifications solidified their legitimacy, PACs proliferated as corporations and single-issue interest groups formed them as a way to direct money to preferred candidates.[11]

It wasn't long before another loophole was exposed, that which allowed individuals, corporations, and unions to contribute unlimited funds to state and local party organizations. Known as "soft money," these unlimited funds became the primary mechanism for big-money interests to influence the system. This led to the 2002 McCain-Feingold campaign finance reform bill, which banned soft money and was hailed by supporters as a major step forward in limiting the influence of money in politics.[12] Nothing could have been further from the truth.

The problem gets worse with each succeeding election cycle. During the 2004 presidential election, outside groups MoveOn.org and Swift Boat Veterans for Truth took turns blasting George Bush and John Kerry, airing a series of harshly negative ads funded by money that fell outside the scope of the McCain-Feingold ban. By the 2006 midterm elections, more of these types of groups had appeared, including VoteVets, the liberal-leaning anti-war group that ran the devastating negative ad targeting my opponent, Melissa Hart. More still would arrive by 2008, combining to spend hundreds of millions of dollars on the presidential and congressional races that year.

Then the floodgates opened. The 2010 Supreme Court decision in the *Citizens United* case helped clear the way for corporations, unions, and other entities to funnel unlimited sums of money into "Super PACs" that could spend the money to influence elections. Super PACs may collect money to spend in support of candidates or issues, but may not coordinate with or contribute directly to campaigns.

Machiavellian political consultant Karl Rove soon found one more loophole, which pertained to politically inclined social welfare nonprofit organizations under section 501(c)(4) of the IRS code. Created for nonprofit advocacy groups that spend less than half their resources directly influencing campaigns, this section of the IRS code allows contributions to these groups to remain anonymous, meaning the names of donors are not publicly disclosed. Money contributed through these nonprofit advocacy groups has become known as "dark money" because their donors are untraceable.[13]

In addition to subverting campaign finance laws, the proliferation of these outside groups has played a major role in increasing the level of political polarization. These types of "private groups," as Jonathan Rauch points out, "are much harder to regulate, less transparent, and less accountable than are the parties and candidates," which only leads to more extremism. "Because they thrive on purism, protest and parochialism, the outside groups are driving politics toward polarization, extremism and short-term gain."[14]

The result has been an unprecedented infusion of money into the political process. An astonishing $3.8 billion was spent during the 2014 midterm elections, a total that was eclipsed in 2016, when more than $4 billion was spent *just on congressional elections*. So much uncoordinated outside money is spent in congressional races that candidates frequently lose control of the message.[15] Even Super PACs that want to help a candidate can sometimes play off-key, airing ads that contradict the candidate's message or focus on issues that don't resonate in the district. This is a concern even among presidential candidates. During the 2016 Republican presidential primary, Senator Ted Cruz voiced frustration that outside groups were running ads that were inconsistent with his message: "I'm left to just hope that what they say bears some resemblance to what I actually believe."[16]

Congressional candidates may spend as much of their own money on their campaigns as they want, but they are only allowed to raise funds through contributions from individuals and regular PACs, both of which are subject to strict contribution limits. To try to accumulate the resources necessary to compete with the flood of outside money, it is not uncommon today for individual candidates to have Super PACs dedicated solely to supporting their own campaign. As of mid-2017, there were approximately 2,400 Super PACs registered to raise and spend money on federal campaigns.[17] As if to make a complete mockery of the requirement that Super PACs and campaigns not coordinate, some so-called "independent" Super PACs are organized and run by family friends or close confidants of the candidate. The problem continues to get worse, with no end in sight.

The proliferation of dark money and our Wild West campaign finance system unquestionably moves our political system toward the extremes. But individual contributions to campaigns also increase polarization. Most Americans never contribute money to a political campaign, and those who do overwhelmingly make only small contributions. Individual donors, especially small donors, are more likely to be ideologically outside the mainstream.

Those at the far extremes of the political spectrum contribute to campaigns at twice the national average.[18] Political scientists

Michael Barber and Nolan McCarty have identified this as one of the biggest drivers of congressional polarization, writing that "an increasing reliance of candidates on ideologically extreme individual donors" will necessitate candidates to move their message toward the extremes in order to raise money.[19] A similar study found "a direct connection between the rise in individual contributions and polarization in American politics." Unsurprisingly, the study confirmed that "the candidates who are most reliant on individual contributions tend to have more extreme voting records."[20]

A comparison of states with different campaign finance regulations showed "there is significantly more legislative polarization in states that allow unlimited individual contributions than in those that place tight constraints on individuals."[21] Given this fact, few would be surprised to learn that votes cast by members of Congress track much more closely to the sources of their campaign contributions than to the views of their constituents.[22] Stanford professor Bruce Cain says this "disconnect between elite behavior and public opinion frustrates many centrist and less politically engaged voters."[23] Truer words were never spoken.

While small donors drive candidates toward the extremes,[24] it is the relative handful of wealthy mega-donors who dominate the campaign finance system. Inequality in campaign contributions is exponentially greater than inequality in income.[25] The percentage of campaign contributions from the super-rich has been going up steadily since the late 1980s, but it has skyrocketed since the *Citizens United* ruling. How rich are we talking about? Consider this: almost 40% of all money contributed to influence federal campaigns is given by those in the top 0.01% of income.[26] Stop and think about that for a moment.

Contrary to popular opinion, contributions from standard PACs—not to be confused with Super PACs, which may not contribute directly to candidates—generally have a far less polarizing effect on candidates than individual contributions. This is because PAC contributions are often motivated by specific policies important to the organizations the PAC represents. Because PACs are also much more concerned than individuals about having access to members of Congress, it is not unusual for PACs to contribute to members of both parties and to change the proportional amounts they give to each party based upon who happens to control Congress at the time.[27] This is one of the reasons why it is problematic that maximum individual campaign contribution limits are indexed for inflation while PAC contributions are not. With each passing election cycle, individual contributions become comparatively more influential.

The proliferation of ideologically driven Super PACs with unlimited resources and the willingness to intervene in primaries has incentivized candidates to move toward the extremes.[28] Today, running a campaign from the center dramatically increases the chance of a well-funded primary challenge.[29] In writing about the wealthy donors who contribute to the Super PACs that fund primaries, Jonathan Haidt accurately points out that the outside money that comes into a district incentivizes "politicians to please wealthy donors and pressure groups that have more extreme views than the voters in their own districts."[30] This leads to more polarization and less room for compromise and moderation in Congress.

The Lion of the Senate

DURING CONSIDERATION OF THE ANNUAL DEFENSE AUthorization bill, I offered an amendment to allow the immediate families of military servicemen and women to use the Family and Medical Leave Act to take time off from work to deal with matters related to deployment. The amendment passed and was included in the House version of the bill but had not been addressed in the Senate. I was named to the House-Senate conference committee, which was tasked with ironing out differences in the bill and agreeing to a final version.

The Defense Authorization bill authorizes funding for the nation's military activities—both foreign and domestic—as well as various national security programs. The nation was engaged in an active two-front war, so timely completion of the bill was critically important. The war in Iraq was at its peak, and during debate on the authorization much time was devoted to America's future involvement in the conflict. The process dragged on for months as votes occurred on a variety of subjects, not all of which were directly related to military issues.

During Senate deliberation of their version of the bill, Senator Edward Kennedy inserted language expanding the federal hate crimes statute to include crimes motivated by a victim's gender, sexual orientation, or gender identity. The language had passed as stand-alone legislation in both the House and Senate, so there was no doubt that a majority of the Congress supported the measure. Nevertheless, a political firestorm ensued, threatening to derail the entire authorization bill.

The controversy was over the fact that Kennedy was using the Defense Authorization bill to try to force President Bush to sign into law a hate crimes provision he opposed. The hate crimes language was not included in the House bill and it wasn't long before President Bush issued a formal veto threat over Kennedy's amendment. As the conference committee met to hammer out an agreement, the fate of the hate crimes language remained a major sticking point. Republicans strongly opposed inclusion of the language, so a special strategy session was called involving only the Democratic members on the conference committee. We gathered in a meeting room in the basement of the Capitol, where the legendary Senator Kennedy settled in for a fight.

The early December meeting had an informal feel, with a group of chairs arranged haphazardly in a configuration somewhat resembling a circle. Right from the start, it was clear the majority of those in attendance wanted to finalize the bill without including Kennedy's hate crimes language. The inescapable fact was we simply did not have enough votes to override a presidential veto. The majority opinion in the room was that including the hate crimes language would guarantee failure and unnecessarily delay the process. Many of us feared that Democrats would be accused of endangering the welfare of our troops in order to pursue an unrelated social agenda. Although most of us supported the goal of Kennedy's language, we did not want to delay the necessary funding and policy changes related to the wars based on an extraneous battle we knew we couldn't win.

Kennedy sat silently as members, one-by-one, offered reasons why the hate crimes language should not be included. He allowed members to speak uninterrupted, but his body language conveyed his fury. He sighed. He fidgeted. His face turned a bold shade of red. He shook his head and looked to the ceiling in exasperation as the same points were made over and over. Finally, he had had enough.

Moving to the edge of his seat, he inserted himself into the conversation: "You all think you know something about politics, and I guess most of you do because you wouldn't be sitting in this room if you didn't." His voice grew louder as he continued. Pointing to his chest and putting slow, deliberate emphasis on the last three words of his next sentence, he bellowed: "But let me tell you something. I know politics!" In no uncertain terms, he informed the group that we were going to include the hate crimes language in the bill and send it to the White House. Let us put George Bush in the position of having to justify delaying the bill over a social agenda. Why did the Democrats have to be the unpatriotic ones when we did our job and sent the bill to Bush? By vetoing it, he is responsible for the delay and the consequences, Kennedy argued.

All good points, but the group voted to remove the hate crimes language. Every eye in the room was on Kennedy as the meeting continued. Without another word, he angrily stared straight ahead, arms crossed in front of him, breathing heavily and shaking his head. After several minutes, he rose from his seat and quietly walked out of the room.

Postscript: The conference committee finalized the bill without the hate crimes language, but Bush unexpectedly vetoed it anyway. The remaining dispute was over disbursement of confiscated Iraqi assets. The bill would finally become law a month later. The hate crimes language also eventually became law, but sadly, Kennedy would not live to see it. He died two months before President Obama signed it into law in October 2009.

In the District

NEARLY EVERY WEEKEND AND RECESS PERIOD, I HELD town hall and "Congress on Your Corner" meetings across the district. I also attended as many community events as I could. The encounters weren't always pleasant.

One Friday night in late March, I traveled home after a long week in Washington. That evening, I took my nine- and six-year-old daughters to dinner at a Lenten fish fry at a Catholic church in a heavily Republican community near our home. After paying the donation to attend, we went through the serving line and were carrying our trays back to our table when an older man I had never met rose from his seat to confront me.

"How dare you show your face around here," he said angrily as he stood in front of me, swaying and steadying himself against a chair as he fidgeted with his suspenders. I told my daughters to continue over to our dinner table, then stayed to listen as the man referenced a few of the recent actions of the new Congress with which he disapproved. He didn't care that I had actually voted the way he would have wanted on most of the issues he mentioned.

"You voted Nancy Pelosi for speaker, so you're just as much to blame as she is," he scoffed. People nearby clapped and nodded in approval. I asked him if it would be okay for me to slide by him to go join my daughters. As I sat down, I noticed one of the church volunteers who had been working the front door was making his way over to me. In my head, I was preparing my response to his inevitable apology. Instead, he leaned down and said firmly: "I think its best that you leave. We've had some complaints and don't want to cause a commotion. This isn't a political event." I asked if we could finish our dinner first. He reluctantly agreed.

When members of Congress talk to constituents across the district, they learn what issues are important to them. These conversations impact the way members approach their jobs in Washington and can bring to their attention new issues that they might otherwise have missed.

Around the same time as the church fish fry, I had a much more pleasant visit to New Castle, spending the day in scheduled meetings with various constituents. I met with a large group of veterans concerned about what they believed to be America's inevitable retreat from Iraq, as well as their outrage about the way returning veterans were being treated. In time, I would win them over as I made veterans' issues a top priority, but in these early days of my first term, they were still skeptical.

Later, I visited with Stephen Vitale, owner of Pyrotecnico, a multi-generational family business that has grown into one of the largest fireworks companies in America. We talked about the impediments to dealing with foreign suppliers, especially the Chinese, as well as the need for more rational regulations for transport of fireworks across state lines. Stephen and I would become friends, and I relied on his sound advice in helping me think through legislative issues related to fireworks. Because it was an important employer in my district, I became one of Congress's leading advocates for the domestic fireworks industry.

I ended the New Castle visit by traveling a few miles outside of town to visit the nearby Amish community. Because the

Amish don't use modern technology, I had one of my friends from New Castle travel there in advance to confirm a late afternoon appointment with Chris Byler, the community's bishop. I first met Chris during my campaign, and we had subsequently built a good rapport. He was working in the shed next to his home when we arrived. Wearing traditional Amish clothing, he removed his hat and invited me and my staff assistant to join him inside his home, as was the custom.

Visiting Amish country truly is like traveling back in time. With electricity strictly forbidden, the bishop's home had the feel of a nineteenth century farmhouse. We met in the "sitting room" near the front door as the bishop's wife was doing her ironing nearby. She excitedly explained that her iron was a "new gadget," apparently meaning it was more "modern" than what she had been using before. I noticed the iron was heated by a lit flame that seemed to me to come too close for comfort to the linens she was pressing, not to mention the kerosene-filled cup attached to the iron. My staff assistant and I glanced at each other with a look of concern. "Should we warn her about this?" we both thought. I decided not to say anything, figuring she knew much more about these newfangled "gadgets" than I did.

Chris Byler does not have the appearance of the prototypical Amish bishop that one might picture in their mind. Slight in build and shy in demeanor, he is unassuming and not the least bit intimidating. During my visits, he always enjoyed talking politics, especially his pet issues of agriculture and trains.

Members of Byler's community do not drive, but they are allowed to ride in cars and trains. He often shared with me printed publications pertaining to the latest controversies over federal funding for Amtrak, with the key parts circled in ink. During this particular visit, he talked about another issue. He spoke with great concern about a proposed federal policy related to a recent outbreak of mad cow disease in Europe. Fearing the requirement to account for the lineage of his cattle would be overly burdensome and an infringement upon his community's religious freedom, he encouraged me to oppose the measure. I told him I would look into it to see what could be done. (It turned out that his concern was widespread and a modification was approved to exempt the Amish from some of the requirements).

I visited Byler about once a year, and we exchanged occasional letters. At election time, I would respectfully ask for his vote and for his help in spreading the word around his two thousand-member community. Because the community is traditionally one of the most conservative areas of the district, I knew my request was a long shot. I never came close to winning there, but I enjoyed the experience and always looked forward to visiting.

Helping a constituent does not always come easy; sometimes even the smallest issues can fall prey to partisan politics. During a late February visit to tiny Springdale Borough along the Allegheny River, I learned of plans that were underway to commemorate the one hundredth anniversary of the birth of Springdale's favorite daughter, the legendary environmentalist Rachel Carson. Best known for her relentless advocacy against the use of chemical pesticides, Carson authored the best-selling book *Silent Spring*, which warned of the dangers of the misuse of DDT. With her May 27th birthday anniversary upcoming, I asked if there was anything I could do to help with the celebration. After discussing various options, I agreed to try to name the borough's small post office building after Carson, who died in 1964. I returned to Washington and introduced a bill to do just that. Little did I realize how big a can of worms I had just opened.

Renaming a post office is almost always noncontroversial. In order for the House to bring the bill to the floor for a vote, it must be cosponsored by the entire delegation of the state where the post office is located. Most post offices are named for deceased officials of local renown, including military heroes or significant historical figures.[31] To be considered, the bill also has to pass out of the committee of jurisdiction, which investigates the appropriateness of the proposed renaming. Only after clearing those hurdles can the bill be brought to the floor for a vote, which by that point is almost always a formality. Bills renaming post offices routinely pass unanimously.

When my bill finally came to the floor on April 23, I expected smooth sailing. There was still more than enough time to get it through Congress and to the president's desk in time for Carson's birthday celebration five weeks later. As the vote transpired, I immediately noticed there was a problem. Dozens of votes were registering against the renaming. Noticing the no votes were all coming from the Republican side, I walked over to the Republican leader, John Boehner, and asked him what the problem was. He chuckled as he told me that some "knuckleheads" on his side had concerns about Carson's record, but that I shouldn't worry because the bill would pass anyway. It didn't make me feel any better when, as I walked away, I glanced up at the tally board and saw that Boehner himself had voted against it.

The bill passed the House 334-53, but languished in the Senate for weeks, the victim of one of the Senate's most infamous practices—the anonymous hold. As May 27 got closer, I began to worry we would run out of time to get the bill enacted before Springdale's commemoration. We did. May turned into June, which turned into July. I found out the source of the hold was Oklahoma's thoughtful but irascible senator, Tom Coburn, who was known to be an immovable block for issues he considered wasteful or inappropriate. After trying for weeks to resolve the issue at the staff level, I finally called Coburn to personally ask him to release his hold.

"Rachel Carson is responsible for more deaths than anyone who ever lived," he said to my utter astonishment. When I asked what led him to that conclusion, he transitioned into a lengthy monologue about the discontinuation of the use of DDT and the subsequent exponential increase in deaths related to mosquito-borne illnesses. Coburn, a physician, was knowledgeable about the subject—at least his version of it—and deeply committed to his position.

I said we were not going to agree on Carson's record, and it wasn't worth arguing the merits of the science because the bill was not about the science. I reminded him that Rachel Carson had been dead for more than forty years, and that renaming the post office wouldn't change history or validate her views. It would not in any way influence the scientific debate. Coburn seemed to be getting my point. "Rachel Carson is the biggest thing that's ever happened to this town of three thousand people, and all they want is to name this tiny building after her," I said in closing. I then asked Coburn to please release his hold so Springdale could take this small step in honoring its most famous citizen.

Soon thereafter, my office received word that the hold had been released and the Senate was going to take up the bill. It passed and was signed into law by President Bush on August 9. Several weeks later, I ran into Coburn at the airport in Washington. I thanked him for allowing the bill to go forward. "You made a good point," he said, claiming he rarely releases a hold. "But I still don't agree with anything she did."

The whole episode was not only an early lesson into how even the most insignificant issues can get wrapped up into larger partisan debates, but also a positive sign that there may be room for agreement and compromise among members of different ideologies if we can just make an effort to understand one another's point of view.

Wolf and Sheepdog

ONE OF THE MOST COMMON CRITICISMS OF NEWT GINgrich as it relates to his role in the escalation of congressional polarization is his decision as speaker to standardize the three-day workweek. Gingrich changed the House calendar so that floor votes were held during the middle of the week, allowing members to spend more time in their districts. He strongly discouraged members from moving their families to Washington, which some have argued has had the effect of curtailing personal relationships between Republicans and Democrats who might otherwise have gotten to know each other socially.[32]

The argument goes something like this: When members and their families used to live in Washington, they became friends as Republicans and Democrats bonded together over the social activities of everyday life. These personal friendships held polarization in check as members genuinely liked and understood one another, and therefore avoided the needless partisan warfare so common in Congress today. If we returned to that type of arrangement, where more members and their families lived in Washington and socialized together, it would help alleviate the animosity between the two sides and take the edge off the bitter partisanship that divides Congress today. It's a nice theory, but I'm not convinced.

It is a misconception that members of Congress from opposing parties don't talk to each other or socialize together. Even during the short workweek, members still hang out together and build friendships that carry beyond the political battlefield. The House gym is one of many examples. Restricted to members only, the gym is a place where both sides can congregate together for a bipartisan morning workout, evening basketball game, or relaxed conversation. The atmosphere is light and cordial, and depending on which time of day you show up, members will be gearing up for what lies ahead or winding down after a long day.

Occasionally, I would retreat to the gym in the evening to do some late-night laps in the swimming pool, which was usually unoccupied at that time of day. I vividly remember one night soon after the 2010 raid that killed Osama bin Laden when I saw then-CIA Director Leon Panetta—a former House member—swimming laps alone in the pool, obviously lost in his thoughts. It was indicative of the fact that Panetta knew it was a place he could go to be among friends.

Congressional travel provides another opportunity to get to know colleagues in a close setting. Known as CODELs, official congressional travel delegations are designed to help members make informed decisions by visiting foreign countries and meeting with leaders to learn firsthand the impact of American foreign policy. Most CODELs are bipartisan, creating the opportunity for members to get to know one another during the long flights and multi-day agendas that accompany such trips, in addition to the intense preparation that goes into a successful visit.

I remember sitting next to conservative Louisiana Republican Charles Boustany, a physician, on the flight back from our CODEL to Iraq. We spent hours chatting about next steps in the war, as well as our shared interest in health policy. We bonded and became friends, and in the years ahead often compared notes about our ideas for health care reform. During the debate on the Affordable Care Act, Charles and I frequently checked in with each other and planned bipartisan discussions about how the two sides might come to agreement. Although the national debate inevitably turned ugly, Charles and I remained friends and often lamented the fact that the opportunity to do bipartisan reform had been lost.

I also maintained good personal relationships with the chairmen of the National Republican Congressional Committee (NRCC) throughout my time in Congress. Like it's Democratic counterpart, the NRCC is always chaired by a current member of Congress, whose job as chair is to win seats for the party in the upcoming congressional elections. The chairmen focus much of their attention on seats currently held by the opposing party, but which have the potential to flip back on Election Day. Because the district I represented leaned Republican, I was a top target of the NRCC every election cycle.

Northern Virginia's Congressman Tom Davis led the NRCC's effort to beat me in 2008, but Tom and I were able to remain friends throughout that election. We were cordial when we saw each other on the House floor and around Capitol Hill, but we both knew that Tom had a job to do when he returned to his office at the NRCC. Sometimes I jokingly tried to pump him for information, but he never fell for it. Perhaps it was easier to stay cordial because my race, a rematch against former Congress-woman Melissa Hart, never tightened. I won by twelve points even though then-Senator Obama lost the district by eleven points in that year's presidential election.

In 2010, my race was close and went down to the wire. It was a disastrous year for Democrats, and there was an active Tea Party contingent in my district fueling my opponent's campaign. Predictably, the campaign turned nasty, and tensions flared back home. But through it all, I maintained my friendship with that year's NRCC chair, Pete Sessions from Texas.

Pete and I shared a mutual interest in football, and we spent many mornings that fall sitting together in the House gym rehashing the previous weekend's gridiron results and chatting about other topical issues. Then we would nod at each other and go about our business for the day, which I knew in Pete's case was figuring out a way to beat me. It reminded me of the *Looney Tunes* sheepdog and wolf characters, who would exchange pleasantries as they clocked into work at the sheep grazing meadow. The sheepdog's job was to protect the sheep; the wolf's job was to catch them. After spending the day brutalizing each other, the shift-change whistle would sound, and the two friends would chat amicably as they walked out, punched out their time cards, and went home.[33]

Like wolf and sheepdog, Pete Sessions and I remained friends through the 2010 Republican tsunami, which I survived, and into the 2012 election cycle, during which Pete again chaired the NRCC. The day after I lost my 2012 Democratic primary, I ran into Pete on the first floor of the Capitol, just outside the Members' Dining Room. Pete asked his staff to excuse him as he walked with me down the hall, out of earshot of the others. With a warm smile and hand on my shoulder, he asked me not to take it the wrong way, but said he had mixed emotions about my loss the night before. "I'm sorry to see you go because you're one of the good guys," he said. "You'll be missed on both sides of the aisle." I was touched by his sentiment. He then said part of him was happy I had lost, because he knew Republicans would now be able to win the seat in the fall. "We had already decided to abandon the race if you had won the primary," he said. "I knew I couldn't beat you and didn't want to waste the money trying."

Bipartisan groups of members socialize regularly on Capitol Hill. A weekly bipartisan Bible study group meets on C Street, near the House office buildings. Members dine together, golf together, and yes, have drinks together. Women members have a bipartisan softball team that plays the women in the congressional press corps. American University political scientist Jennifer Lawless led a 2016 study of the differences between male and female members of Congress when it comes to bipartisanship. She found that congressional women cultivate bipartisan relationships with each other, not only through the softball game, but through "trips to the theater, bowling nights and baby showers." The purpose of the study was to test the conventional wisdom that: "Because Democratic and Republican women are friends with each other outside the chamber, they are more likely to trust and cooperate with one another inside the halls of Congress."[34] The results may surprise you.

Lawless and her coauthor, University of Texas professor Sean Theriault, conducted an exhaustive study, looking at four different categories of information. They researched 9,732 overseas CODEL trips taken by members of Congress over a 35-year period. They compared the frequency with which every member of Congress since 1993 crossed the aisle to cosponsor legislation introduced by a member of the opposing party. They analyzed nearly 14,000 procedural votes dating back to 1973 to test voting patterns of every member of Congress during that time. And they scrutinized the results of the votes on all 4,488 amendments offered on the House floor between 1993 and 2014 that received a recorded vote. As it turns out, there was no evidence that friendships among members in any way diminished partisanship on the job. Additionally, women were just as partisan as men, and in some cases, more so.[35]

What does all this mean? It means socializing away from the job doesn't help reduce partisanship. Keeping members and their families in Washington won't make a difference. There are multiple reasons why polarization on Capitol Hill is at an all-time high, but the fact that most House members live back home in their districts isn't one of them.

CHAPTER 5

EXTREME
LETDOWN

—— .•. ——

An Education in Relationships

THERE ARE TRADE ASSOCIATIONS AND LOBBYING GROUPS
representing every imaginable constituency. There is even an
association of association executives. Outreach between interest groups and members of Congress has become quite so-
phisticated. Some of that outreach involves financial support
to campaigns, but the most effective organizations have also
perfected the art of relationship building. No group in Washington does a better job of cultivating relationships with members
of Congress than the American Israel Public Affairs Committee,
commonly known as AIPAC.

Contrary to what the acronym implies, AIPAC is not a political action committee. With the goal of strengthening US-Israel
relations and promoting strongly pro-Israel policies in Congress, AIPAC empowers activists across the country to become
politically engaged and to build relationships with members
of Congress. The organization claims more than one hundred
thousand Americans are active with AIPAC, working through a
network of regional offices which report up through the group's
national headquarters in downtown Washington DC.[1]

Both in their home districts and on Capitol Hill, AIPAC
volunteers meet with members of Congress and their staff to
educate them on issues related to Israel. Although AIPAC as

an organization does not contribute directly to candidates, the group's volunteer activists are extremely politically active, hosting fundraising events that raise money from like-minded donors in the congressional district. AIPAC's annual Washington, DC conference is one of the premier events in the nation's capital, culminating with a gala dinner that attracts hundreds of members of Congress and more than ten thousand guests, usually including the Israeli prime minister.

The cultivation begins well before a candidate is elected to office. During a campaign, when it becomes clear a candidate has a good chance to win, AIPAC springs into action. Groups of activists from the district reach out to request an introductory meeting to discuss AIPAC's key issues. The initial meeting may or may not be connected to a fundraiser, but either way, the candidate is left with the unmistakable impression that having a positive relationship with AIPAC can be politically beneficial. Attendees at the initial meeting will often include a national AIPAC representative, in addition to a group of local activists who will inevitably stay in close touch with the candidate throughout the race. At the beginning of each new session of Congress, AIPAC's Washington office will assign one or more of their lobbyists to each newly elected member, with the expressed purpose of building a trusting friendship with the member and their staff.

During the month-long August recess, groups of freshman members of Congress are invited to visit Israel on an eight-day trip funded by a supporting charitable foundation of AIPAC. The lavish trip is considered a rite of passage for new members of Congress.

Spouses are invited, so my wife Kelly traveled with me. AIPAC staff led an amazing journey around the country, mixing historical sightseeing with informational briefings and meetings with high-level Israeli officials. We met with then-Israeli Prime Minister Ehud Olmert in Jerusalem and separately with former-Israeli Prime Ministers Shimon Peres, Benjamin Netanyahu, and Ehud Barak. We traveled to Tel Aviv, where we received intelligence briefings from top Israeli security officers, mostly about Iran's nuclear ambitions and the progress of its weapons program. Separate from the AIPAC-scheduled events, the members of Congress in our group also took a side trip to the West Bank to meet in Ramallah with Palestinian Authority Prime Minister Salam Fayyad.

The AIPAC trip included tours of Israel's borders with Jordan, Lebanon, and Syria, including a lengthy overview of the strategic importance of the Golan Heights. We talked with residents of Sderot, a southern Israeli town along the Gaza border, and viewed the high-tech fencing on the Israeli border with the West Bank. We had guided tours of various sites of historical and religious significance, including the Old City of Jerusalem, the Sea of Galilee, the presumed sites of Jesus's baptism and crucifixion, the Western Wall, and the Dead Sea, where we were invited to float in the sea's miraculously buoyant waters. No expense was spared to make sure our group was able to view the geography, learn the policy issues, and experience everything Israel has to offer.

One morning during the trip, I broke away from the group to have a private breakfast in Jerusalem with Daniel Levy, an Israeli political scientist and close associate of Bill Benter, my campaign supporter from Pittsburgh. Levy and Benter are not aligned with AIPAC's political views, so Benter had earlier put me in touch with Levy and asked me to meet with him during my visit to Israel. Levy asked my impressions of the trip so far, and he seemed disappointed as I described with great enthusiasm the amazing experience we were having. I told him I found the information I was learning on the trip to be quite persuasive, but Levy wanted to make sure I realized there were different points of view about the political issues relating to Israel, and that I should be cautious about accepting AIPAC's positions as the consensus of Middle East policy experts. Levy said he and Benter were involved in establishing a new political group that they hoped would rival AIPAC's clout and influence.

Less than a month later, Benter and Levy paid a visit to my Washington office. They wanted to make sure I had not been swayed by AIPAC's dog-and-pony show in Israel. We discussed pending Middle East issues, but it was clear that we were unlikely to be on the same side on many of them. Displaying the literal definition of a "poker face," Benter showed no emotion as he listened to me explain why I would be opposing his position. The meeting was uncomfortable for me because I didn't want to disappoint Benter on an issue about which he cared so deeply.

The subject of his prior support of my campaign never came up during that or future conversations, but it didn't have to. Both of us recognized it was quite likely I would never have been elected to Congress in the first place were it not for his generous early support.

Levy and Benter told me about the new organization they were helping to create. Called "J Street," it would draw clear policy distinctions with some of AIPAC's priority issues. The group would also attempt to counter AIPAC's powerful nationwide grassroots advocacy network.[2]

A liberal-leaning organization that supports a two-state solution to achieve Middle East peace, J Street differs from AIPAC on some issues, such as the future of Jerusalem, how to respond to Iran's nuclear program, and the relationship between Israel and the Palestinian territories.[3] Established as a direct challenge to the Jewish political establishment, the group was initially quite controversial. As a favor to Benter, I attended some of J Street's early events and always took meetings with their representatives. It was clear to me Benter was closely involved with the group, but it was not until much later that I learned just how closely.

Three years after J Street was founded, a leaked IRS document generated a political firestorm when it was revealed that George Soros, the billionaire liberal activist known for his controversial views about Israel, had been one of J Street's top donors and fundraisers. Media reports about the IRS document also focused on another revelation.[4]

"Nearly half of J Street's revenue during the time frame . . . came from a single donor," reported the *Washington Times*, referring to an obscure Hong Kong businesswoman named Consolacion Esdicul.[5] When questioned about the donation, J Street executives admitted the overseas contribution had been solicited by Benter, a business associate of Esdicul.[6]

The issue of J Street's funding became so controversial[7] that the organization had to create a "Myths and Facts" section on its website to respond to concerns about the mysterious Hong Kong donor and the involvement of Soros. The website explained that Benter had "committed to contribute and help raise substantial funds" for J Street, and the Esdicul donation was only one contribution he helped raise.[8] While all perfectly legal, the episode brought to light the fact that Benter from the beginning had been one of J Street's largest financial support-ers—probably the largest.[9]

In time, Benter would become more visible as a major donor to liberal political causes, with special emphasis on his person-al interest in the politics of the Middle East. In addition to his support for J Street, he has contributed hundreds of thousands of dollars to fund the operations of left-of-center nonprofit orga-nizations such as Media Matters and the Center for American Progress.[10] He has also given enormous sums directly to Demo-cratic candidates and Super PACs,[11] and he played a leading role in bankrolling the advertising campaign in support of the 2013 nomination of J Street favorite Chuck Hagel as defense secretary.[12]

Although we remained friends, my relationship with Bill was never quite the same after my decision to align more closely with the AIPAC foreign policy agenda. Whenever an issue concern-ing the Middle East was debated, particularly issues related to Iran's nuclear capabilities, Bill would always call or email me to discuss the specifics and encourage me to support J Street's position. More often than not, I disagreed with his position and would end up voting the other way. Although he never involved himself in attempts to fund a primary challenge against me, he was clearly disappointed at my centrist voting record, and his enthusiasm for my campaigns declined precipitously.

Superdelegate Showdown

NO EVENT BETTER EPITOMIZES THE THEATRICAL PARTI-sanship that exists in Washington than the annual State of the Union address. It is the Super Bowl of Capitol Hill—the day when the cream of the crop from the world of media, celebrity and politics come together for a pre-scripted show designed to demonstrate both unity and division.

Before the speech, congressional Democrats and Republi-cans meet separately to strategize about how to message their respective response. The White House makes it easy by provid-ing an advance copy of the speech, embargoed to the press so the text doesn't leak.

In addition to the discussion of the evening's talking points, the pre-speech meeting also provides an opportunity for the House sergeant-at-arms to discuss safety protocols that will be enforced throughout the day, including potential evacuation procedures in case of an emergency. Occasionally, the ominous presentation turns downright scary, as occurred during one meeting I recall where staff provided a physical demonstration of the proper use of the emergency gas masks that are available in the case of chemical attack during the president's speech.

The buildup to the State of the Union also includes one of the most amusing traditions in Washington—the battle for the aisle seats. Because the House chamber is cleared for a security sweep hours before the speech, some of the more ambitious members will leave personalized pieces of paper on their preferred seats in the hopes of claiming a position along the center aisle or in view of the cameras that pan the chamber during the speech. When the chamber is reopened after the sweep, the members who have been waiting outside will rush back in to claim their seats, where they will literally sit for hours until they are seen greeting the president just prior to the speech.

Republicans generally sit on the right side of the aisle, with Democrats on the left. The attending justices of the Supreme Court sit silently up front as each side of the chamber takes turns standing to cheer and applaud mentions of their preferred policy priorities. References to the military or American greatness will bring both sides to their feet. Afterwards, members from both parties walk the few steps to nearby Statuary Hall, which will be jam-packed. Members line up at designated cameras where interviewers from various media outlets listen as member after member repeats the identical talking points.

The dynamic within the chamber during the 2008 State of the Union speech was particularly interesting because of the presence of three senators who had realistic aspirations to be standing at the presidential podium the following year. From my seat in the middle of the chamber, I watched intently as Senators John McCain, Hillary Clinton, and Barack Obama stared up at President Bush, invariably thinking that, next time, they would be the one delivering the State of the Union speech.

Before the 2008 speech, during the time when members of Congress mill around together on the House floor talking informally to one another, I approached Senator Obama to say hello. Referencing our ongoing conversations about his presidential campaign, he jokingly asked if I was finally ready to endorse him. I told him I still had no plans to endorse anybody, then laughed as he playfully clasped his hands in front of him and said with a smile, "What do I have to do, Altmire? What do I have to do?"

Obama had been working feverishly for months to win the endorsements of Democratic members, each of whom was also a "superdelegate," meaning they were free to vote at the national convention for any candidate they wanted, regardless of who won their home state or district. Hillary Clinton, his primary opponent, made little effort to cultivate congressional endorsements until she fell hopelessly behind Obama in the delegate count.

Obama first reached out to rank-and-file members of Congress to formally discuss his presidential campaign on February 28, 2007, hosting a breakfast meeting at the Democratic National Committee headquarters, just down the street from the Capitol. I was one of only a small handful of members who took the time to attend, mostly because it was so long before the election, in addition to the widely held belief that Obama was making a mistake to consider a challenge to Clinton, the clear frontrunner. He made a compelling but unremarkable pitch, supplemented by supporting commentary from a few members of the Illinois congressional delegation. In all, there were probably twenty people in the room.

Afterwards, I spoke to him about my desire to see more bipartisanship and collaboration in Congress and with the administration. Obama followed up with a note, thanking me for attending and writing that he was interested in "moving beyond old ideological divisions, bringing independents" into the fold in a way that "no other candidate can."

He called me in June to give me an update on his campaign. He again reminded me of his desire to move beyond partisan politics, stressing one more time that he was the only candidate capable of doing that. I asked why he was calling me since I was only a freshman congressman from Pennsylvania, a state that was irrelevant to his campaign because its late-April primary would be nearly four months after the Iowa Caucus. He said the race would be close, and Pennsylvania was going to be important. He also asked for my endorsement as a superdelegate, claiming it would help build momentum for his campaign, which at the time was polling double digits behind Clinton. I told him it was too early for me to think about a convention that was more than a year away, but we agreed to stay in touch.

In October, I was invited to attend a speech Michelle Obama was giving to a group of businesswomen at the Lowes Hotel in Philadelphia. As I watched the speech with my top campaign advisor, Rachael Heisler, we were asked to come backstage to speak with Mrs. Obama after she concluded. Patrick Murphy, one of my freshman colleagues in the House, was already in the room when we arrived. When Michelle entered a short time later, the four of us spent the next half hour speaking informally about the presidential campaign.

Michelle leaned forward from the edge of her seat as she sipped from a bottle of water, excitedly talking about the momentum she felt was building for the campaign. In response to my question about the path to victory given the fact that Obama was polling so far behind, she transitioned into a detailed explanation of exactly how she expected the campaign to unfold.

"The key for us," Michelle said, "is we have people on the ground in every state." She said the Obama campaign was "in it for the long haul," and once the campaign moved beyond the early states, they would capitalize on Clinton's lack of organization in the later states and "get on a roll" that would seal the nomination. "That's why we need your help," she said, referencing Pennsylvania's April 22 primary.

I said I was impressed by her presentation and appreciative of the opportunity to discuss the campaign. Like her husband had done after our February meeting, Michelle followed up by sending me a note referencing some of the things we had discussed. It was clear they were touching every base.

The race unfolded almost exactly as Michelle had predicted, with Obama winning state after state and Clinton falling further and further behind in the delegate count. By the time the campaign calendar reached the end of February, it was too late for Clinton to realistically catch up. Knowing her only chance to secure the nomination was to garner the support of enough uncommitted superdelegates to overcome Obama's insurmountable lead in elected delegates, Clinton finally began contacting superdelegates to ask for their support.

Hillary Clinton left me a voice mail on the evening of February 29, saying she hoped she could count on my support. We spoke briefly when I called her back the next day. She was about to speak at an event but said she looked forward to catching up soon.

Bill Clinton called me three days later to discuss Hillary's victories in the Texas and Ohio primaries, and to ask that I not make any endorsement until he had the chance to talk to me in person. He asked how I thought Hillary would do in the general election in my conservative district. I said I thought it would be difficult because I had the sense that she was not popular there among Republicans or even conservative Democrats.

"How did I do there," he asked, surely knowing the answer. I responded that he had carried the district twice during his 1990s presidential campaigns.

"Well, there you go," he said triumphantly. After pausing to think of the most appropriate way to respond, I said, "But, Mr. President, with all due respect, you're not on the ballot this year."

The silence was deafening. He then talked at length about Hillary's popularity in Arkansas during his time as governor and how she had won over the conservative skeptics who had originally doubted her. He also said that during her two Senate elections, she had done particularly well in the rural, upstate parts of New York, territory where Democrats running statewide usually get clobbered. He said this was evidence that she could appeal to conservative voters in my district, just as she had done in New York and Arkansas.

As we were wrapping up the call, he reminded me of what he considered to be an old favor—that I had served on a working group of Hillary's health care reform task force in 1993. The appointment came when I was a twenty-five-year-old Capitol Hill staffer, just learning the ropes of the health care industry that would later become my career. The comment was subtle and made in passing, but I got the message. He concluded by saying he would be calling again, and he looked forward to having the opportunity to talk in person when he was in Pennsylvania.

Two weeks later, Obama was in my district, spending the day campaigning in the blue-collar Ohio River Valley. His campaign invited me to spend the day with him while he spoke to a large rally, met with a group of local dignitaries, did a national press conference, and sat for a lengthy interview with PBS political analyst Gwen Ifill. We then walked together to his waiting SUV, where we sat in the back while a driver and security officer occupied the front seats.

As we made our way along the thirty-minute route to Pittsburgh International Airport, Obama relaxed and made polite small talk, talking about life on the campaign trail and the effect it was having on his family. We each have two daughters about the same age, so we compared notes about parenting and discussed their personal interests. Then he moved on to the specifics of his campaign.

With the Pennsylvania primary still a month away, he asked me how he thought he would do in my district and what issues were most important there. I responded honestly, saying that while I expected he would likely win the nomination, conservative Western Pennsylvania was probably not going to be his strongest area. Our car pulled into the airport complex and made its way toward his campaign plane sitting on the runway.

"You may be right about that, but I'm going to win this race, and I'm going to be your president," he said. "And I'd love to have your support." We began to wrap up the conversation as the car came to a stop near a stream of reporters climbing up the back steps of the plane. Obama nodded to the two men sitting in the front, each of whom got out of the car and stood outside with their backs turned against the windows. We stayed inside the car and continued talking.

In the midst of an onslaught of bad press about his relationship with the controversial Reverend Jeremiah Wright, Obama the following day would be in Philadelphia to give a major speech about race relations in America. As we were saying good-bye and the officers were opening the doors, I wished him luck with his speech. With a glance that obviously meant "close the door," Obama looked back at the officer on his side. After the doors were closed, he leaned towards me and squinted his eyes with a flash of anger and a look of steely determination.

"Don't worry about me," he said confidently. He then defiantly listed a number of obstacles he had overcome throughout his lifetime. In referencing what up to that moment he considered to be the capstone of the list, he closed with: "They told me I couldn't beat Hillary Clinton, and I'm beating both Clintons. Don't worry about me, I'll be fine." With that, he knocked on the widow behind him, the doors opened, and he exited the car. Moments later, he ducked his head back in, flashing his trademark smile. "Thanks for your hospitality, Congressman. I could really use your support!"

Within a few days of Obama's visit to my district, Hillary Clinton invited me to her home in Washington as part of a group of about twenty uncommitted superdelegates. An impressive selection of hors d'oeuvres ran the length of her dinner table, while guests circulated around the first floor of her elegant home, engaging in conversation with Clinton and her staff in a cocktail-party setting.

After about an hour of mingling, Clinton invited the undecided members to join her in the living room for a question and answer session, during which I asked why she believed superdelegates should vote for her even though Obama was likely to win a majority of votes, states, and elected delegates. She said that superdelegates had an obligation to make an independent decision, choosing the candidate they believe is most qualified irrespective of what the voters have said. She seemed to be implying that overturning the will of the people was an acceptable option, which didn't make much sense to me.

Both candidates and their campaigns kept in touch with me and my staff as the primary approached. As I traveled around my conservative congressional district, it became clear that Hillary Clinton was going to win big in the Democratic primary, but neither Obama nor Clinton would do well in the general election. For the past several weeks, I had been telling both candidates that I would not be endorsing any candidate during the primary season and would wait until every American had had the chance to vote. I hated the superdelegate system, which I considered silly because it gave so-called party elites a more influential role than everyday Americans in choosing the nominee. Still, the candidates persisted.

Prior to Bill Clinton's visit to my district four days before the primary, his staff called my office to arrange for a meeting while he was there. Our staffs agreed that the most convenient way would be for us to ride together during the drive between Clinton's two speaking engagements in the district. As we rode the forty miles between Hickory Township and Beaver Falls, he focused on our mutual belief that Hillary was going to win the primary in Pennsylvania and in my district. He said I had a responsibility to support my constituents. He noticeably cringed when I pointed out that I represented everyone in the district, not just the Democrats. He talked at length about his experience as a new president and how he believed Hillary was much more qualified to take the reins of power than Obama, who had been a state senator only four years before. I reiterated that I would not endorse anybody before the primaries were over in every state.

The day after the Pennsylvania primary, I was on the House floor when a note was handed to me saying Senator Clinton wanted to meet with me at the Democratic National Committee office building at 9:30 p.m. that evening. She had won my district by thirty-one points the night before, so I knew she would once again be asking for an endorsement. When I arrived, staff led me into the second floor conference room, where two chairs had been pulled away from the table, facing each other. After some awkward small talk and discussion about my visit with Bill Clinton the previous weekend, I congratulated her and commented about how impressed I was by her relentless campaigning.

"You know, Jason, over the past six weeks I've traveled all over the state," she said as she leaned back in her chair. "I've met with party leaders, elected officials, fundraisers—people that I think could be very helpful to you if you ever ran for statewide office in Pennsylvania . . ."

"Senator," I interrupted. "As I have told you and President Clinton, Senator Obama, and for that matter everyone else who has asked, I'm not going to make an endorsement. . . ."

Cutting me off in mid-sentence, she stood up, put out her hand, and half-heartedly thanked me for coming. The meeting was over five minutes after it began.[13]

Only Two Years to Do This

AFTER A SECOND CONSECUTIVE DEMOCRATIC WAVE election in 2008 added a whole new class of centrists, House Democrats had a seventy-eight-seat majority and momentum at their backs. With Barack Obama in the White House and control of a filibuster-proof sixty seats in the Senate, Democrats saw their opportunity to create a new era of progressivism on a scale not seen since the days of LBJ's Great Society and FDR's New Deal. The first order of business was to clear a potential roadblock by removing the venerable John Dingell as chairman of the powerful Energy and Commerce Committee. This was critically important for Pelosi because Energy and Commerce was the committee through which bills dealing with her priority issues—climate change and health care—would have to flow.

The eighty-two-year-old Dingell was revered on Capitol Hill. Watching from the visitor's gallery as a teenager, he had personally witnessed FDR's famous speech to Congress following the attack on Pearl Harbor. He was elected to Congress during the Eisenhower Administration, replacing his father in a Detroit-area district. Dingell would eventually become the longest-serving member of Congress in American history, and by the time he was challenged for his chairmanship, he had been the top Democrat on the Energy and Commerce Committee for an astonishing twenty-eight years.

Henry Waxman, who announced he would challenge Dingell for the committee's gavel, had been a member of the historic "Watergate Class" that was swept into Congress in 1974 following President Nixon's resignation. From his perspective representing a district anchored by Santa Monica and Beverly Hills, Waxman saw the world quite differently than Dingell. A close ally of Speaker Pelosi, Waxman had established a record of liberal accomplishment over his more than three decades in the House, especially in the areas of environmental and consumer protections, as well as health care regulation. Although Pelosi never formally announced a position in the race for the committee's chairmanship, it was widely known that she supported Waxman.

In conversations with colleagues prior to the caucus vote, Waxman pitched himself as the more dependable champion of Pelosi's progressive agenda. He also argued that the unique opportunity Democrats had before them—with complete control of the reins of power—would not last long. "We only have two years to do this," he told me and many others, referring to the sweeping policy changes he, Pelosi, and their allies hoped to pass through Congress.

Waxman was keenly aware of the historical trend of new presidents losing seats in Congress during midterm elections.[14] He also realized the liberal policies he and Pelosi hoped to enact would not be popular in swing districts like the one I represented. By stressing the need to move quickly and push through an ambitious progressive legislative agenda before the next election, Waxman seemed to many of us centrist Democrats to be implying that we were expendable commodities.

I supported Dingell, but Waxman won the Energy and Commerce Committee chairmanship by a 137-122 vote. It didn't take long before he engaged in a series of epic clashes with centrist Democrats that would leave scars on both sides and result in the worst electoral defeat suffered by congressional Democrats in seventy-two years.

The Democrats held the majority in the House due to the fact that dozens of centrist Democrats had been able to win seats previously held by Republicans. This infusion of centrists inflated the ranks of the two House coalition groups designated for moderates. Called the Blue Dogs and the New Democrats (New Dems), the two groups cater to different constituencies.

The Blue Dogs focus on fiscal conservatism, with a stated goal of finding common ground and building consensus between the two parties. New Dems, on the other hand, exist to modernize and strengthen the Democratic Party by focusing on issues not traditionally priorities for liberals, such as foreign trade, technological innovation, and business-friendly tax and financial services reforms. Neither group takes a position on hot-button social issues. Blue Dogs are more willing to confront party leadership over ideological differences, while New Dems try to work within the party leadership structure to affect change and push their pro-business agenda. As a result, some tension exists between the two groups, although some members join both, as I did during my time in office.

The New Dems are skeptical of Blue Dogs and their tactics and sometimes criticize them as being too willing to work with Republicans. Many New Dem members who are not also Blue Dogs tend to vote uniformly with party leadership on most issues. *Washington Post* writer Dana Milbank questions whether New Dems can fairly be called moderates at all, given the fact that the average liberal rating of New Dem leaders has at times been calculated to be higher than that of the House Democratic Caucus as a whole.[15] Blue Dogs, on the other hand, are always atop the list of Democratic members most willing to break ranks with party leadership.

Centrists are vulnerable to the wrath of liberals within their own caucus. Lynn Woolsey, then-chairwoman of the Progressive Caucus, the coalition representing the most liberal House Democrats—which is unsurprisingly the largest coalition in the Democratic Caucus—waited all of nine months into the new Democratic majority before calling for primary challenges against her centrist Democrat colleagues. This infuriated the Blue Dogs, but it was indicative of the frosty relationship that existed between the diverse Democratic groups.[16]

Liberal bloggers and activists detest the Blue Dogs, often supporting their primary challengers and rejoicing in their demise. New Dems don't fare much better with the activists, who have been known to refer to New Dems as "corporatists" and as the Blue Dogs' "kissin' cousins."[17] One prominent liberal writer compared the relative levels of treachery of the two groups, finding the New Dems' mission to be "completely different than the Blue Dogs. Except for the fact that it's the same."[18] She then advocated for Democrats to abandon the idea of supporting centrists in pursuit of the majority, calling the whole idea "a horrible Frankenstein experiment gone wrong," adding to her view that it was better for centrist Democrats to go "quietly into extinction before they permanently damage the [political] ecosystem."[19] I wonder if she thinks the Democratic Party is better off now that she has achieved her goal of purging nearly all the Democratic moderates from Congress, giving Republicans complete control of Washington under President Trump.

Dying Breed of Bridge Builders

THE PROBLEM OF POLITICAL POLARIZATION HAS BEEN EDItorialized across the country, often in the ironic context of each side blaming the other for the problem. In 2004, a full five years before the birth of the Tea Party, even Nancy Pelosi's hometown *San Francisco Chronicle* weighed in with an article titled, "Where Did the Middle Go? How Polarized Politics and a Radical GOP Have Put a Chill on Measured Debate."[20]

Since then, the problem has only gotten worse. Today, congressional centrists are all but extinct, and as the *Chronicle* article references, this has had a devastating impact on the ability of members to work with each other. Few members are willing to reach across the aisle because compromise has become a dirty word. Those who do work with the other side will face criticism from party activists, and will draw the ire of the partisan Super PACs that help fund primary challenges.

Centrist members are also guaranteed to become familiar with the favored terminology of the many influential partisan bloggers who detest compromise. The derisive titles RINOs and DINOs are reserved for any member of Congress with the audacity to bring thoughtful moderation to their work in Congress, rather than simply following their party's leadership on nearly every vote.

I and many of my centrist colleagues personally experienced these attacks from our left flank, which eventually resulted in the loss of nearly every Democrat in the country who represented a conservative-leaning seat. On the Republican side, moderate members, such as Congressman Richard Hanna from New York, have been driven out of Congress for not being conservative enough.

Hanna, who represented one of the few remaining evenly split congressional districts, had a centrist voting record and regularly talked about his willingness to work with Democrats. He fended off Tea Party primary challenges with the tag line "Compromise is not treason." First elected in 2010, Hanna chose to retire from Congress after only three terms in office, frustrated with the animosity that exists toward centrists.[21] In 2016, few were surprised when he became the first Republican member of Congress to endorse Hillary Clinton for president over Donald Trump.

Hanna and I served in Congress together and were part of a truly rare breed. In 2012, my last year in the House, Richard and I were 2 of only 15 of the 435 House members to have a truly centrist voting record, according to a comprehensive calculation by political scientists.[22] Today, most of those 15 members are no longer in Congress.

Scholars have observed that, however one measures party unity, members of Congress are voting with their party caucuses much more frequently than they used to. Near unanimous party line votes are commonplace, and the two parties disagree to a much greater extent than before.[23]

In the mid-1970s, moderates made up 37% of the House. By 2005, when I began my first campaign for Congress, that number had dropped to 8%. By 2016, the middle had nearly disappeared altogether.[24] Members of Congress from every region of the country have moved away from the center, heightening the polarization, and making it almost impossible to come to an agreement on major legislation.[25]

Ohio governor John Kasich, who served in the House for eighteen years, accurately blames Congress's gridlock on the fact that "we're putting in people who don't understand compromise."[26] Even necessary legislation that used to be routinely reauthorized, like agriculture and transportation bills, are now held hostage to partisan bickering.[27]

Political scientists have also proven through research what might be self-intuitive to some: "The greater the polarization of the partisan elite, the greater the frequency of legislative gridlock."[28] Cross-party coalitions have become nearly impossible, as there are almost no members left in the middle in either chamber of Congress.[29] The fewer the moderates, the less productive the Congress.[30]

Ron Brownstein puts it more succinctly, "Congress is an institution of individuals, and when the number of bridge builders in it declines, so does the number of bridges that are built."[31] The opposite is also true—the more centrists there are in a divided Congress, the less legislative stalemate.[32] Referring to the fact that moderates in the electorate tend to be the least politically interested Americans, journalist Jill Lepore says of congressional centrists: "In Congress, moderates aren't people who don't know much about politics. Moderates are people who get laws passed."[33]

The lack of an activist political center moves Congress further to the extremes and makes members reluctant to do anything that might irritate their base voters back home.[34] Particularly in the House, where two-year election cycles have members constantly looking over their shoulders, this has led to a strong disincentive to reaching agreement on issues. Although political activists sometimes claim they want bipartisan compromise, their definition of it is if "you accept my position, then we've compromised." Any actual movement toward the center is often met with hostility among the activists.

In March 2016, conservative Republican Senator Jerry Moran was speaking before an audience that should have been friendly territory for him—a Rotary Club in his home state of Kansas. Moran made the mistake of saying that he believed the Senate should *hold a hearing* on President Obama's Supreme Court nominee, Merrick Garland. Condemning Moran's "outrageous behavior," Tea Party activists threatened to support a primary challenge to the senator in retaliation for his heresy. Moran quickly issued a statement confirming his opposition to Garland's nomination.[35]

The distrust of the other side, even of members of the same party deemed not to be extreme enough, has led to historic public disapproval of Congress. Members then go back home and criticize the partisanship in Congress, resulting in the famous

"Fenno's Paradox," where people like their own representative but hate Congress.[36] The real paradox is the inability of partisans to recognize the generally centrist distribution of public opinion while pursuing overreaching policies that appeal only to their party's base voters.[37] The resulting midterm wave elections wash away the moderate members who gave the party the majority in the first place.

Few know more about the inner workings of Congress than former Senate Majority Leaders Tom Daschle and Trent Lott. Each served in the House before moving to the Senate, and each rose up through the ranks within their respective parties, holding high-ranking Senate leadership positions in both the majority and minority.

Writing about the demise of centrists in their 2016 book, *Crisis Point*, the two leaders observe, "It's actually extremely difficult to survive as a moderate in Congress . . . Parties have pulled further apart and it has been exacerbated by primaries . . . There are far more Republicans in Congress on the far right, far more Democrats on the far left." Daschle and Lott agree that the most "risky" place for members of Congress is "in the middle: compromising positions, reaching halfway, making deals with the other side." The electoral implications for being a centrist are severe. "Becoming a moderate has simply become too high a price to pay . . . Many careers have gone down in flames due to attacks from the more extreme sides of the party—what's now called getting 'primaried.'" It is much easier to engage in rhetorical battles on partisan issues, which leads to gridlock. "The knock-down, drag-out fights never really lead anywhere in terms of legislation; what they do is shore up party support, raise money and rally the base."[38] Although neither could accurately be called a centrist themselves, the two leaders certainly understand the difficulties experienced by congressional moderates and why this "dying breed" is almost extinct.

Working with the Enemy

THROUGHOUT MY FIRST TERM, I WORKED HARD TO BUILD bipartisan relationships, earning me a reputation as a centrist who worked openly with both sides. During one mid-summer recess period, I teamed with my Republican colleague, Pennsylvania's Tim Murphy, to do two bipartisan town hall meetings—one in his district and one in mine. Murphy represented a neighboring congressional district and was often a target of national Democrats hoping to win back the seat.

When our town hall meetings were advertised in advance, House Democratic leaders asked me to reconsider, saying Murphy's seat was on their target list. They feared that appearing with me would make Murphy appear moderate to independent and Democratic swing voters who were going to be seeing a lot of television ads in the fall painting Murphy as a far-right conservative. Tim later told me that his leadership had a similar conversation with him, asking him to skip the town halls because the events would negate Republican attempts to paint me as a liberal acolyte of Nancy Pelosi. We laughed it off as "politics as usual" and went ahead with the town halls.

More concerning to me was the fact that some of my liberal constituents were upset that I was appearing with Murphy, not because they were afraid it would help him, but because they didn't want me to work with Republicans at all. To the liberals, the events confirmed their fears that I was really just a Republican in Democrat clothing.

I had built a moderate voting record and was solidifying a reputation as a bipartisan centrist. To general election voters, this was a positive. But to the left-wing partisans, my continued moderation was a cause of great concern.

The town halls were exceedingly well attended, drawing overflow crowds and media coverage at both venues. Tim and I had agreed to discourage political confrontations or overly partisan "gotcha" questions. As it turned out, the crowds were well behaved and both meetings generated the kind of thoughtful give-and-take absent in most town halls. At both events, we saw many new faces in the crowd, leading both Tim and I to conclude that many of those in attendance were people who would not normally attend a political event. They came out specifically because it was a bipartisan discussion. This is the type of outcome that gives me optimism that some people who disengage from politics because they are disgusted with congressional polarization can regain interest if they have confidence that genuine bipartisanship is possible.

The following week, I organized an even more rare bipartisan discussion. Typical debate on the House floor is highly scripted and scheduled in strictly enforced time increments. Rarely do members have anything more than a cursory back and forth with each other, and when they do, time often runs out to halt the discussion. Special Orders speeches, on the other hand, are scheduled in one-hour time blocks, which is why they have become a vehicle for some of the most vitriolic House commentary. Special Orders time is often reserved by small groups of the House's most partisan members, who proceed to take turns lambasting the policies of the other party, all with C-SPAN's cameras rolling. Occasionally, a bipartisan group will gather during Special Orders to talk about a subject upon which everyone agrees, such as a victorious sports team in their home region or commemorating a retiring colleague. Not since 1995 had the House had an unrestricted bipartisan Special Orders debate over an issue about which members of the two parties disagreed.

At the time of our bipartisan Special Order, gasoline prices had skyrocketed to the highest levels in American history, peaking at a record national average of $4.11 per gallon. To no one's surprise, the two sides politicized the issue to the fullest extent possible. Democrats blamed the policies of President Bush, while Republicans had taken to calling rising gas prices the "Pelosi Premium," referencing the role they believed Speaker Pelosi's anti-drilling environmental policies had played in the price increases. Americans became more frustrated with each passing day, and the issue became standard fodder on the campaign trail for candidates across the country. A previously little-known Alaska governor named Sarah Palin would soon take the country by storm with her familiar catch-phrase, "Drill, baby, drill!" Given the intensity of public sentiment on both sides, the possibility of a rational bipartisan debate seemed highly unlikely.

But it was precisely because there was a legitimate and easily defined difference of opinion between the parties that I believed this issue provided the perfect opportunity to bring the two sides together for a legitimate debate. Speaking privately with my ultra-conservative Republican colleague Lynn Westmoreland of Georgia, I broached the topic of bringing the two sides together during Special Orders hours to have an unscripted debate. Westmoreland was one of the leaders in the "Pelosi Premium" crowd, frequently taking to the floor to harshly criticize Democrats for their opposition to expanded oil drilling off

America's coasts. We agreed to test the idea among our respective colleagues and reconvene to discuss the details. Over the next few weeks, we finalized plans for what would become the only truly bipartisan Special Orders debate the House has seen in more than twenty years.

At the moment when nationwide gas prices were at their peak, we gathered on the House floor for two back-to-back Special Orders sessions, effectively giving us two-hours of free-flowing debate time. Westmoreland and I had arranged for the participation of the key leaders on the committees with jurisdiction over off-shore drilling, federal lands, and energy policy. I controlled time for the Democrats, while Texas congressman Joe Barton, the top Republican on the Energy and Commerce Committee, controlled time for the GOP. For two full hours, both sides carried on a serious discussion about the issue and the pros and cons of various solutions. The session was fun and informative, and it helped bring about a better understanding of each side's position. We proved that, even on the most incendiary issues, it is possible to bring both sides together for a respectful debate.

Media Madness

ONE OF THE BEST PREDICTORS OF PEOPLE'S POLITICAL leanings and voting behavior is their media content preference—what they watch and where they get their news. It should come as no surprise to learn that Republicans, particularly extreme conservatives, are highly overrepresented among consumers of conservative media, while they utilize mainstream media at rates far below the national average. Democrats prefer mainstream media, while independents are underrepresented among nearly all types of political and news media.[39] As for cable news channels, the more ideological the content, the more ideological the audience.[40] No surprise there. A 2014 Pew Research Center study shed new light on how the media habits of liberals, conservatives, and centrists help shape their politics.

The good news is that it is becoming more difficult to live in a completely isolated ideological bubble. The bad news is that those on the political extremes are doing their best to stay in those bubbles. Pew estimates that the 21% of Americans populating the far ends of the political spectrum have information streams that are completely distinct from each other. The only thing they have in common is that they are much more likely than political moderates to closely follow government and political news.[41]

The Pew research shows that these partisans have a disproportionate impact on the political process, as "the most ideologically oriented and politically rancorous Americans" create "a more ideologically extreme electorate." Other studies have confirmed that when the electorate is "made up primarily of impassioned partisans, political leaders will have fewer incentives to pursue the compromises that are the antidote to political gridlock."[42]

The Pew survey also showed that those with consistently conservative views predominantly get their political information from Fox News and talk radio. No other media source was listed by more than 5% of consistently conservative respondents. Liberals offered a much wider range of responses when asked to name their sources of information, focusing on a mix of CNN, NPR, MSNBC, and the *New York Times*. Those in the middle of the political spectrum list CNN as their main source for political news. These moderates also list among their preferences news aggregation websites Google and Yahoo, as well as local television news.[43]

A multitude of studies have shown that, when presented with a choice, partisans will seek out like-minded news sources. This applies even when the news doesn't really come from those sources. In one study, articles were randomly assigned different partisan news labels and offered to the study participants. Regardless of the content of the article, Republicans chose articles purported to be from Fox News, while Democrats chose articles allegedly from NPR and CNN. Similar results appeared when studying the browsing behavior of people in a waiting room with partisan magazines arranged strategically in front of them.[44]

Utilizing "selective exposure," people with access to hundreds of partisan media outlets will use them to find evidence confirming their pre-conceived views.[45] With that confirmation comes greater distrust of the other side. Unfortunately, once partisans find a program that aligns to their views, they stop looking for alternatives.[46] Commentators from these media sources preach to the choir, further convincing the activists that they are absolutely right and the other side is completely wrong.

This causes greater polarization on the political extremes but does not impact those in the middle, because they pay less attention to partisan media.[47] The partisans who are impacted represent a relatively small portion of Americans, but they are more likely to vote and participate in politics, giving them a disproportionate influence on the political process.[48]

President Trump's confrontational approach to the media has sent cable news ratings soaring. Nevertheless, viewers of partisan programming represent a proportionately small number of Americans. For most of the past two decades, Fox News has had the largest primetime cable news audience, attracting two to three million viewers[49] on a typical evening in a nation of 220 million eligible voters. Talk radio has a loyal following, especially among conservatives, but the listening audience still makes up only a small fraction of voters.[50] For those on the extremes, exposure to partisan media causes partisans to trust their opposition less and increases the animosity they feel towards members of the other party.[51] Unsurprisingly, there is a deep partisan divide about which sources of information to trust.

When asked in a survey to list the sources they trust most, nine different media sources were named by liberals, while only four sources were named by conservatives. There was no overlap. Interestingly, the three most trusted sources for liberals were all public news organizations: NPR, PBS, and the BBC. The remaining most trusted sources for liberals were the *New York Times*, CNN, MSNBC, and the three major network newscasts. Conservatives overwhelmingly trusted Fox News, followed by Sean Hannity, Rush Limbaugh, and Glenn Beck. A majority of those in the middle listed only CNN and the three network newscasts.[52]

It is easy to see the problem here. This is true polarization. Thirteen different news sources were mentioned without a single point of agreement between liberals and conservatives.

Again, the consumers of partisan media are the political activists, and they have a disproportionate impact on our elections. Is it any wonder there is polarization among the people they are sending to Congress?

CHAPTER 6

LESSONS IN GROUP DYNAMICS

———— ·•· ————

Indoctrinating the Children

ONE OF THE MORE RIDICULOUS EXAMPLES OF A CONTRO-
versy driven entirely by partisan media occurred when the
Obama administration announced in 2009 that the president
would deliver a back-to-school speech to students at a Virginia
high school. The topic of the speech was nonpolitical—encouraging students to "work hard, set educational goals, and take
responsibility for their learning." Public schools across the
country were given the opportunity to show the speech to their
own students through a live Internet link. The idea was not
unique. President George H. W. Bush had made available to
schools a similar speech to students during his time in office.[1]

When Obama's speech was announced, almost nobody contacted my office to discuss the topic. Then, a few days before the
speech was to be given, talk radio and conservative websites took
up the cause, accusing the president of a plot to "indoctrinate
their children with socialist ideas."[2] Suddenly, hundreds of calls
and emails were coming into my office from concerned parents
and school administrators. According to the *New York Times*,
similar complaints poured into congressional offices and local
schools across America. The complaints rose to absurd levels.

Rush Limbaugh discussed with a guest on his radio program
how the plan to livestream the president's speech to students

was similar to the manipulative tactics that had been used by Iraqi dictator Saddam Hussein.[3]

A local talk-radio host in Kansas City told listeners that he "wouldn't let my next-door neighbor talk to my kid alone; I'm sure as hell not letting Barack Obama talk to him alone."[4]

The chairman of the Republican Party of Florida issued an error-filled statement in which he said, "President Obama has turned to American's (sic) youngest children to spread his liberal lies, indoctrinating American's (sic) youngest children before they have a chance to decide for themselves."[5]

A sobbing parent in Colorado fought through tears during a CNN interview to say that students "having to listen to that just really upsets me. I'm an American. They are Americans, and I don't feel that's okay. I feel very scared to be in this country with our leadership right now."[6]

The president delivered his seventeen-minute speech on September 8, but many school districts—including several in the district I represented—opted not to show it. Some parents residing in school districts that did show the speech chose to keep their children home for the day. The whole episode would be funny if it weren't so sad.

Polarization is a Group Effort

IT IS SELF-INTUITIVE THAT MOST PEOPLE WHO REGULARLY access partisan media already hold polarized political attitudes. This has been proven time and again through experimental research. Perhaps more disheartening is what the research shows happens when partisans are provided credible information offering an alternative viewpoint. No matter how factually accurate, opposing information is often deemed by partisans to be unfair or biased. Rather than rethinking their position, partisans may actually become *more* polarized after hearing different opinions. Encountering differing perspectives only strengthens their resolve and motivates them to build counter arguments. They view exposure to the other side of the story as opposition research rather than fact finding.[7]

Even neutral news coverage won't change a partisan's mind. When shown unbiased news coverage of political issues, partisans are likely to view the coverage as hostile to their viewpoint, focusing their attention on the parts of the story that don't conform to their own thinking. When newscasts present both sides of the story equally, most partisans will accept only the points they agree with and dismiss contradictory claims.[8] Centrists are turned off by partisan programming, but they view mainstream news as credible and can be influenced by it—if you can get them to watch it.[9]

One way to get partisans to consider alternative viewpoints is by convincing them that opinion leaders in their own party are doing so. Partisans will reject evidence disproving their beliefs if that evidence is presented by the opposing party. Partisans will also reject evidence provided by nonpartisan groups if it contradicts their own views. The most effective way to get partisans to reconsider their views is for an elite from their own party to speak in opposition to the partisans' own beliefs. The party affiliation of the source of the new information is the factor that best determines whether people will rethink their positions.[10]

When shown an opinion column written by a fictional author, participants in an experiment were more likely to reconsider their position on controversial issues. Why? Because they were told the author was a highly credible leader in their party or "frequent contributor" to either Fox News or MSNBC, depending on the political affiliation of the respondent. On controversial issues like banking regulation and environmental policy, the fictional author made a strong case in opposition to conventional party doctrine. Study participants found the argument persuasive if it was offered by someone ideologically similar to themselves.[11] Of course, this reconsideration did not last long. When the study was over and participants went home, it was back to the echo chamber. But for that one moment, there was doubt. Could there be room for encouragement there?

Throughout my time in Congress, I found that partisans generally arrive at their positions on policy issues based largely upon what their party or ideological leaders are saying. Proving politics no longer stops at the water's edge, for many partisans, the decision about whether to support or oppose a foreign policy issue is based almost entirely upon the party affiliation of the president proposing those policies.

Some issues are morally or religiously oriented, which of course requires a more personal introspection outside of ideological considerations. But for most political issues—economic policy, oil drilling, education reform, etc.—the opinion of party leaders plays a major role in an individual's decision.[12]

In Congress, this applies even on issues where members have themselves taken the opposite position in the past, a phenomenon that frequently occurs after a change in administration or party control of Congress. Examples of these flip-flops include the periodic votes to raise the debt limit, opposition to the use of presidential Executive Orders, the threat of a government shutdown to achieve political goals, and the appropriateness of the use of procedural delaying tactics to stall legislation. Each of these issues provides opportunity to find scores of members of Congress whose positions changed based solely upon who was calling the shots at the time.

One of the most notorious examples occurred in 2010 during Senate consideration of a bipartisan bill to establish an eighteen-member task force that would have been charged with crafting a comprehensive deficit reduction plan. Within a week of introduction, more than one-third of the entire Senate had cosponsored the bill, including twenty-one Republicans and thirteen Democrats. Senate Republican leader Mitch McConnell praised the proposal, which appeared headed for passage. Then something happened that changed everything; President Obama endorsed the Senate bill. Within hours of Obama's announcement, Republican cosponsors began to withdraw their support. In all, seven Republicans withdrew as cosponsors. The resolution to bring the bill to the floor fell seven votes shy of the sixty votes necessary to overcome a filibuster. McConnell himself voted against the resolution.[13]

After the vote, *Washington Post* opinion editor Fred Hiatt wrote, "No single vote by any single senator could possibly illustrate everything that is wrong with Washington today. No single vote could embody the full cynicism and cowardice of our political elite at its worst, or explain why problems do not get solved. But here's one that comes close."[14]

For the 80% of House members occupying safe seats, deciding how to vote is quite simple. Do what your leader does. This is especially true among House Democrats, where the purging of moderates from the party's ranks has made the caucus's message sound particularly unified. In the case of Republicans, "leader" is a relative term because Freedom Caucus and mainstream Republicans have distinctly different opinions about who is leading their respective movements. Sometimes a locally relevant issue may change the calculation, but for the most part, members of Congress from safe seats fall in line behind their leadership, be it congressional or ideological.

Congressional leadership messages are conveyed to rank-and-file members during the weekly caucus meetings, where each party gathers in the Capitol with their respective leaders. The tone of the two meetings could not be more different. In contrast to most Democratic Caucus meetings, the Republican gatherings can be quite raucous, as Tea Party-backed members and traditional Republicans spar with one another over pending legislation and the direction of the party. The rift spilled out into the public during the ugly fight over the House bill to repeal and replace the Affordable Care Act. The Freedom Caucus has now moved so far to the right that the group engages in open warfare with members within its own party.

Democrats have a more unified message in their caucus meetings because few centrists remain to occupy seats in the room. This gives Democratic House members a certainty the American people are with them, because they rarely hear an opposing viewpoint in caucus meetings or at home in the district. If anything, the growing points of dissention in Democratic meetings revolve around liberal frustration as to why party leaders do not take a more aggressive approach in promoting an even more liberal agenda. The resurgence of the far-left has been emboldened even further by supporters of Senator Bernie Sanders, who overperformed expectations in the 2016 presidential primary with his populist message. Today, the raging debate within the Democratic Party is not whether to moderate their message to better appeal to centrist voters, but how far to the left the party should go in messaging and recruiting candidates.

Party leaders also designate surrogates to speak over the airwaves. Designated members on each side will appear on news and political programs, sticking with the talking points and directing their message to the partisans who pay attention to those shows. Local political activists across the country will then use those talking points to decide which position to take and how to articulate their view. The more polarized Congress is on an issue, the more firmly their partisan constituents will stick to those talking points, no matter what the facts say.

My favorite study about this is a 2013 experiment[15] that exposed participants to arguments that either support or oppose legislation pending before Congress. Some participants received a strong argument, while others were provided particularly weak arguments to support their position. In addition, participants were told whether or not members of the two parties in Congress were in agreement on the issue or opposed to each other along party lines.

Study participants who were told the two parties were in agreement generally accepted only the strong arguments, even if those arguments did not align with the individual's own ideology. So, if a partisan split did not exist on the issue, respondents were willing to consider the facts. There was a significant difference when respondents were told that Congress was polarized on the issue. In that case, respondents tended to accept only the arguments that supported their own party's position, regardless of whether those arguments were strong or weak. Knowing there was a clear difference of opinion between the parties, this time respondents were not interested in hearing alternative points of view. Wanting to make sure they supported the politically correct side, they would accept even the flimsiest supporting evidence, while rejecting stronger arguments to the contrary.[16] These results are consistent with my experience talking with the partisan constituents who attend town hall meetings and call congressional offices.

When I attended political forums in the district, I found the issues constituents would bring up were almost always determined by what the talk radio or cable news shows happened to be talking about at the time. Even on complex policy issues, people's positions were reliably predictable if you knew what the talk show hosts were saying.

On the way to town hall meetings, I would always listen to talk radio to get a sense of what issues would come up. My staff used to have fun with the fact that talk radio would drive the volume of calls into my office throughout the day. Like clockwork, when the Rush Limbaugh radio program concluded each afternoon, the phone lines in my office would begin to light up with callers from Republican areas of the district. Mimicking whatever Limbaugh had said that day, the callers would talk to my staff about those same issues, using the same terminology. Sometimes my staff would ask if the constituent had been listening to talk radio. The callers would usually be reluctant to admit they had been listening to Limbaugh, insisting instead that they had spontaneously come to these conclusions all by themselves.

An important part of being a representative is to be cautious about giving too much weight to these types of calls. It is important to know whether or not callers are truly representative of the district or only a small but vocal minority. The same held true for form letters and orchestrated email campaigns, as well as information received from activists who rallied at my office or attended town hall meetings. These constituents were making the most noise, but I had a responsibility to gauge how much their message was consistent with the majority view of the 750,000 people I was elected to represent. That's why it was so important to visit with people across the entire district. Unlike most congressional districts where public opinion is relatively consistent, the swing district I represented was sometimes evenly split on issues. It was also not unusual for the mood of the overall district to be noticeably different than the opinions of the activists with the loudest voice.

No public event provides a more accurate view into the window of human behavior than the political town hall meeting. Town halls are meant to give any member of the community an opportunity to learn about pending legislative issues, as well as to ask questions of their elected representative.

During my three terms in office, I held countless town halls and public meetings in every part of the district. Those who participate in these types of meetings tend to be those with the most extreme views and the most confidence in their opinions. Centrist constituents and those with moderate political views don't make up the majority of attendees of town halls, and in most cases don't even bother to attend at all. The town hall is therefore left to partisans who use the meeting not as a forum to exchange ideas, debate public policy, and learn new information, but instead to join their like-minded compatriots in trying to disrupt the meeting and create as big a media firestorm as possible.

Although the few remaining congressional swing districts contain voters on both sides, often those citizens are geographically sorted and live in clusters, so political events held in different parts of the same district can attract wildly different types of crowds. Such was the case with most of my town hall meetings. Depending on where I held the meeting, the crowd could be almost entirely Democrat or entirely Republican, with little overlap. The one thing that remained consistent wherever I held the meeting was that those who took the time to attend usually represented the extreme wings of their parties.

Town hall meetings can be quite a show. Social norms that are accepted in every other area of society do not apply to politics. People who might never muster the courage to speak on their own are comfortable shouting at an elected representative they've never met. Attendees at town halls remind me of an English-speaking American asking directions in a foreign country, speaking louder and louder as if the increased volume will somehow overcome the fact that the other person doesn't understand English.

Democrats in 2017 have mobilized their most extreme partisans to create an even more incendiary environment at public meetings.[17] Organized by left-wing groups like MoveOn.org and patterning their behavior on the Tea Party protests of 2009, Democratic activists have used similarly disruptive tactics to confront Republican members of Congress.[18] Some Republican members take advantage of the opportunity by highlighting the wackiest of the protesters. In a process akin to how *The Price is Right* gameshow selects it's contestants, the most eccentric liberal activists are plucked from the crowd and placed near the television cameras. Cable news programs gleefully run the clips of Republican members being berated by these activists, often with socially inappropriate signage nearby. Both sides believe this visual plays to their advantage because it stokes the passions of their respective partisans.

Staunch conservative Republican Congressman Tom Mc-Clintock has held numerous public forums in his California district, skillfully using the events to draw attention to the most disruptive members of the audience. Protest organizers have grown frustrated by McClintock's tactics, accusing him of purposely making outrageously partisan statements in order to enrage liberals in the audience. Video clips from the congressman's town halls often make the rounds on social media and cable news channels, and his events have grown so raucous that on at least one occasion he had to be escorted out by police. Unfortunately, such mayhem is not isolated to McClintock's district.[19]

In Florida, Republican congressman Ted Yoho was repeatedly jeered, interrupted, and ridiculed by hundreds of angry Democratic protesters at an April 2017 town hall in his district. Yoho called the event the most unruly he has experienced in his career, which is significant given the fact that only weeks earlier a man was arrested for punching an attendee in the face outside another Yoho town hall.[20]

Partisan disruptions at town hall meetings have become the new normal, with political reporters and other attendees often tweeting real-time play-by-play of the mayhem. Meanwhile, centrist Americans remain on the sidelines, growing even more disenchanted by the ever-increasing polarization they see all around them.

Results of the many social experiments that have been carried out to test the power of the group on an individual's thinking can be both amusing and frightening. One of the leading experts on the impact of group dynamics, Jonathan Haidt, says,

> DECADES OF RESEARCH on public opinion have led to the conclusion that self-interest is a weak predictor of policy preferences . . . Rather, people care about their groups, whether those be racial, regional, religious or political . . . In matters of public opinion, citizens seem to be asking themselves not 'What's in it for me?' but rather 'What's in it for my group.' Political opinions function as 'badges of social membership.'[21]

In the same way sports fans evaluate a referee's call based upon whether or not the call went against their team, political partisans evaluate the strength of a policy argument based upon whether or not that argument is promoted by a member of their own political party. As Harvard psychologist Steven Pinker has observed, "we don't want the truth to prevail, we want our version of the truth to prevail."[22]

If you ever decide to research this topic, which I highly recommend because it's fascinating, you'll stumble upon a 2004 experiment conducted by psychologist Drew Westen.[23] In the landmark study, Westen and colleagues at Emory University used an MRI machine to monitor the brain activities of political partisans from both sides. During the heat of the contentious presidential election, the partisans went under the brain scanner one by one. Each was provided information showing blatantly hypocritical statements made by Senator John Kerry and President George W. Bush. As an example, the partisans were shown quotes from President Bush heaping praise upon the business practices of then-Enron CEO Ken Lay, using him as the example of how Bush wanted to run the country. With the MRI monitoring their brain activity, the partisans were then given information about the calamitous fall of Enron and Bush's later embarrassing reluctance to mention anything about Ken Lay. Finally, participants were shown a slide explaining that Bush had felt betrayed by Lay and was shocked to learn of the corruption of Enron's leadership. Similarly conflicting information was provided about statements that had been made by Kerry.[24]

Each of the partisans had been provided initial information casting Bush and Kerry in a negative light, followed by further information that clarified the circumstances in a way that absolved the candidates of their perceived hypocrisy. What did the brain scan show while all of this was going on? The partisans felt threatened when their preferred candidate looked bad, as demonstrated by the activation of the areas of the brain that control negative emotion and response to punishment. They later experienced a sense of relief as the situation was explained to their satisfaction. Unsurprisingly, the partisans were also excited and felt pleasure when their nonpreferred candidate was made to look bad.[25]

Here is the scary part—the experiment demonstrated that extreme partisanship is mentally blinding and literally addicting. The study participants processed the information they were provided, but their brains ignored the evidence incriminating their own candidate. While the sections of the brain controlling emotion and pleasure lit up during the experiment, the sections controlling reasoning and objectivity stayed dark. Study participants paid no attention to the facts of what they were being shown. Instead, they spent their mental energy either dismissing negative information about their own candidate or relishing in the negative information about the opposing candidate. As Westen describes the results: "We did not see any increased activation of the parts of the brain normally engaged during reasoning . . . When confronted with potentially troubling political information . . . the brain registers the conflict between data and desire and begins to search for ways to turn off the spigot of unpleasant emotion."[26]

To make matters worse, the brain actually rewarded study participants for ignoring negative information about their own candidates. When participants were convinced their own candidate had been absolved of hypocrisy, the MRI scan showed participants' brains activated in the area of the ventral striatum, a part of the brain that controls reward through emission of the neurotransmitter dopamine.[27]

In discussing this phenomenon, Haidt points out that heroin and cocaine are addictive because they artificially trigger this type of dopamine response. In his study of partisan brain activity, Westen found that participants got a small hit of dopamine when they realized their candidate had been absolved. Alarmingly, the study proved that partisanship is literally addicting. It makes you feel good. This does not bode well for finding a resolution to political polarization.[28]

A similar experiment was conducted by neuroscientists at the University of Southern California in 2016. Forty self-described liberals agreed to an MRI scan to show how their brains responded when their political beliefs were challenged.[29]

Study participants were presented with strong counterarguments to both political and nonpolitical statements with which they agreed. As it turned out, they could be persuaded to change their minds on nonpolitical statements but refused to budge on political matters, such as immigration, military budgets, and gun control.

When presented with evidence that contradicted their political beliefs, their brains activated in the areas involved in perceiving threat and anxiety related to self-perception. The participants considered the political counterevidence to be a direct challenge to the way they viewed themselves based on their political beliefs. They could not bring themselves to change their minds, because doing so would not only go against their view on the issue but also how they viewed themselves.[30]

Dr. Jonas Kaplan, lead author of the USC study, explains: "Political beliefs are like religious beliefs in the respect that both are part of who you are and important for the social circle to which you belong. To consider an alternative view, you would have to consider an alternative version of yourself."[31]

David Blankenhorn, president of the Institute for American Values, recognizes that polarization is made worse by group behaviors. He says, "Humans form in-groups, 'us' in opposition to 'them.'" This leads to "intellectual habits such as binary thinking and negatively exaggerating and stereotyping the views of outsiders."[32]

In *The Big Sort*, Bill Bishop gives an informative history of the study of group dynamics—what he calls "the psychology of the tribe."[33] The first known experiment in social psychology related to group interaction was conducted in 1897 by Indiana University professor Norman Triplett. Using two thousand bicyclists as subjects, Triplett famously proved that individuals peddled faster when racing against others than when racing against the clock. In proving that groups change individual behavior, Triplett's research initiated more than a century of experiments into the effects of groups on individuals.[34]

Bishop describes a study of German school children who followed the lead of popular children in breaking the rules, then blamed their bad behavior on the unpopular students. In another study, both American and Turkish college students were asked to rank from one to sixteen a list of famous authors. The students were then given sixteen different paragraphs that they were told had been written by each of the noteworthy authors, but in reality had all been written by the same author. The students' rankings unsurprisingly coincided with their own rankings of the well-known authors.[35]

In another study, subjects in a group were shown strips of paper of varying lengths. As part of the study, a few actors had been placed in the group to argue that all the strips were the same length. Even though study participants could see with their own eyes that the strips were different lengths, 75% of them eventually agreed that the strips were all the same length. The need to conform with the group outweighed the need to provide accurate information.[36]

Later experiments moved into the concept of extremism in groups and the unwillingness to consider alternative points of view. A University of Michigan study showed that groups welcome those who change their position on an issue to conform with the group consensus, but shun those who take an opposing position, eventually excluding them from the group altogether.[37] A later study demonstrated that, when evaluating whether an overmatched chess player should engage in a series of increasingly risky moves with little chance of success, the group consistently recommended a riskier move than the respondents recommended individually .[38]

Author Rick Shenkman has observed, "An individual, on his own, will refrain from taking an extreme position on an issue. But put him with a group of like-minded people . . . and pretty soon he and the other members will drift inexorably toward more and more extreme positions. If they drive the dissenters out, they'll go even more extreme."[39] Group behavior can also drive people to make irresponsible and unethical decisions.

Duke University behavioral economist Dan Ariely conducted a unique study of group behavior using college students in Pittsburgh. Carnegie Mellon is a private university considered to be one of the most prestigious science and technology schools in the world. The neighboring University of Pittsburgh accepts a majority of applicants[40] and has a comparatively less distinguished academic reputation. The two schools could not accurately be called rivals, but many Carnegie Mellon students are notoriously skeptical of the academic credentials of their neighboring students at the other end of Pittsburgh's Forbes Avenue.

To assist with the study, Ariely hired an acting student from CMU's highly ranked School of Drama. The actor sat among a group of CMU students who agreed to participate in an experiment conducted by a math professor. The students were given a difficult math exam and paid for each problem they solved correctly. The acting student flagrantly cheated on the exam and pocketed the money. Observing what had happened without consequences, the others followed his lead and cheated as well.[41] Ariely described it as giving "social justification for a new social norm to emerge about cheating."[42] But here's where it gets interesting. In a second experiment, the acting student wore a University of Pittsburgh sweatshirt. This time, almost nobody followed his lead. The CMU students in the room resisted the urge to cheat and completed the exam honestly. Why the difference? The sweatshirt identified the actor as an outsider, not part of the group.[43] Ariely theorizes what the CMU students thought: "This is cheating. This is what the other people in the bad school are doing. This is not what we're doing."[44] Groups follow the actions of their own members, which drives them to extremes.

When partisan bias is mixed with the psychology of group dynamics, the results can be combustible. Human reasoning has evolved in a way that encourages people to assess facts not to learn new information, but to help bolster their own arguments—and to manipulate those facts to persuade others. Cognitive scientists Hugo Mercier and Dan Sperber explained it this way: "Skilled arguers . . . are not after the truth but after arguments supporting their views."[45] Haidt points out that "each individual reasoner is really good at one thing: finding evidence to support the position he or she already holds . . . We should not expect truth-seeking individuals to produce good, open-minded, truth-seeking reasoning."[46]

Haidt focuses his research on ways to bring different people together to form groups with ideological and intellectual diversity, thereby increasing the chances of civility and thoughtful decision making. Perhaps that might work, but it is not what happens in town hall meetings.

Shouting Down a Nun

I ALWAYS HAD THE MOST FUN IN TOWN HALLS LOCATED IN areas of the district where the meeting could attract people from both parties. Like the "Congress on Your Corner" event where two attendees argued with each other about whether it was Nancy Pelosi or George Bush who pulled my puppet strings, it never failed in the politically mixed events that I would be criticized from both extremes. I always took it as a compliment, because it confirmed my record was right down the middle.

Frequently, the different sides of the district would be split on an issue. But sometimes public opinion across the district was completely one-sided.

One of my most memorable town halls was held in Shaler Township, a politically divided middle-class suburb where studio wrestler turned union leader John DeFazio was the Democratic chairman. Immigration reform was the hot topic in Washington and on talk radio, and an overflow crowd had come to voice their opinion. I knew which side they would be on, because the hundreds of calls that had come into my office skewed overwhelming against legalizing undocumented immigrants. With the exception of the Affordable Care Act, no issue during my time in office drew a more heated response from constituents.

With DeFazio looking on, constituents rose one by one to convey their opposition to amnesty for "the illegals." Union workers feared loss of jobs, despite the fact that Pittsburgh had the lowest number of immigrant workers of any region in the country. Other attendees gave romanticized versions of how their parents and grandparents had immigrated from Europe decades before, but had done so "the right way"—learning English, "working hard," and refusing taxpayer benefits. I noticed an elderly woman sitting alone in front, nervously fidgeting as the rhetoric grew more intense. Finally, she raised her hand and stood up.

Visibly shaking as she leaned against the banister in front of her, she took a deep breath and identified herself as a Catholic nun. Her voice quivered as she implored the audience to avoid using the term "illegals." She said these were just people who came to this country to make better lives for themselves and their families, just as so many relatives of those in attendance had done for their own families so long ago. She gave an impassioned defense of America, saying the welcoming of immigrants represents the values upon which this nation was founded. I could feel tears welling up in my eyes as she bravely defended a position she knew was unpopular. Then the crowd interrupted her and shouted her down.

"They're illegals!" an enraged man yelled, cutting off the elderly woman in mid-sentence. "What don't you understand about the word illegal?" called out another. People began shouting over one another. I asked the crowd to allow her to finish, but she shook her head and sat down, indicating she had said all she could say. She sat silently for the rest of the meeting, listening as one person after another argued against "amnesty."

After the meeting, I asked the woman to stay so I could speak with her privately. I thanked her for coming and for having the courage to voice her concerns. I told her I was inspired by her remarks and that it was especially important for her to be there because the district I represented was very one-sided on the issue. I said it was good to have in attendance a constituent who could so passionately present a different point of view. Then came the kicker; she was not a constituent at all. She lived far outside the district but had driven in for the meeting because she had seen me quoted in the news about how opposed the district was to the immigration bill. Of all the people who spoke that night, she had been the only one to speak favorably about the bill.

Another town hall meeting highlighted for me the absurdity of some of the misinformation that people use to form their opinions and how difficult it is to break people from those opinions even after they are presented with facts. The meeting was held in a public library in a strongly Republican suburban community where I knew there would be a sizable Tea Party presence. More than a hundred people crammed into a room that sat sixty, and the crowd was boisterous in their criticisms of Washington. I had come to know most of the people there because they were regular attendees at my town halls in that part of the district.

One man sitting in front criticized the "fact" that members of Congress don't pay Social Security taxes. I corrected him, saying that all members do in fact pay into Social Security, just like everybody else. Others in the audience took his side, saying they had seen their version of the truth "in the news" or "on the Internet." I responded that I would happily send them a letter and a Congressional Research Service report verifying the facts, but they said they already knew the facts so there was no reason for me to send the report. Exasperated, I said that short of showing them my W-2 tax form, I didn't know what else I could do to prove I paid Social Security taxes. The meeting continued and I never did convince them.

One of the most vocal women among the group mentioned that she was going to be in Washington soon and wanted to meet with me. I agreed, although I knew the meeting would be unpleasant because she was one of my harshest and most unwavering critics. Leading up to the meeting, my staff heard through the grapevine that the woman had been bragging to her circle of Tea Party activists how she was going to take full advantage of the opportunity and really let me have it. Meeting in my office, there would be no distractions and no way for me to avoid her inquisition.

When she finally visited my office, we had a civilized discussion. The woman was respectful and listened intently as I conveyed my point of view. We discovered that we agreed nearly as much as we disagreed. Most interesting was her reserved demeanor, which was quite different from the show she could put on when she attended public meetings with her activist friends. If anything, she came across as shy and reserved, which seemed out of character but was probably her real personality. It highlighted for me how group dynamics can ignite passions and prevent thoughtful discourse, even among otherwise reasonable people.

Judging Ignorance

STORIES ABOUT THE FACTUAL IGNORANCE OF AMERICANS are well-known. We have all seen the news reports about what percentage of Americans would fail the standard citizenship test that immigrants must pass (38%).[47] The dismal lack of knowledge Americans possess about the basic facts of civics, government, and politics—combined with their delusional confidence in their own opinion—is downright depressing. Let's do a reality check.

The American Revolution Center conducted a national survey of adults to gauge knowledge about the American Revolution. In response to the first question, 89% of respondents believed they could pass a basic test about the Revolution. By the end of the survey, 83% had failed. One-third of respondents did not even know the century in which the Revolution took place. If it makes you feel any better, 90% believed it was important for Americans to know the history and principles of the nation's founding.[48] So, there's that.

Other surveys show equally alarming results. A majority of American adults inaccurately believe Christianity is written into the Constitution.[49] Only 45% can correctly identify what the Republican Party's GOP initials stand for.[50] Three-quarters of Americans don't know the length of a senator's term, while only 20% know how many senators there are. Twice as many people can name two characters in the popular cartoon show *The Simpsons* than can name two rights guaranteed in the First Amendment. Less than half of Americans know that Herbert Hoover was a president.[51] When Americans were asked to identify the percentage of the federal budget that goes to foreign aid, the average response was 27%. When asked what percentage of the budget they thought it should be, the average was 13%. (It is actually less than 1%).[52]

Americans' knowledge of the Supreme Court is particularly unimpressive. Less than half can name even a single justice. Almost nobody can name all nine. In fact, of the 1,032 people surveyed in a 2017 C-SPAN poll, none could.[53] The coups de grace?

Ten percent of Americans think television's Judith Sheindlin (Judge Judy) is on the Supreme Court.[54]

The Lake Wobegon Effect

IT DOESN'T TAKE A POLITICIAN LONG TO RECOGNIZE THAT most partisan activists have deeply held opinions. More often than not, those opinions are only loosely related to the facts. Political activists believe they are right, and they are not at all interested in hearing a different point of view or a nuanced policy position.

As a centrist looking for compromise and middle ground on issues, I was always frustrated about how people look for easy answers to complex problems. This criticism applies to both sides of the aisle. Most of the time, partisans aren't actually looking for answers—they are certain they already know the right answer. It is impossible to get people to consider compromise when they believe their side is 100% right and the other side is 100% wrong. For them, to compromise is not only to move away from their principles, but also to move away from what they perceive to be the facts.

What is it about the way people think that makes them so certain they are right and so unwilling to consider different opinions? As with the other types of cognitive biases that lead to hyperpartisanship and polarization, science provides an answer—and it isn't pretty.

In *Political Animals*, Rick Shenkman argues the problem stems from human evolution having programmed into our brains certain biases that were helpful thousands of years ago at a time when the ability to make quick decisions based upon intuition could be the difference between life and death. Today, people still make quick decisions with little to no information to go on, and they have an irrational certainty that those decisions are correct.[55] Unfortunately, this results in flawed public policy and resistance to compromise.

One bias that is extremely detrimental to thoughtful public policy is the Availability Bias. This stems from the unwillingness of people to admit, even to themselves, that they don't know the answer. Or at least that they don't know enough about the question to arrive at a thoughtful conclusion. People want to believe they are qualified to give an answer even when the information available to them is laughably limited.

If you were given only a photograph and the name of a person you have never met, would you be able to provide key details about that person's life and behavior? According to one study,[56] when presented with only this limited information, many people are willing to give a definitive opinion about specific details of the life of the person in the photograph, including how the person would behave under certain circumstances.

A second control group in the study had the opportunity to meet and interview the people in the photographs before offering those opinions. As you might expect, the results showed that the group that had met the people in the pictures were much more accurate in their predictions. But the results also showed that study participants who had not met the people in the photographs were almost as certain that their predictions were correct as those who had interviewed the people in the photographs. It doesn't matter how much information people have to form their opinions—deep depth of knowledge or just a hunch—they still have confidence they are right.[57]

Even worse, it is extremely difficult to move someone off of their opinion once they arrive at it, even when they are shown contradictory evidence. This is called the "Perseverance Bias." People stick with what they believe, even if they are unable to remember exactly where they learned the "facts" that led them to that conclusion. Like the study involving the photographs of people they've never met, many partisans will immediately form an opinion about information they've heard in only superficial detail. Then they forget where they heard it in the first place. Social scientists call this "Source Confusion"—a person's inability to recall where they learned the information about which they are so confident.[58]

Voters use mental shortcuts to compensate for lack of information.[59] For example, voters will use a candidate's party affiliation, a friend's recommendation, or the position of a candidate's name on the ballot as a source of information to determine their vote when they have limited information about the actual candidate. Unfortunately, studies have also shown that voters make worse choices in a polarized environment.

Political scientists determine "opinion quality" by measuring the accuracy of information voters use to determine their vote.

As author Jill Lepore describes it, opinion quality is "the match between what we know and how we vote. If you know a lot about something and apply that information to a vote that matches your policy preferences, your opinion quality is high."[60]

Noted political scientist James Druckman tested this in a survey of more than six hundred voters, each of whom was provided varying information about drilling for oil and gas. Druckman found the opinion quality of voters decreased as the information provided to them became more partisan. "They found that in a more polarized environment voters make worse choices and have more confidence in them."[61]

Perhaps the least surprising of all cognitive biases is "Superiority Bias," also known as the "Lake Wobegon Effect"[62] in reference to radio celebrity Garrison Keillor's imaginary place "where all the women are strong, all the men are good-looking, and all the children are above average."[63] Superiority Bias is the human characteristic where people think they are better at things than they really are.[64]

When asked to rate themselves in any number of categories, most people will always rank themselves above average.[65] The scientific literature is overflowing with bewildering examples. Large majorities place themselves above the median in all sorts of categories, including leadership skills, athletic prowess, and ability to get along with others.[66] Americans in every demographic category rate themselves as above-average drivers.[67] In evaluating their own performance, people think their jokes are funnier and they use better grammar than others.[67] They think their logical reasoning skills are more advanced and their potential for future success is better than most everybody else.[68] University professors consistently rate themselves above the median, including the 95% of University of Nebraska faculty who rated themselves above average in teaching ability.[69] This certainly adds color to the old joke that the "N" on the Nebraska football helmet stands for "knowledge."

As with other types of biases, Superiority Bias is addicting. In one study, scientists took a group of volunteers and studied their brain activity using both an MRI test and a Positron Emission Tomography (PET) scan. The results showed that the brains of those with more complimentary views of themselves produced higher levels of dopamine than the brains of those with more realistic self-appraisals.[70] This outcome presented scientists with some important information about how to treat people with depression, but it gives us little hope of finding a realistic way of helping people get an accurate understanding about their own levels of political and factual misinformation.

Superiority Bias plays an important role in politically polarized attitudes. It is partly attributed to metacognition, where those with lesser knowledge are unable to accurately understand their level of misinformation because they don't know what they don't know.[71] A common example is a student who learns Newton's three laws and therefore believes herself to be highly literate in physics. We have all encountered people like this in the political world, such as the small businessman who considers himself to be an expert on macroeconomic policy because he pays taxes and balances his own budget.

Social experiments have shown that those with the lowest level of ability often have the most inflated estimation of their own talents. Furthermore, the less a person knows about something, the less accurate they are in judging other people's knowledge in the same subject.[72] It is not hard to see the direct correlation with political polarization.

Partisans often fall victim to the related bias of asymmetric insight, which in effect means they believe they know their own internal and moral convictions better than their political opponent knows theirs. As blogger Thorin Klosowski has explained,

> BECAUSE OF ASYMMETRIC insight, in a political debate you don't believe the other side will ever understand your point of view. At the same time, you believe you understand their point of view, but you're so smart you know they're wrong. For example: 'I'm too smart to believe those Democrats,' you tell yourself, 'I understand everything about the Democrats and disagree with them. They don't even try to understand us Republicans. If they could understand us, they'd be on our side.' (And vice versa).[73]

Unfortunately, all of this tends to work to the advantage of the ideological activists, as studies have also shown that being right is not what wins arguments. What matters most is being the most obstinate and the most certain of the correctness of your position. More often than not, the one who is most determined to argue through all the challenges and ignore contrary points of view is also the one who is able to bring others over to their side. The opposition just gives up, even when they are correct.[74]

Given all of this, it is no wonder why politicians tell voters what they want to hear. Voters simply are not persuaded by the facts. Haidt says it best:

> WE CIRCLE AROUND sacred values and then share post hoc arguments about why we are so right and they are so wrong. We think the other side is blind to the truth, reason, science, and common sense, but in fact everyone goes blind when talking about their sacred objects. . . . If you ask people to believe something that violates their intuitions, they will devote their efforts to finding an escape hatch—a reason to doubt your argument or conclusions.[75]

So how do you engage in a political debate with someone who is so certain of their position that even facts won't persuade them? Steve McIntosh of the Institute for Cultural Evolution believes the key is to acknowledge that you have listened to and considered the views of the other side. Refusing to accept any legitimacy in the other side's position undermines any opportunity to work together to find common ground. McIntosh says, "The partisans of any given position are far more likely to listen to and respect the opinion of opponents who are willing to affirm at least some of the strengths of their position."[76]

In his 2017 journal article, *How to Convince Someone When Facts Fail*, author Michael Shermer asks, "If corrective facts only make matters worse, what can we do to convince people of the error of their beliefs?" He largely agrees with the approach advocated by McIntosh, recommending against injecting emotion or confrontation into the debate, while focusing on an understanding of the other person's position. Perhaps most important, Shermer recommends trying "to show how changing facts does not necessarily mean changing worldviews."[77]

Research shows people are more likely to accept new evidence if it is presented to them in a way that doesn't trigger a defensive or emotional reaction. Yale professor Dan Kahan has found that people are more open to receiving new information if it doesn't threaten their overall political view. For example, Kahan found that conservative climate change skeptics were more likely to accept the fact that humans are causing global warming when they are presented up front with politically palatable solutions, like expansion of nuclear energy. Once partisans realize the other side doesn't automatically "win," they are more likely to move outside of their ideological comfort zone.[78]

Perhaps most encouraging is a University of Illinois study that showed it is possible to disrupt the tendency of partisans to be blinded by bias. The researchers found that: "Liberals and conservatives who are politically polarized on certain subjects become more moderate when reading political arguments in difficult-to-read font." When presented identical arguments in easy-to-read font, partisans became much more polarized than those in peer groups who had to slow down and read through the same material in a more challenging-printed font.[79] According to researchers writing in the *Journal of Experimental Social Psychology*, this study shows "that subtle manipulations that affect how people take in information can reduce political polarization." Ivan Hernandez, who led the study, said, "We showed that if we can slow people down, if we can make them stop relying on their gut reaction—that feeling that they already know what something says—it can make them more moderate; it can have them start doubting their initial beliefs and start seeing the other side of the argument a bit more."[80]

Concessions

WHEN POWER IS DIVIDED IN WASHINGTON, CONGRESSES with more centrists tend to be more productive. Centrists can also play a key role even when one party controls both Congress and the White House, as is the case today. Without compromise, even issues that may seem tangential to much larger initiatives can hold up passage of major legislation.

One example in which I was directly involved was the Omnibus Public Land Management Act of 2009, a massive piece of legislation that incorporated more than 150 different bills that had been considered but not passed in previous Congresses over a period of many years. In terms of total geographic reach, the scope of the bill was nearly unprecedented. It covered two million acres of wilderness areas and greatly expanded national parks, forest lands, heritage areas, and thousands of miles of public trails along the National Wild and Scenic River System.

The bill dealt with multiple agencies within the federal government and touched upon issues ranging from oceanic research to livestock replenishment to decades-old interstate water jurisdictional disputes. It was an enormous undertaking that was years in the making.[81]

Using the threat of a filibuster, the mercurial Oklahoma Senator Tom Coburn had held up consideration of the bill during the previous session of Congress, but in 2009 the Senate was finally able to pass the bill over Coburn's opposition. After a strong bipartisan vote in the Senate, the bill was sent across the Capitol for consideration in the House, where it unexpectedly fell two votes shy of passage. At issue was the concern among sportsmen's groups that, with encroaching development, increasing population and the demand for open space, the bill could result in the closure of land that had traditionally been popular territory for the shooting sports.[82]

Because I had heard both sides of these same concerns from constituents in my district, I knew a compromise was possible. Working with Republican and Democratic colleagues, as well as a diverse set of interest groups representing environmental activists and sportsmen's organizations, I was able to craft an amendment to break the deadlock. The amendment prohibited any effort to close the lands covered under the bill to hunting, fishing, trapping, and the shooting sports. As with any compromise, not everyone was satisfied, and some groups still opposed the bill even after it was amended. Nevertheless, the amendment broke the logjam and added enough support to pass the bill and send it to the president, who signed it into law.

I enjoyed working with both sides of the aisle in effort to find common ground. I hated the game playing that so often occurred on the extremes, where winning a political fight is more desirable than solving a problem. One of the reasons I was able to build a trusting relationship with so many of my Republican colleagues was the fact that I had a demonstrably centrist voting record.

At about the same time the public lands bill was moving through Congress, the respected nonpartisan public policy magazine *National Journal* was publishing its annual list of congressional vote rankings. Published every year since 1981, the *National Journal* rankings list every member of Congress along the ideological spectrum based upon their votes on the most substantive issues debated in Congress over an entire year. The magazine uses a computer-generated composite score to calculate the percentage of House members who are more liberal and conservative than each of the other 434 members. I was pleased to learn that the magazine identified me as the most centrist member of the entire House. My voting record placed me exactly in the midpoint. I was more liberal than 50% of my colleagues and more conservative than the other 50%.[83] It was exactly where I wanted to be.

It wasn't where John DeFazio wanted me to be. He often expressed disappointment that I wasn't voting more often with the Democrats, and like many other union leaders, he also had concerns about my membership in the Blue Dogs (whom he regarded as anti-labor) and the New Dems (who supported free-trade policies anathema to unions).

During one conversation, I expressed to DeFazio my view that Congress would be better off if the two parties would work together and try to find compromise. He used a different word. "Concessions? We don't need no concessions." In his opinion, because Democrats were now in charge there was no need to "give in" to the Republicans.

DeFazio's partisan views were colored by his experience as a union negotiator during the downfall of the steel industry in Pittsburgh nearly three decades earlier. Contemporary accounts relate how DeFazio believed he had been lied to by corporate lawyers at the bargaining table. He had learned his lesson the hard way, through an early 1980s agreement the steelworkers signed with U.S. Steel. DeFazio was convinced the agreement contained an ironclad "Buy America" clause. When U.S. Steel began importing foreign steel—and successfully justifying before Congress their decision to do so—DeFazio had forever lost faith in the negotiations.[84]

Although those days were long gone, DeFazio's demeanor when I spoke of compromise—and his use of the word concessions—were indicative of the fact that my attempts to work with both sides were not particularly well received among the union leaders. Another sign of things to come.

CHAPTER 7

A TEA PARTY AND
AN EARTHQUAKE

—— .•. ——

The Blue Dogs Have Their Day

WHEN PRESIDENT OBAMA TOOK OFFICE, THE ECONOMY
was in complete freefall. Hundreds of thousands of jobs were
being lost every month, and the economy was contracting at an
alarming rate. To stop the bleeding, the president's first order of
business was enactment of his $787 billion economic stimulus
plan, which came on the heels of the $700 billion Wall Street
Bailout that had passed four months before Obama took office.
The public was nervous about the economy and frustrated about
the unprecedented levels of spending that had been approved.
Other perceived "bailouts" were proposed, such as those for the
struggling auto industry and for homeowners who had suffered
the consequences of gambling on high-risk mortgages.

Through it all, Obama made clear that the focus on the
economy would not distract him from pursuing comprehensive
health care reform. Conversations about the topic had begun
during the presidential transition, even before Obama officially
took office. Six weeks into his first term, the president convened a bipartisan White House meeting of 150 political and
health care leaders representing all sides of the industry.[1] The
televised forum made clear that Obama considered health care
reform a priority and that he was determined to succeed on an

issue where so many of his predecessors had failed. The debate quickly shifted to Congress.

Throughout the spring and summer, White House officials negotiated with the same industry special interests that had derailed President Bill Clinton's health care reform bill a decade and a half before. At the same time, the Senate spent months trying to piece together a bipartisan compromise, despite the fact that Democrats in the chamber had a filibuster-proof majority. Meanwhile, House leaders were taking the opposite approach by measuring how far to the left they could push the issue. Three separate committees took up a proposed House bill, which Speaker Pelosi initially hoped to pass before the August recess.[2]

I served on the Education and Labor Committee, which was one of those three committees of jurisdiction. The issue came to a head on a hot July night, when the committee worked nonstop into the next morning during a round-the-clock mark-up session. Going line by line through the bill in what proved to be a tense debate, committee members considered amendments and argued about various provisions of the bill. Two amendments I offered were added to the bill, one dealing with personal care attendants and the other pertaining to diagnostic tests performed in independent labs. After twenty hours of debate, the committee finally passed the bill by a vote of twenty-six to twenty-two.

I voted against the committee's bill due to concerns about the failure to address health care costs. I opposed the bill's price tag—which was then north of $1 trillion—as well as the proposed income tax increase for individuals and small businesses, and the cuts the bill would make to Medicare. Because I represented a district that had the fourth-most Medicare beneficiaries of any district in the country, that last point was no small concern. I was hopeful that changes could be made as the bill progressed through the legislative process, but for now I was unable to support it.

As the August deadline approached, opposition by centrist Democrats threatened to derail the entire process. A group of seven Blue Dogs serving on the Energy and Commerce Committee were united in opposition to several provisions in the bill. Without the support of at least some of them, Chairman Henry Waxman would not have enough votes to pass the bill out of his committee. Negotiations soon grew acrimonious as the two sides openly criticized one another in the media and participants stormed out of closed-door negotiating sessions. Democratic activists were furious and turned the focus of their anger squarely on the Blue Dogs.

Bloggers and pundits excoriated the so-called obstructionists, while liberal radio and television commentators criticized the Blue Dogs as traitors. Union-funded interest groups ran television attack ads in Blue Dog districts, while other left-wing groups called for primaries against Democrats who failed to support the bill. Cable news hosts gave out over the airwaves the office phone numbers of the Blue Dogs, asking their viewers to call and berate the recalcitrant members.[3]

Speaker Pelosi convened meetings of the entire Democratic Caucus to discuss the stalemate, with one member after another rising to speak against the tactics of the centrists within their ranks. House members pleaded with Pelosi and Waxman to hang tough, vowing to stay through the August recess until the bill was passed.

For their part, the Blue Dogs convened almost daily meetings of the fifty-two-member group to hear updates about the progress of the negotiations. Mike Ross, an Arkansas pharmacist, led the group of hold-outs on the committee, whom he proudly referred to as "The Magnificent Seven." He used the meetings to inform the rest of the Blue Dog Coalition about the progress being made on the remaining points of disagreement. Among the issues under negotiation were the overall cost of the bill, the tax increases, the public insurance option, and the treatment of small businesses.[4]

An agreement was finally reached between Waxman and the Blue Dogs, but the floor vote was delayed until after the August recess.[5] This gave members the opportunity to hear from their constituents. And hear from their constituents they did.

Even before Obama held his first health care meeting in March, the seeds had been sown for the growth of the Tea Party movement that by August had become one of the most powerful political insurgencies in American history. The Tea Party began in the most unlikely of places, led by perhaps the most unlikely of people.

Keli Carender was a thirty-year-old Seattle teacher with a degree from Oxford and a ring through her nose. On February 16, 2009, she led what is considered to be the first Tea Party protest, gathering 120 people to express their opposition to the stimulus bill.[6] Three days later, CNBC's Rick Santelli took to the floor of the Chicago Mercantile Exchange to call for a "Chicago Tea Party" to protest economic policies that he believed "reward bad behavior" by providing taxpayer funds to the "losers" who will only squander the money.[7] Santelli's infamous rant would appear tame in comparison to the antics that would occur at congressional town hall meetings across the country during the 2009 August recess.

Because my professional background was in the health care industry, I focused much of my attention on the issue throughout my career in Congress. Lowering health care costs was a staple of the platform upon which I ran my first campaign, and I spoke about the issue in almost every public forum.

The district had a strong conservative tilt, so support on many issues trended toward the right. When I was in Democratic areas like New Castle and the working-class towns along the Ohio and Allegheny Rivers, I would hear proportionately more support for Democratic positions; but even then, on the health care issue it was tempered by moderation. Nevertheless, a small but vocal group of union leaders and activists held left-of-center views and kept in close touch with me and my staff. They also organized rallies at my office and blogged about their dissatisfaction with my centrist voting record.

Meanwhile, the right-wing activists that had dogged me throughout my time in office had by this time morphed into a vibrant Tea Party chapter. Like the liberal union activists, the Tea Party crowd made their presence known in every possible way. The two extremist groups may have tried to be the most visible, but I knew neither was representative of the district as a whole. That's why I spent so much time attending events where I knew I would run into people who were not political activists. That's where I learned what was really on the minds of most constituents in the district.

Everywhere I went, people approached me to discuss the health care bill. When I walked through large events like county fairs, summer carnivals, and car cruises, it never failed that a group would form around me as people stopped to listen and add to the conversation. Constituents stopped me in the grocery store and at restaurants as I dined with my family. Neighbors turned off their lawnmowers and walked over to talk to me on the sidewalk as my wife and I strolled around the neighborhood. With most issues, I had a pretty good idea what side people would be on based upon where I was in the district. With health care, it was becoming increasingly clear that most people were on the same side—in opposition to the bill.

Tea Time

AS MEMBERS OF CONGRESS TRAVELED BACK TO THEIR DIS-tricts at the beginning of August, there was a sense among all of us that the combustible atmosphere would make for an interesting and eventful recess. Over the summer, the Tea Party had organized large protests at town hall meetings, causing disruptions that in some cases led to physical altercations and arrests.

In June, discussion at a town hall meeting in suburban New York became so heated that the event was cut short and police were called to escort Congressman Tim Bishop to his car. Further upstate in Syracuse, protesters were arrested after police were called to restore order to Congressman Dan Maffei's town meeting. In Florida, more than a hundred sign-waving protestors disrupted Congressman Allen Boyd's seemingly innocuous small business development forum in Panama City.[8]

With opposition growing by the day, it was no mystery why Speaker Pelosi had hoped to finish work on the health care bill before the August recess. Having missed that deadline, her worst fears were about to be realized.

Within a week, the disruptive behavior of attendees at town halls across the country would dominate the news. The opening paragraph of an August 7 *New York Times* story summarized it perfectly:

> THE BITTER DIVISIONS over an overhaul of the health care system have exploded at town-hall-style meetings over the last few days as members of Congress have been shouted down, hanged in effigy and taunted by crowds. In several cities, noisy demonstrations have led to fistfights, arrests and hospitalizations.[9]

Attendees videotaped the chaos, uploading homemade movies that would receive hundreds of thousands of views. Right-wing talk show hosts stoked the flames, calling for attendees to disrupt the meetings. "Become a part of the mob!" read a banner atop Sean Hannity's website. "Attend an Obama Care Town Hall Near You!"[10] C-SPAN covered some of the town halls live, while news channels did live cut-ins of meetings that were experiencing particularly egregious breaks in decorum. Some of the most incendiary exchanges even received international news coverage.[11] Seemingly every day, new stories would emerge about increasingly outrageous behavior.

An overflow crowd of 1,500 people attended Congresswoman Kathy Castor's town hall in Tampa, where scuffles broke out and protestors shouted down Castor as she tried to speak. In Wisconsin, Congressman Steve Kagen encountered angry heckling during a tense town hall session. In Texas, Congressman Lloyd Doggett organized a "Congress on Your Corner" event at a local grocery store and was greeted by dozens of boisterous protestors, one of whom was carrying a faux tombstone with the congressman's name inscribed on it. Taking it a step further, a Maryland rally in opposition to the health care bill featured an effigy of Congressman Frank Kratovil being hanged. In Georgia, a swastika was painted outside the office of Congressman David Scott, who is black. In St. Louis, police arrested six people outside a high school gymnasium as members of the Service Employees International Union (SEIU) fought with members of the local Tea Party at a health care town hall.[12]

The incident that came to epitomize the rage overflowing at town hall meetings involved Pennsylvania's five-term senator, Arlen Specter. During a televised meeting attended by hundreds of activists, Specter wandered through the crowd, microphone in hand. Tensions rose as constituents began to direct their anger at one another in addition to the senator.

An irate man stood to confront Specter, angrily pointing and shouting into the senator's face about his belief that Specter was "trampling on our Constitution." Another constituent in the audience shoved the man, yelling at him to sit down. Security rushed in to restore order, but the audience applauded loudly as the man struggled and continued yelling and pointing at Specter, saying, "God is going to stand before you, and he's going to judge you!"[13]

Against this backdrop, I held an August town meeting in Farrell, Pennsylvania, a decaying steel town along the Ohio border. Because the district had both an active Tea Party group and a vocal union presence, I knew the meeting would draw a large crowd and had the potential to become volatile. Approximately one thousand people attended, representing both extremes of the political spectrum. For nearly two hours, I fielded questions about various provisions in the bill and my position on health care reform. Because I had made a point to be especially visible and accessible during the August recess, many of the people in the audience had already met with me or heard me speak about the issue.

The meeting began ominously. As a courtesy, I asked the town's Democratic mayor to greet the crowd to open the meeting. Although I had asked her to refrain from politics, she diverted from the introduction and transitioned into a spirited defense of President Obama and the health care bill, drawing loud boos from the audience. I then gave an overview of the issue, conveying my belief that we needed to find a way to lower the cost of health care while keeping intact the many parts of our health care system that were working well.

For nearly two hours, I took questions from the audience. It quickly became clear that both sides were represented but the crowd was heavily skewed in opposition to the bill, even though the meeting occurred in the most solidly Democratic area of the district. By the time of the meeting, I had done enough public appearances—and seen and heard enough political talk shows—to know which issues were most likely to come up in the discussion. I was prepared for the usual questions about tort reform, the public option, taxation of benefits, and even the so-called "death panels" that Sarah Palin had made up out of whole cloth. When a constituent opened the meeting with what was a standard Tea Party-themed question, I was ready.

After a lengthy monologue about the inefficiencies of government and her perception that the bill represented a "government take-over" of our health care system, the constituent dared me to name even one social program that Congress had initiated that worked well and was worth the cost. The audience cheered loudly as the woman sat down, confident that she had scored points for her side. I paused deliberately, leaning toward the microphone for dramatic emphasis. The audience was silent as I slowly gave my well-rehearsed answer: "The GI Bill."

Stunned, the Tea Party contingent looked at each other in bewildered silence, wondering what to say next. I had gone off-script with a program I knew they couldn't oppose. I saw some of them look at each other and shrug as if to say, "Well, can't argue with that." Just then, from the far back of the auditorium, a man yelled out, "Name another one!" The comment initiated a round of laughter from the audience that helped break the tension.

The meeting was spirited and somewhat heated at times, but it lacked the out-of-control pandemonium that had oc-curred in other areas of the country. My key takeaways from the town hall and other meetings I had during the recess were that: 1) Few people on either side really understood what was in the bill or how it would impact the district; 2) Republicans were nearly unified in their opposition to the bill, while Democrats were at best evenly split; 3) Discussion points on the issue were driven almost entirely by external forces, such as talk shows and social media. I heard very few unique points of view, but it was clear that the upcoming vote on health care had generated a level of passion rarely seen in national political debates.

As members returned to Washington in September, Presi-dent Obama called both houses together for a nationally tele-vised Joint Session of Congress. The White House scheduled the speech as a way to regain control of a message that had fallen hopelessly off track during the month-long recess. Media coverage focused on the public's growing opposition to the bill, and Republicans pounced on the opportunity to use that oppo-sition to their advantage. As members gathered for the speech, tempers were raw, and an aura of bitterness hung in the air.

The president used much of the speech to refute what Dem-ocrats believed were false accusations about the content of the bill. One of the most prevalent and damaging claims was that the bill allowed illegal immigrants to qualify for free health care. It was a frequent talking point of Tea Party activists and Fox News commentators. Obama highlighted the issue during his speech, saying: "There are also those who claim that our re-form effort will insure illegal immigrants. This, too, is false—the reforms I'm proposing would not apply to those who are here illegally."

"You lie!" yelled one House member in the hushed cham-ber. Obama looked startled as he glanced in the direction of the shout. Members in attendance gasped. I was sitting next to the gentile Tennessee Democrat Jim Cooper. Looking across the chamber to the area where I heard the shout, I asked Cooper if he knew who it was. He said, partly in disbelief, that he thought it might have been Joe Wilson. I said it couldn't have been Joe, because it was so out of character for him to conduct himself in that manner. But in fact it was him.

Representing a conservative, Bible Belt district in South Carolina, Joe Wilson spoke on the House floor often, usually about military and national security matters. I had a cordial relationship with Joe and always found him to be gentlemanly. He later apologized for his outburst, but that didn't stop him from raising more than $2 million in online political contributions from conservatives delighted at his expression of disrespect to the President of the United States.[14] The episode came to epitomize the growing animosity in Congress and the confrontational tactics of the Tea Party.

Pelosi Works Her Magic

KNOWING THAT REPUBLICANS WERE UNLIKELY TO SUPport the bill, Speaker Pelosi needed to win over some of her wavering Democratic members in order accumulate enough votes to pass it. A master at doing just that, she slowly put the pieces together in individual conversations with members who were on the fence. She often approached me and other undecided centrists on the House floor to ask our opinion of various provisions under consideration. In phone calls and face-to-face conversations, she asked my concerns and what it would take to get me to yes. I reiterated my opposition to the tax increases, Medicare cuts, and the lack of cost containment.

A month before the bill came to the floor, I received a late-evening phone call from the speaker's office asking me to join a meeting that was occurring in her office. I walked over to the Capitol and entered her office suite, arriving at approximately 10:00 p.m. I was directed to a conference table with Pelosi at the head and three House members sitting on each side. The six members were evenly deadlocked about the effective date of an obscure provision of the bill dealing with the construction of specialty hospitals. Pelosi knew that I had worked in the hospital industry before being elected to Congress, so she asked for my opinion. I framed my answer in the context of cost reduction, and the final bill brought to the floor included my recommendation. The incident was indicative of how far Pelosi was willing to go to entice Democrats to vote for the bill.

In October, two weeks before the final vote, I was back in Pennsylvania for a Friday night public meeting on the campus of the University of Pittsburgh. I was part of a three-person panel discussion including my neighboring Republican Congressman Tim Murphy and Paul O'Neill, who served as Treasury Secretary under President George W. Bush. The topic of the panel was health care reform, but the meeting lacked the outrageous antics that had plagued the August town halls around the country. During a ninety-minute bipartisan discussion, the three of us debated the merits of the pending legislation and took questions from an audience of several hundred people. I felt good about the event until my staff showed me the flyer that was being circulated to attendees as they left the meeting.

Produced by the liberal group Health Care for America Now, the flyer depicted an unflattering profile view of me next to the same photo facing the opposite direction. Titled "The Two Faces of Jason Altmire," the message was that I was turning my back on my constituents and was merely a tool of the insurance industry. I thought it was an unusual way to encourage me to support the bill, but the same organization had also aired a hard-hitting television attack ad featuring a similar message, so I was not surprised by their combative approach.

Two days before the vote, I had an informal dinner in Washington with my House colleagues Chris Murphy from Connecticut and Tim Ryan from Ohio, both partisan Democrats. The two House members asked me to join them so they could make one final pitch for why I should support the bill. Riding in a car on the way to the restaurant, I received another call from Pelosi. I explained to her that it had become clear my district leaned in opposition to the bill. In addition, the previous concerns I had raised remained largely unaddressed. I was leaning towards a no vote, I told her for the first time. Then she played the final card in her deck.

Pelosi knew I enjoyed presiding over the House as speaker pro tempore, an honor that I had served for a cumulative total of 150 hours during the 3 years I had been in office. She said that she would like me to serve as speaker pro tempore for the "historic vote." I was flattered but responded that I was confused by the offer, because it was my understanding that the presiding officer—as the designee of the speaker herself—would be expected to vote in support of the speaker's agenda. "Well, yes," she said sternly. "To do it you would have to vote for the bill." I respectfully declined.

During dinner, Murphy and Ryan, who were two of my closest friends in Congress, discussed with me both the politics and the policy of the bill. We had a productive conversation, but I told them I had all but decided to vote no.

The following day, I received a phone call from President Obama. He was noticeably downhearted, telling me he had spent much of the past two days dealing with the aftermath of the Fort Hood mass shooting, which had occurred the previous day. An Army major had killed thirteen and wounded more than thirty at the Texas military base. Obama slowly transitioned into the purpose of his call, which was to make one final pitch for the health care bill. We discussed my policy concerns, as well as the unpopularity of the bill in my district and around the country.

I referenced the gubernatorial election that had just occurred in Virginia, a swing state where the Democratic candidate had been trounced in a campaign that had been waged largely over the issue of "Obamacare." The president rejected the correlation, dismissing the viability of the Democratic nominee, then a member of the Virginia House. "We had a weak candidate," the president told me, emphasizing that I shouldn't put too much stock in the outcome of that race. I told him my vote was a difficult decision, but I was leaning in opposition.

Later that same day, I sought out Pelosi to tell her that I would definitely oppose the bill. I talked with her on the House floor as the chamber was clearing out after a vote. She was visibly disappointed but did not challenge my decision. The next day, the bill passed the House by a vote of 220-215.

It wasn't until Christmas Eve that the Senate finally passed their version of health care reform. Unlike the House, the Senate had at least attempted to craft a bipartisan bill before abandoning the effort in order to focus on the holdouts within the Democratic Caucus. In the end, Majority Leader Harry Reid had to cut deals with moderate senators Joe Lieberman, Mary Landrieu, and Ben Nelson to finally achieve the sixty-vote filibuster-proof majority. Among other things, the deals resulted in the removal of the public option, delivering a crushing blow to liberals.

An International Incident

ON THE EVENING OF TUESDAY, JANUARY 12, 2010, NEWS reports across America focused on the devastating earthquake that had just struck Haiti near the capital of Port-au-Prince. The magnitude 7.0 earthquake caused massive destruction that killed more than 200,000 people. Buildings that were damaged or destroyed included the Presidential Palace, National Assembly building, and the Port-au-Prince airport, jail, and cathedral.

The next morning, my always diligent district director, Jim Ferruchie, arrived early for work in my district office. As was his routine, he started the day by checking the office voice mails for constituent messages that had come in the night before. He heard a message that was anything but routine. He listened intently as a panicked caller named Diane McMutrie said her daughters lived in Haiti and she was frantically trying to contact them. Jim sent me an email with details of the call, saying he would be reaching out to Mrs. McMutrie and the State Department to try to ascertain the facts and determine how we might be able to help. The facts turned out to be quite complicated.

Diane McMutrie had two adult daughters, Jamie and Ali, who ran an orphanage in Haiti. The two women, ages thirty and twenty-two, and the children under their care had all survived the earthquake. After checking with the State Department, Jim called Diane to relay the good news that, as American citizens, her daughters were allowed to leave anytime they wanted and we would be able assist in their timely departure. But there was more to the story. Diane told Jim that her daughters didn't want to leave Haiti without the fifty-four orphan children under their care who were in the process of adoption to American families. Thus began what would become the most remarkable week of my time in Congress.

It soon became clear that it would not be easy to gain State Department approval for the orphans—ranging in age from eleven months to fourteen years—to leave the country. In addition, the Haitian government was not going to allow the children to leave without confirmation of their adoptive status, a process that could take weeks or months and would be slowed even further by the loss of some of the orphans' records and the fact that some of the Haitian government's physical and telecommunications infrastructure had been damaged in the earthquake. Dealing with the worst natural disaster in their nation's history, the Haitian government justifiably wanted to protect its most vulnerable citizens during a time of unprecedented chaos.

Upon learning of these impediments, that afternoon I called Rahm Emanuel, who was then President Obama's chief of staff. I explained the situation and asked for his advice about how to get approval to bring the Haitian orphans to the United States. He said he was sure this could all be worked out and that we should continue to work with the State Department while Rahm brought this issue to the attention of Denis McDonough, then a senior national security aide assigned by the White House to manage the relief efforts on the ground in Haiti. The day that had begun with an emotional voice mail from a concerned parent had ended with direct involvement of the White House in what would soon become a riveting international news story.

The plight of the McMutrie sisters quickly went viral. A Facebook site was established to build support for the sisters, and local bloggers provided continuing updates on the latest rumors related to the orphans and ongoing attempts to rescue them. The websites quickly became inundated with comments ranging from offers of help to pleas for government intervention. By Thursday, two days after the quake, a new wrinkle was added to the story when Pittsburgh's high-profile former United States Attorney, Mary Beth Buchanan, tried to intervene on behalf of the orphans.

A partisan Republican, Buchanan's recent tenure as US Attorney was notable mostly for her skilled use of the media to promote her agenda and raise her visibility. Having been out of office for only two months, Buchanan was publicly mulling a challenge to me in the upcoming election. Sensing opportunity and working with a local political blogger who was one of my harshest critics, Buchanan began to piece together what she hoped would be a private rescue mission. Together, Buchanan and her media savvy associates kept the local news and social media community abreast of every detail of her actions as she phoned immigration officials, organized medical supply teams, and worked to secure an aircraft—an effort that never got off the ground. As Buchanan operated from her kitchen table and held meetings in the conference room of her husband's law firm, I continued my work in Washington to find a solution and get the orphans home.

By the end of the week, Pennsylvania Governor Ed Rendell was also involved, working with the University of Pittsburgh Medical Center (UPMC) and various relief organizations to get assistance to the orphans. On Friday, January 15, CNN aired a segment recorded at the orphanage, including interviews with the McMutrie sisters. Media around the world subsequently reported on the saga.

With all of this happening simultaneously, a public outcry ensued as rumors began to spread about the deteriorating condition of the orphans, who were said to be running out of food and water. To make matters worse, machete-wielding looters were roaming the streets of Port-au-Prince, and an orphanage run by two young women presented an inviting target for desperate people willing do anything to get their hands on supplies. McMutrie family members tried to reassure the public: "The proper people at the highest levels are working on it," read one Facebook post from the family. "We have the most qualified people in the world offering to go down and save them."

On Saturday, January 16, I spoke by phone with Jamie McMutrie, who was at the orphanage in Haiti. She said they were almost out of fresh water, and some of the children—especially the younger ones—were starting to get sick. The orphanage had been damaged in the earthquake, so the sisters and the orphans had to stay outside. She was strong but scared, expressing fear that the looters could arrive at any moment. I told her that we were very close to finalizing a plan to bring the orphans to the United States.

That same Saturday night, Governor Rendell spoke to the Haitian Ambassador to the United States, who secured approval from the Haitian government for an American rescue mission to enter the country. While Rendell also sought approval from officials from the Department of Homeland Security, I confirmed with Rahm Emanuel that we were planning a trip to Haiti to personally negotiate the situation. Rahm told me Denis McDonough would be ready to assist us when we arrived.

The key final pieces of the puzzle were put into place by Leslie Merrill, a senior UPMC official with whom I had worked during my time there. Leslie had been in frequent contact with the McMutrie family, had organized a team of medical personnel to accompany us on the trip, and worked with Republic Airways to make available an Embraer 170 commercial jetliner for our group to use. To confirm the final details, Leslie convened a meeting late Sunday night at a small Chinese restaurant near my home in Wexford, Pennsylvania.

The meeting included several of the medical personnel planning to accompany us. The owner closed the restaurant but allowed us to stay as we talked until almost midnight. Finally, we adjourned the meeting and agreed to meet a few hours later at the Pittsburgh International Airport, where our flight was scheduled to take off at 6:00 a.m. Monday morning.

As our group arrived at the airport and prepared to leave, we were informed that a landing spot would not be available in Haiti until Monday afternoon, so our plane would be delayed several hours. As we waited for clearance to leave, word of the rescue mission leaked out, and media began arriving at the airport, cameras in tow.

At about 9:00 a.m., my staff called to inform me that an international adoption official who had worked closely with Mary Beth Buchanan on her rival rescue plan had called my office to threaten legal action if we went through with our mission to "kidnap" the orphans. She also told my staff that she had alerted the national media about our "illegal" actions and was trying to get the airport to prevent our plane from leaving. Nevertheless, later that morning our plane departed Pittsburgh loaded with medical supplies and thirty-one passengers on board.

Our plane finally landed in Port-au-Prince at approximately 6:30 p.m. The State Department allowed us only one hour to complete our mission, after which our plane would be required to leave, freeing up the valuable spot on the landing strip for another of the continuous stream of military and international supply planes that circled above. As our plane taxied down the lone ten thousand-foot runway, the scene outside looked exactly like what it was—a disaster area.

We rolled to a stop as the plane pulled up to the terminal, which had been vacated after sustaining serious damage in the earthquake. Nobody was allowed inside, so the runway and areas outside the terminal were jammed with hundreds of people roving around the grounds of the airport. The door to the plane was opened, and Rendell and I descended into the chaos. After a quick survey of the tumultuous situation, we agreed that the medical personnel and others joining us on the trip should stay on the plane. Leslie Merrill joined us on the ground as we tried to ascertain first steps. We agreed that Rendell would contact the State Department, Leslie would track down the McMutrie sisters, and I would find Denis McDonough.

The US Air Force was in charge of managing operations at Port-au-Prince airport in the days after the earthquake. Because the control tower had collapsed, air traffic control operations were led from a small folding table set up just off the runway. There were people everywhere. Homeless Haitians with nowhere else to go, foreign nationals hoping to find their way home, media correspondents with bright lights shinning and cameras rolling, military personnel, humanitarian relief organizers, and flight teams waiting hours for their planes to arrive.

A handful of impromptu parking spots had been created along the sides of the lone runway to provide room for arriving supply planes to unload quickly before flying back out. The smell of garbage and jet fuel was unmistakable. The airport that normally handles only a few flights a day was now experiencing hundreds of landings and departures, all designed for quick turnaround to keep air traffic moving.

I made my way through the crowd, looking for McDonough, whom I had never met. After several minutes, I located some US military personnel, who pointed me to the Air Force operations center, just off the runway. Once there, I shouted above the roaring jet engines, asking if they knew Denis. Yes, they knew him, but they didn't know where he was, they shouted back. From there, one of the Air Force officers walked around with me, looking for Denis, whom we eventually found near the terminal. Denis and I made our way to the plane to discuss the situation with Rendell.

McDonough is calm and cool, always in charge, and not easily flustered. He was helpful from the onset. Arriving back at the plane, we encountered Governor Rendell and Leslie, both of whom were talking on their phones and appeared to be upset. Rendell had been told by the State Department that it would take hours to sort through the adoption status of the orphans, particularly several whose paperwork was missing. Leslie had learned that the sisters were exasperated with the embassy and were about to give up and return to the orphanage. Jamie's husband Doug, who had joined us on the trip, was livid, directing his anger mostly at Rendell and Leslie. As everybody yelled at each other, McDonough pulled me aside. "You're going to need more time to sort this out. I'll see if I can get an extension," he said, referring to our one-hour time limit. He headed back into the crowd, while the rest of us tried to save the mission.

Leslie told the sisters by phone to wait at the embassy while a group from our team rode out to meet them. After several failed attempts to find transportation, we were joined on the runway by an embassy official who was stationed at the airport to assist Americans trying to leave the country. McDonough had sent him to help us resolve the paperwork issues with the orphans' adoption status. Upon learning about the new plan, he agreed to drive the group to the embassy, but still there was no car.

As Leslie went off in search of a vehicle, McDonough arrived back to say that he had secured another ninety minutes for our plane to remain on the runway. Leslie returned with an SUV she had somehow commandeered, and she and a few other members of our group piled in and quickly drove off to the embassy. Rendell and I stayed behind with McDonough, standing by our plane on the crowded and noisy runway.

The next few hours involved multiple layers of intense negotiation. The group at the embassy talked the McMutrie sisters out of leaving, eventually getting them to agree to come to the airport in an embassy convoy that would include all fifty-four orphans. Rendell continued his discussions with the State Department, mostly talking by phone with Huma Abedin, a top aide to Secretary of State Hillary Clinton. Abedin told Rendell that forty-seven of the orphans were cleared but the remaining seven would not be allowed to leave. The sisters refused to return to America with anything less than all fifty-four children, but they agreed to travel to the airport, just in case. By the time they arrived, our plane was gone.

While the group was at the embassy, McDonough came over to speak to me and Rendell. He brought along a couple of Air Force officers, who had some bad news. Our plane had to leave. We said we couldn't leave because we didn't have all of our group. The increasingly testy Air Force officers pointed up to the sky, asking if we saw all those dots of light circling above. "Those are relief planes from all over the world waiting for your plane to leave so they can bring supplies. If you don't leave now, you're going to cause an international incident!" one of them shouted.

Knowing there was no room for negotiation, we unloaded from our plane the medical supplies and remaining members of our group. As we all stood together in our corner of the runway beside a mountain of boxes, linens, and medical equipment, we watched helplessly as our now-empty commercial jetliner rolled down the runway, took off, and slowly disappeared into the dark Haitian sky. Rendell and I stood next to each other, watching silently as the lights from our airplane disappeared into the distance. We glanced over at each other and shrugged.

An unsung hero of the eventual success of the mission was my chief of staff, Sharon Werner. She had spent the past several days working tirelessly on this issue, which had begun as a constituent request for assistance. She worked late into the night every day that week, making valuable contacts with relevant government agencies and the White House. During my time on the ground in Haiti, I kept in close touch via email with Sharon, who was working the phones with her contacts at the State Department and McDonough's staff at the White House. This proved invaluable, as the connection between the two entities soon became extremely important.

Throughout the ordeal, the State Department would not budge. They refused to clear the remaining seven undocumented orphans without paperwork. McDonough and the Air Force officers informed us that a military C-17 cargo plane would soon be landing with supplies that would need to be unloaded. We could then board the C-17 and return back to America—with or without the orphans.

Just then, the convoy arrived from the embassy, carrying the sisters, the orphans, and the remaining members of our group. The sisters became enraged upon learning that the plane had already left. It got even worse when they found out that seven orphans still had not been approved to leave. As tempers flared, the orphans were escorted off their bus and began to run around in the area where we were standing. This was the first time we had seen them, which was exciting for everybody. They appeared to be in surprisingly good condition, wearing mostly T-shirts and shorts. Now, with everyone together, success seemed so close—but still no approval for the last seven orphans to leave.

The C-17 landed, and we were told the final moment for a decision had come. We would either leave with forty-seven of the orphans or none at all. The sisters remained adamant. They were not leaving unless all fifty-four orphans came with them.

As the supplies on the enormous cargo plane were unloaded on the runway in front of us, it appeared the failure of our mission was inevitable. Members of our medical team were evaluating the children while Rendell and I pleaded with the Air Force officers for more time. I sent one last email to Rahm, explaining how everything was falling apart while we seemed so close to success. McDonough asked the Air Force officers to allow all the children on the plane, saying that the details could be worked out later. They refused.

With the C-17 now unloaded, the time had come. With the screaming back and forth exacerbated by the combination of aircraft noise and inflamed tensions, the Air Force officers insisted we either get on the plane now or it was leaving without us. Just then, when all seemed lost, McDonough glanced over at me with a subtle smile as he tapped into his blackberry device.

Other aircraft could not land while the giant cargo plane sat on the runway. As the yelling continued, McDonough was still fidgeting with his blackberry. Suddenly, a broad smile appeared across his face. Holding his blackberry up to the faces of the two Air Force officers, he calmly said, "Read this." The shouting stopped as the two men leaned in, squinted, and read the message. They looked at each other, then stared back at McDonough. "Who is that from?" one of them asked. "The Office of the President," came McDonough's matter-of-fact reply. The two officers looked stunned. "The commander in chief?" one of them responded. McDonough, still holding up the blackberry, nodded silently. The two officers looked at each other, then one of them pointed at the children, wheeling his hand around with a circular motion as he pointed back to the plane. "Load 'em up!" he yelled. Members of our group hugged each other and jumped up and down as Rendell and I high-fived. After five hours of unpredictable ups and downs, we were finally going home with all fifty-four orphans.

Hurriedly, our group began putting the children on board the plane along with some of the supplies. Assisted by Air Force personnel, we strapped the children into their seats around the edges of the cavernous interior of the massive cargo plane and locked down the remaining supplies in the middle. Ali and Jamie did a quick headcount.

"Fifty-three," came the response.

"That can't be right!" screamed Ali.

With the engines revving and the pilots strapping themselves into their cockpit seats, others joined in a second panicked headcount, then a third. Every count came in at fifty-three.

The sisters looked at each other and yelled simultaneously, "Emma!"

Without a word, Jamie ran out the back of the plane and disappeared into the darkness, searching for the missing two-year-old. Others, including Ali, ran after her. The Air Force officers said the plane had to take off immediately, with or without anyone who might not be on board.

Ali returned, distraught and nearing a breakdown. Jamie stayed behind at the airport as the door closed and the plane slowly began its move down the runway. The plane picked up speed and took off, leaving behind Jamie and little Emma, who had not yet been located. What had moments before been a wild celebration had turned into a stunned silence broken only by Ali's hysterical cries of concern for Emma.

The plane was headed to Sanford Airport in Orlando, Florida. There, the passengers would unload and spent the night in the airport while our original commercial airliner, which was overnighting in Miami, returned to pick us up. During the three-hour flight, the children were singing and playing games with each other, while the adults tended to the younger children. I held one of the sleeping toddlers in my arms.

As soon as we landed and the plane was taxing to a stop, Jamie's husband Doug checked his emails and yelled, "They found her! Emma's okay!" Still strapped into our seats, our group cheered loudly, and many cried, knowing once and for all that the mission had been a complete success. Jamie would travel with Emma to Pittsburgh the following day.

We landed in Orlando in the middle of the night, staying the next several hours in the airport. We were packed into small rooms, where some of the children fell asleep sitting up. Later that morning, our original Republic Airways plane arrived. We rounded up the children and began boarding the plane. I was in line behind a young boy, maybe ten, who was tightly clutching to his chest a blanket and a square object. I had noticed that he had been doing this from the moment he had gotten off the embassy bus at the Port-au-Prince airport. As we boarded the plane in Orlando, one of the volunteers helping us at the airport asked the boy if she could hold his items while he made his way up the outdoor stairs of the airplane. The boy refused and clutched the items even harder, holding them tightly against his chest with both arms. Half way up the steps, he slipped slightly and reached out to grab the railing to prevent himself from falling. The square item fell from his grasp onto the step below him. Panicked, he looked back at me for help. I reached down and picked it up. It was a framed photo of his adoptive family in the United States. This put in perspective our rescue mission and all the work of that entire tumultuous week. Tears streamed down my face as I handed him the picture.

Back in Pittsburgh, local news covered the events of the rescue around the clock, breaking into regularly scheduled programing when our plane arrived. National television networks reported live from the scene. The children were taken to the hospital for evaluation and were eventually united with their adoptive families.[15]

In the years to come, whenever I walked in the July 4th parade through the McMutrie family's neighborhood, Jamie and Ali's parents would always stand outside to greet me. Waiting along with them would be Fredo, the Haitian orphan they themselves had adopted. It truly was a happy ending.

It wasn't long before politics reared its odious head. The bloggers and media that had breathlessly reported about Mary Beth Buchanan's attempts to piece together a rescue plan now openly criticized me, insinuating I only went on the mission to upstage Buchanan, a potential political rival. Ironically, as would be the case throughout my political career, the criticisms came from both the left and the right. Liberals still angry about my vote against the House health care bill joined Republicans who supported Buchanan's fledgling campaign for Congress. They derided my efforts as little more than political grandstanding. Nevertheless, the Haitian orphan rescue mission is probably the most rewarding experience of my political career, if not my entire professional life.

CHAPTER 8

SURVIVING A
TIDAL WAVE

———— ·•· ————

Obamacare

ON JANUARY 19, 2010, REPUBLICAN SCOTT BROWN WON A
special election to fill the remainder of the term of the late Senator Edward Kennedy. Brown's victory in the Democratic bastion
of Massachusetts was largely attributed to the unpopularity of
the pending health care bill, providing further evidence of the
toxicity of the issue at the ballot box. Now, with only fifty-nine
Democratic votes, it would be impossible for the Senate to overcome a filibuster on a negotiated health care agreement with
the House.

During this time, I and other centrist Democrats continued
to engage in conversations with our Republican colleagues to
try to find a way for the two parties to come together on health
care. Over the next several weeks, President Obama held high-
profile talks with Republican House members, as well as with a
bipartisan group of congressional leaders. In the end, attempts
at bipartisanship would fail, and the decision was made to try
to pass the bill with only Democratic votes.[1]

The House would have to vote to approve the Senate bill,
then vote on a second package of budget-related amendments
that were not subject to the Senate's filibuster rules. By using the "budget reconciliation" process, Senate Majority Leader
Reid would need only fifty-one votes to approve the House

amendments. As the calendar turned to March, the effort was in full swing, and the nation watched as Congress moved toward a final vote on the controversial heath care overhaul.

Republican victories in gubernatorial races in New Jersey and Virginia—coupled with Scott Brown's stunning upset in Massachusetts—caused some centrist Democrats to get cold feet. Some of those who had voted for the House bill in November now announced they would oppose the legislation on final passage. To win the House vote, Pelosi would have to convince some Democrats who had voted against the bill the first time to now support the Senate bill and related House amendments. National media outlets focused their attention on the small handful of potential vote-switchers, including me.

Back in the district, feedback from my vote against the November bill had been overwhelmingly positive. Not a day went by without multiple people approaching me to thank me for my vote. Republicans and Democrats alike called and wrote my office to express their support for my decision. If anything, opposition to the bill had grown more intense as the debate dragged on. I remained confident that I had made the right decision and that my vote represented the majority view of my district.

Some left-of-center Democrats felt differently. Small groups of liberal and union activists expressed their disappointment in my vote and organized meetings to discuss a primary challenge for me in the upcoming election. The liberals remained unaware that they made up only a small fraction of the conservative-leaning district.

The activists commissioned a poll to gauge support among Democrats in the district to run a primary challenge against me. They must have been disappointed in the results, which showed 53% of *Democrats* in the district supported my decision to vote against the health care bill. Given the fact that nearly all Republicans supported my position, it was difficult to make the case that my vote was unrepresentative of the district.

As the final vote neared, President Obama personally spoke to dozens of wavering House members in the hopes of winning their support. Similarly, Speaker Pelosi meticulously worked her way through the list of House members whose votes were up for grabs.[2] Although liberals in her caucus expressed their disappointment over setbacks on issues like abortion, the public option, and the so-called "Cadillac tax" on generous health care benefits, eventually that group fell in line. The centrist Democrats would now be the decisive votes.

In the three weeks leading up to the vote, the White House left no stone unturned in wooing those centrists. During this time, President Obama called me twice, and I was invited to the White House five times. Although health care was not always the scheduled topic of the visit, I knew the conversation was going to turn in that direction.

Under the guise of celebrating passage of deficit reduction legislation that had been enacted months earlier, I was invited to join a group of centrist members at a small White House reception in the ornate Blue Room. With a captive audience of wavering Democrats, President Obama worked the room in search of health care votes. As I chatted informally with two colleagues and Vice President Biden, the president approached. Referencing the topic of the reception, Obama noted that the health care bill would be an even better way to reduce the deficit. Turning his back to the rest of the group so that he and I could chat privately, he rattled off a series of provisions in the bill that he believed would help trim the cost of health care. I responded with a few policy concerns but focused on the fact that my district was opposed to the proposal.

As we ended our conversation and the president walked away, Rahm Emanuel came over to give me the hard sell. I expressed my discomfort with the heavy-handed pressure tactics that were being applied. Just then, I felt two arms come over my shoulders from behind me. It was Biden. "Just say yes," the vice president whispered in my ear, arms still locked around me. "If you just say yes, this all goes away."

Walking back to Capitol Hill from the White House, I received a call from Senator Al Franken. Recalling the fundraiser he headlined for me at Bill Benter's home in Pittsburgh during the final days of my first campaign, Franken let me know that a lot of the people who supported me would be disappointed if I voted against the president's signature legislation. I understood his point but reminded him that I represented the entire district, not just the minority of Democrats who supported the bill. He said that even if I lost my seat because of it, I would be proud for the rest of my life of a vote in favor of this historic legislation.

Walking across the darkened National Mall on that chilly March evening, I held the phone to my ear as I considered what the senator had just said. After several seconds of silence, Franken began to laugh heartily. I asked what was so funny, because I must have missed the humor in our quite serious conversation. He said he laughed because he was picturing himself a year from now, sitting at his desk in the Senate, fondly remembering what a hero Congressman Altmire had been, even though he was thrown out of office. He realized that vision did not seem so appealing to me.

I attended an Oval Office meeting the following day with five other members of the pro-business New Dems. The president focused on the market-oriented reforms in the bill, insisting that the legislation would eventually become popular as voters and business leaders learned more about it. Although that particular talking point was a stretch, it was a standard message delivered by the president and advocates of the bill during those frenzied final days before the vote.

There was nowhere I could go to escape the pressure. The week of the vote, I attended the annual Washington fundraiser for the American Ireland Fund, which supports various charities related to Irish peace and reconciliation. Not long after I arrived, I saw Dan Rooney surrounded by well-wishers. The seventy-seven-year-old Rooney was the United States Ambassador to Ireland and longtime owner of the Pittsburgh Steelers. I had gotten to know Rooney through community circles in Pittsburgh and had the utmost respect for his kind demeanor and soft-spoken manner. He approached me and asked that we step into a corner of the room where we could speak privately.

"They asked me to talk to you about this health care bill," he said in his distinctly Pittsburgh accent. "How are you going to vote?" I explained my concerns and said that I had not yet made a final decision. "Well," he responded, "let me give you one piece of advice." I listened intently as Rooney looked around the room to make sure nobody else was within earshot.

"I have found that, in football and in life, if you just do the right thing, it all has a way of working out for the best," the ambassador began. "You do what you think is right and everything will be okay."

I was touched by his candor and genuine understanding of my dilemma. "Mr. Ambassador," I responded, "of all the people they have had talk to me about this, you just made the most sense of anybody."

Four days before the vote, I found myself back at the White House for a bill signing ceremony at the Rose Garden. As I suspected, my presence at the event turned out to be just one more opportunity for supporters of the bill to lobby me.

I traveled to the White House with a group of House members who were going to watch the ceremony from seats arranged in front of the president's signing desk outside the West Wing. As we arrived, I was unexpectedly directed away from the group and taken inside the White House to the Cabinet Room, where Nancy Pelosi, Harry Reid, Chuck Schumer, and other House and Senate leaders were waiting. I was told that I would be standing with the leaders behind the president during the ceremony. As we were led outside to the Rose Garden, I saw a familiar face. Denis McDonough, the Deputy National Security Advisor and hero of the Haitian orphan rescue mission stood at the door. I said I was surprised to see him because the bill being signed was a domestic policy initiative far outside the scope of McDonough's responsibilities at the time.

"I came over to see you," he said.

We reminisced about the excitement of the Haitian rescue mission two months earlier. I thanked him again for his help and said the orphans were all doing well and that those who had completed the adoption process were now officially American citizens.

"American citizens?" he asked slyly. "Are you going to get them health care?"

It was not entirely a surprise that McDonough had played the Haiti chit, as both Rahm Emanuel and President Obama had also recalled the favor during their recent conversations with me.

As I stood with the others behind Obama at the bill singing, I watched as he used several different pens to sign his name, as is the tradition when the pens are to be given away as keepsakes for those participating in the ceremony. When he had finished signing the bill, the president reached down to grab the pens and give one to each of us.

"I'll decide who gets the pens," Pelosi said as she scooped all of them up for herself. The group laughed as Pelosi glared at me.

That night, the language of the health care amendment was finalized, setting in motion the promised seventy-two-hour waiting period to allow members time to read the language upon which they would be voting. The final vote was set for Sunday evening, March 21.

In reading through the language, it was clear that many of my concerns had still not been addressed, so I decided to vote against the bill.

Meanwhile, back in the district, things had gotten down-right bizarre. Phone calls came in by the thousands from all over the country. My staff did the best they could to handle the onslaught, prioritizing local calls in an attempt to accurately report to me public sentiment. Calls ran more than five to one against the bill during that last crazy week.

Signs and billboards appeared throughout Western Pennsylvania encouraging me to vote against the bill, while tone-deaf Democratic activists continued to openly advocate a liberal election challenge against me. A small plane circled over downtown Pittsburgh streaming a message from a trailing banner: "Tell Altmire To Vote No." Both sides threatened to remove me from office if I voted against their position.

Tea Party activists organized a rally outside my office in the Democratic stronghold of Aliquippa, a union-dominated former steel town. The rally grew so large that the crowd circled around the corner and lined the main street through town. Cars honked approvingly as they drove past the hundreds of rowdy protesters who lined both sides of the street for blocks. People screamed and waved the ubiquitous yellow *Don't Tread on Me* flags while others held signs indicating their opposition to the bill. One sign listed the names of the unsuccessful Democratic candidates in the recent New Jersey and Virginia gubernatorial elections, as well as the Massachusetts Senate race. My name was listed below the three losers with all four of our names crossed out with a deep red line. Another protester held up one of my campaign signs with the words "Take Out The Trash" painted across my name.

For their part, union activists tried to counter the Tea Party onslaught. First, they gave my personal cell phone number to union members across Pennsylvania. The move did not have the desired impact, as several of the union callers left voice mails asking me to ignore their leadership and vote *against* the bill. Of the calls in support, most came from area codes in the Philadelphia region, three hundred miles away. A few days later, after I had announced I would vote against the bill, about thirty union members visited my office to deliver a petition expressing their disappointment. The next day, while I was in Washington for the vote, a dozen union members drove to my neighborhood and walked in a picket line circle in front of my home while my young daughters, Natalie and Grace, played in the front yard.

I put a lot of thought into the best way to let my constituents know how I planned to vote. On Friday morning, I awoke early and decided I would write a statement explaining my decision. Still in my 420-square foot apartment two blocks from my Capitol Hill office, I emailed Rahm Emanuel at approximately 7:00 a.m. to inform him that I was soon going to announce my opposition to the bill.

"Don't do it!" came the immediate reply.

Not hearing anything more, a few hours went by before I called him from my office. After a heated discussion, I agreed to hold off on my announcement until later in the afternoon. At 4:00 p.m., I posted my statement of opposition on my congressional website, then spent the next several hours talking by phone with constituents and supporters to explain my decision. At 7:30 p.m., I was sitting at my desk when President Obama called.

"What's the matter, didn't we give you enough attention?" the president began tersely.

I said I appreciated all that had been done, but in the end my decision was based on what I believed was the best vote for the district I represented. The president said he knew I had already put out a statement and wasn't going to change my mind. He asked me to consider how I was going to feel after the bill passed, knowing I wasn't "on the team." I agreed that I would likely feel a sense of disappointment that I had let him down, along with some of my early supporters. But again, I believed I was making the right vote for my district.

The call ended cordially, although it was clear to me the vote count was still not enough to guarantee passage of the bill. Work would continue into the weekend in a desperate search for enough votes to put the bill over the top. By Sunday, Speaker Pelosi had the votes she needed, so the bill was brought to the floor.

The nation watched as the House engaged in an all-day debate, leading up to the vote on final passage that occurred just before midnight. In the end, 34 Democrats joined all Republicans in voting against the bill, which passed 219-212. As jubilant Democrats celebrated passage, I leaned along the railing in the back of the House chamber, taking in the scene and thinking about the history I was witnessing. Just then, I was approached by a sobbing Michele Bachmann, mascara running down her face.

Fighting through tears, she thanked me for voting against "this monstrosity," complaining that "the country as we know it is now over." As I watched my Democratic colleagues hug and high-five one another, the conversation made me queasy. As Obama had predicted, I didn't feel like part of the team. But I remained satisfied that I had made the right vote.

With an eye toward the 2010 elections, Republican leaders unified in opposition to the Affordable Care Act. They traveled the country stirring up the Tea Party and recruiting candidates who could win back the swing districts that had given Democrats the majority. Left-wing groups, donors, and organized labor took the opposite approach. Rather than recognizing the importance the centrist Democrats had played in giving Democrats the majority, the liberals vilified them and openly bragged about their ongoing work in waging primary campaigns against Democrats who had voted against the bill.

Groups like Blue America PAC, MoveOn.org, and FireDogLake aggressively recruited and raised money for progressive challengers to centrist Democrats. The effort continues to this day, but in a bitterly ironic twist, there are few conservative Democrats left in Congress for progressives to oppose. They have been replaced, not by champions of the liberal cause, but by Tea Party-backed Republicans solidly entrenched in those districts—now with Donald Trump in the White House.

As it turned out, the health care law did not, as many supporters had hoped, become more popular by the time the election rolled around in November. To the contrary, public sentiment ran decisively against it. Democrats lost an astonishing sixty-three seats that fall, their biggest electoral disaster in seventy-two years.

Bucking this trend, I won a hard-fought race against a Tea Party-backed opponent, hard-working local attorney Keith Rothfus, who had unexpectedly defeated former US Attorney Mary Beth Buchanan in the Republican primary. Rothfus tried desperately to convince voters I was merely a pawn for the wildly unpopular Pelosi, but it was a difficult case to make given my voting record and the fact that liberals in the district had so loudly expressed their disappointment in me. I was also helped by the fact that I ran television commercials featuring constituents—both Republicans and Democrats—thanking me for my political moderation.

I had friends on both sides of the aisle, which helped immensely. As the election tightened, I was approached on the House floor by then-Indiana Congressman Mike Pence, who told me he was about to visit Pittsburgh to headline a fundraiser for Rothfus. Pence wanted to let me know in advance that he was visiting in his capacity as a member of the House Republican leadership, but that he would refrain from saying bad things about me personally. He kept his word. In his speech at the event, which raised $40,000 for Rothfus, Pence never criticized me. When encouraged to do so by the press afterwards, he offered only complimentary remarks.[3] The following week, Pence again approached me on the House floor, giving his perspective of the event and the state of the race. He wished me luck and said he hoped there were no hard feelings. I appreciated his approach and valued our relationship. In the end, I survived a close race, but many of my colleagues were not so lucky.

The powerful 2010 Tea Party tidal wave washed away Democratic candidates all across the country. It did not miss my district. Pennsylvania's Democratic candidates for senator and governor were both routed, losing my district by a whopping thirty-eight thousand and fifty-six thousand votes respectively. Democrats in Pennsylvania lost both races, in addition to five seats in Congress. It was an electoral disaster, but I survived. Having seen firsthand the deep resentment that existed in the district over passage of the Affordable Care Act, there is no doubt in my mind that I would have lost by double-digits had I voted for it.

Downgrading Credit Where Credit is Due

AFTER THE 2010 ELECTIONS, SEVERAL COMPETING DYNAMics got underway in Congress. The emboldened Tea Party wing of the Republican Party pulled the GOP further to the right, organizing and plotting for the confrontational approach that would become its trademark. Incoming Speaker John Boehner would soon find out that corralling his two-headed monster of a majority was nearly impossible. For their part, House Democrats would circle their wagons, inexplicably returning to leadership the entire slate that had presided over one of the most comprehensive electoral defeats in American history. I disagreed with this approach, voted against Pelosi as Democratic nominee for speaker, and went on several national television programs to call for a change in leadership. Needless to say, this did not ingratiate me with Democratic House leaders.

The Blue Dog Coalition had been nearly eviscerated in the electoral tsunami of 2010. Looking for a way out of the wilderness, several of us traveled to New York City in February 2011 to meet with political leaders of all stripes to discuss the role of centrists in the new Congress and beyond.

We had separate meetings with New York Mayor Michael Bloomberg, former President Bill Clinton, and Donald Trump. Each lamented the polarization in Congress and offered thoughtful advice on how to wield the greatest influence under the circumstances. Offering comments that would prove eerily prophetic, Clinton discussed in detail how congressional Democrats were in danger of seeing the Rust Belt region go the way of Kentucky and West Virginia as Republicans continued to make headway with blue-collar workers.

Our meeting with Trump was even more interesting. As we sat around a conference table in his enormous Trump Tower office suite, Trump harshly criticized both parties and said the country was leaderless as both the White House and Congress had failed the American people. He surprised us by saying he was seriously considering running against Obama in 2012, then launched into a populist rant about the many ways he perceived America to be in decline. In discussing what he would do as president, he proceeded to make a series of increasingly outrageous statements that we assumed were being offered for shock value. We left the hour-long meeting struck by his enthusiasm and entertained by his performance, but none of us believed he was serious about actually running for president.

While Congress worked through the transition of power, an even more consequential series of events was occurring outside the beltway. State legislatures across America had been flipped from blue to red as part of the 2010 shellacking of Democrats. As Congress dithered and fought to an embarrassing stalemate, state legislatures turned their attention to redrawing the lines that form the borders of every congressional and state legislative seat in the nation. The result would be to solidify Republican majorities for a decade as the vanquished Democrats were reduced to mere bit players in the drama.

As the new GOP-controlled Congress got underway, Speaker Boehner made a genuine attempt to reach out to the few remaining centrist Democrats to gauge support for across-the-aisle compromise. He brought together a group of about eight of us for clandestine meetings in the historic "Board of Education" room on the first floor of the Capitol, directly underneath the House chamber.

The room received its nickname because of its use by the legendary Sam Rayburn during his time as one of the most powerful House speakers in history. Rayburn used the room as an office and was known to call wayward Democrats there so they could be "educated" on Rayburn's views on pending issues. Since that time, the room has served various purposes but Boehner had it set up in the style of a conference room with a well-stocked bar in the corner for use during after-work meetings such as those to which the centrist Democrats were invited.

Joined by his chief of staff as well as Iowa's conservative Representative Tom Latham—one of Boehner's top lieutenants in the House—the speaker presided over the informal discussions during the first half of 2011. After everyone had made themselves a drink, the group would sit around the table to chat. Boehner never failed to emphasize the need for secrecy, stressing that if word of the meetings leaked out they would be discontinued. If anything, the conversations were awkward and unproductive. Although the meetings went a long way toward building a trusting relationship with the speaker, they never resulted in any serious legislative discussion. It soon became apparent that Boehner was becoming increasingly concerned about his right flank, as Tea Party freshmen caused him one headache after another. He was justifiably more worried about the confrontational tactics of the eighty-seven-member Republican freshman class than he was about the few centrist Democrats sitting with him under the chandelier in Rayburn's Board of Education room. By the half-way point of Boehner's first term as speaker, the bipartisan meetings fizzled out.

The first major sign of trouble came in the spring, when the House debated the budget for the upcoming fiscal year. At issue was the budget proposal of the Republican Study Group (RSG). The RSG had been created decades before as an informal group of conservative members hoping to pull congressional Republicans to the right. Over time, the group grew so large that by the time Boehner became Speaker, the RSG's members made up more than two-thirds of all Republican House members.[4] The group put forward a budget that made draconian cuts to numerous popular programs, cut benefits and raised the retirement age for Social Security and Medicare, and froze overall discretionary spending at unrealistically low levels.

Passage of the RSG budget would have been a public relations disaster for the GOP, which was of no concern to the newly elected Tea Party contingent in the House. This was the first of many times Boehner would have to scramble to prevent the extremists in his caucus from driving the Republican bus off a cliff. Eventually, the more confrontational members of the already ultra-conservative RSC would break away to form the House Freedom Caucus, which provided a home for three dozen of the House's most far-right extremists. The group would keep moving to the right, driving Boehner from office and making life miserable for his successor, Paul Ryan. As congressional scholars Mann and Ornstein have written, the fact that some leaders of the Freedom Caucus believe that even their own group is not sufficiently confrontational or conservative is "beyond absurd" to most observers and lawmakers.[5]

Over the past decade, as House conservatives have strengthened their clout and pushed Republican members to the right, Democrats in the House have moved further to the left. The ranks of the Blue Dogs have dwindled, shrinking to little more than a dozen by 2017. The New Dems have remained relatively steady at sixty-one members.

The Republican counterpart to the New Dems is the Tuesday Group, which has fifty-four members and also purports to represent moderates. Like the New Dems, most members of the Tuesday Group have historically been hesitant to break ranks and have voted almost in lock step with their party's leadership. But this may be changing, as the continuing effort by Republican House leaders to placate the Freedom Caucus may have finally reached a breaking point, causing a bitter rift that has made governing the Republican majority almost impossible.[6]

Periodic attempts by the New Dems and Tuesday Group to join forces to empower centrists have stalled.[7] Party leaders on both sides strongly discourage such talk, which undermines party leaders' ability to control the message and agenda of their respective sides. However, in truth, efforts to align the New Dems and Tuesday Group have failed primarily because only a small handful of House members in each party can truly be called centrists in today's Congress. It is not an accident; in fact, it is an outgrowth of a concerted effort to take advantage of the public's frustration with Washington.

In the months leading up to the 2010 Republican landslide, the seeds were sown for the embarrassing budgetary confrontations that would crater public support for Congress, shut down the government, lead the treasury to the brink of default, and result in the first-ever credit downgrade for the United States. Believing that previous and current GOP leaders lacked sufficient backbone, a group of House Republicans plotted to recruit highly ideological candidates that would be more interested in confrontation than compromise.

Coinciding with the growth of the Tea Party, the effort sprouted conservative candidates who were able to tap into public anger in a way that reinforced voters' cynicism about Congress. With technical and financial support from Washington, the candidates focused their attention on the debt limit and perceived out-of-control government spending. Mann and Ornstein have noted that these candidates made the debt limit a core issue, "frequently misrepresenting a vote to raise it as a vote to add more debt."[8]

While these candidates used Washington-issued talking points to fan the flames of public resentment, conservative leaders in Congress plotted to use the debt limit—and the catastrophic consequences of failing to raise it—as the ultimate weapon against the status quo. Once elected, the Tea Party-backed House freshmen flexed their muscles by provoking repeated games of chicken each time a budget deadline loomed. The brinksmanship caused a downgrade in both Congress's public approval and the nation's credit rating.

Four months into the new Congress, Treasury Secretary Tim Geithner notified congressional leaders that the nation would face default if the debt limit was not raised by August 2, 2011. The Tea Party had their first deadline.

According to Mann and Ornstein, the debt limit had already been raised seventy-eight times between 1960 and 2011, under both Republican and Democrat administrations.[9] Raising the debt limit does not authorize new spending; rather, it authorizes payment for debts already incurred. In the history of the country, the United States has never defaulted on its debt obligations, which is why the term "full faith and credit of the United States" carries maximum weight throughout the world.

Notification of the August 2 deadline spawned a series of bipartisan negotiations involving congressional leaders and the White House. After some promising leads melted away, Boehner, Obama, and Harry Reid became directly involved, working tirelessly to forge a major budget compromise that could appease both the right and the left. The three leaders set a goal of reducing federal spending by $4 trillion over ten years in a deal that would leave no sacred cow untouched. Details of a bipartisan "Grand Bargain" emerged, including major tax reform and reductions in the growth of discretionary spending and entitlements such as Medicare and Social Security. The deal fell through when Boehner failed to convince his new Tea Party freshmen—along with some more senior Republican members—to agree to tax increases in exchange for spending cuts.[10]

The House and Senate traded proposals as Boehner and Obama tried one last time to strike a compromise. Every attempt at a deal collapsed as hard-liners in the Republican Conference refused to yield. In the end, it became clear the Tea Party held all the cards. No matter what the other players in the game did, it was they who would have the last word.

Finally, the country avoided default at the eleventh hour when a package was approved that included spending cuts with no tax increases, and the creation of a bipartisan twelve-member "super committee" that would recommend a plan to achieve more than a trillion dollars of additional debt reduction. If the super committee failed to reach agreement or its recommendation was rejected by Congress, automatic across-the-board cuts would be enacted.

Tensions finally boiled over at a meeting of House Democrats attended by Vice President Biden, who had been sent to the meeting in an attempt to appease Democrats infuriated at having been outmaneuvered by the upstart Tea Partiers. During the meeting, which I attended, Biden engaged the Democratic members in a lengthy and candid discussion about the tactics used by Republicans to take advantage of the debt limit deadline. When one furious member referred to the Tea Party as "terrorists," Biden agreed with the sentiment. The incident was widely reported in the press, further increasing the antipathy between Republicans and Democrats.[11]

At a public town hall meeting in Iowa two weeks later, President Obama himself was heckled by a Tea Party activist. The man stood up and interrupted the president, shouting questions about whether Biden had used the term "terrorists" in reference to the Tea Party. After the event, Obama and the man continued the argument in a close encounter that was described by another attendee as "extraordinarily rude" and press reports as "a heated back and forth."[12]

Following the debt-limit fiasco, Standard & Poor's downgraded the credit rating of the United States from AAA to AA+. Specifically referencing the "political brinksmanship of recent months," the ratings agency blamed political dysfunction, justifying the downgrade by saying it "reflects our view that the effectiveness, stability and predictability of American policymaking and political institutions have weakened . . ."[13] It was the first time American credit had been downgraded since ratings began in 1917.[14]

In doubting Congress's ability to repair its crippling dysfunction, Standard & Poor's would be proven right time and again. The so-called super committee would fail spectacularly,[15] and in 2013 yet another budget impasse forced a sixteen-day government shutdown that cost the economy $24 billion and decreased the country's Gross Domestic Product by more than half a percentage point.[16]

Message Votes

WHY DON'T MEMBERS OF CONGRESS DIRECT THEIR ATtention to diagnosing the causes of congressional polarization and fixing the problem? The most obvious answer is that members of the two parties strongly disagree on the causes, preferring instead to cast blame on the other side. But more importantly, there is no evidence that congressional leaders or even rank-and-file members pay a political price for polarization. Scholars have speculated that "congressional reforms are more likely to be undertaken when sufficient numbers determine that their own interests would be best served by altering the institution. Without such immediate benefits of reform, legislators will be unlikely to invest the time in devising reforms or to succeed in securing them."[17] Members of Congress won't challenge the status quo until their own constituents make it the decisive factor in their votes, and that's not happening.

In considering whether polarization is bad for American democracy, some have argued that the increased political involvement by activists—as evidenced by participation in election activities—is a benefit to the country.[18] If more people talk about politics, put up yard signs, vote in presidential elections, and participate in online discussions about political affairs, is that necessarily a bad thing? The problem is, the people who are participating are the partisan extremes, while the rest of America goes about their daily business. The effects reverberate throughout Congress.

Polarization affects the way party leaders interact with each other and encourages legislative strategies that inflame partisan passions. As Mann and Ornstein have written:

LIKE-MINDED PARTY members representing more homogeneous constituencies are willing to delegate authority to their leaders to advance their collective electoral interests, putting a premium on strategic partisan team play. Building and maintaining each party's reputation dictate against splitting the difference in policy terms. It's better to have an issue than a bill, to shape the party's brand name and highlight party differences.[19]

Many of the votes taken in Congress are simply "message votes" designed more to make a political statement than to pass legislation. Party leaders will craft amendments designed solely to put the other side in a difficult position, and sometimes even instruct their own members to vote in ways that seem counterintuitive.

One of the most egregious examples of partisan legislative tactics is the "Motion to Recommit" (MTR). The MTR is a procedural maneuver where the minority party is able to call for one last vote before a bill's final passage. The MTR contains a potential amendment to the bill or sends the bill back to committee for further review. Part of standard House rules in some form since the first session of Congress, the MTR has become the primary vehicle for the minority party to force the majority to vote "on the record" on controversial issues.[20]

MTR votes are targeted at members who represent swing districts where the controversial topic of the MTR would have particular resonance. "Sometimes we offer motions to recommit to improve legislation—sometimes it's to force Democrats in marginal districts to make tough choices," admitted then-Minority Leader John Boehner.[21]

I found the MTR votes to be an amusing annoyance. Although the continual partisan game playing frustrated me, I always looked forward to the MTR because the language was usually kept strictly confidential until the very moment it was introduced on the floor. This prevented Democratic leaders from planning their response and from having the opportunity to corral wayward centrist members and explain why it would be a bad idea for them to support the MTR. It was always fun to watch leadership aides scrambling around the House floor when the language of the MTR was unveiled. A successful MTR could mean the bill goes back to committee and dies, so majority party leaders do their best to keep their members in line.

Some examples of particularly manipulative MTRs offered during my time in office:

- During debate over a Democratic proposal to give the District of Columbia a vote in Congress, Republicans offered an MTR amendment repealing the District's strict gun control laws. Knowing she didn't have the votes to prevent an embarrassing defeat, Speaker Pelosi withdrew the entire bill from consideration.[22]

- A 2009 student aid bill was amended by an MTR that prohibited funding for the controversial community organizing group ACORN, which was in the news at the time regarding violations of campaign law. In offering the MTR, Republicans failed to mention that the education bill being debated did not actually provide any funding to ACORN. Nevertheless, the MTR passed overwhelmingly and ACORN disbanded soon thereafter.[23]

- A 2010 bill to improve American competitiveness by increasing funding for math and science education died when 121 Democrats joined Republicans in voting for an MTR barring federal employees from being paid if they were found to be watching pornography at work. The issue had not been brought up at any point during the hearings that had been held on the bill or when amendments were considered on the floor. The only way the bill could have proceeded to a final vote would have been to vote against the MTR; however, doing so would have exposed Democrats to accusations that they were in favor of using taxpayer dollars to support government subsidized porn.[24]

The last example was a particularly stinging defeat for Democrats. When Pelosi withdrew the bill following the successful MTR vote, House Republican leaders openly celebrated.[25]

While in the minority, Democrats have used the MTR to their advantage. But during Nancy Pelosi's time as speaker, Republicans refined the MTR process to an art form. Unfortunately, such cynical abuse of procedural tactics for partisan gain remains standard fare today, occurring in both houses of Congress.

Former Senate Majority Leaders Lott and Daschle wrote in 2016 about "politically radioactive votes that could hurt senators with their party or home state." They lamented that, like the House, "Senate tactics frequently include adding amendments to bills in order to force members on the other side into a corner with their vote."[26]

The most discouraging part of all this is the fact that it is the few remaining centrists who are impacted by such maneuvering. Those members who occupy safe seats need not worry about the implications of a creative thirty-second ad based upon a ridiculous MTR vote, but moderate members who represent swing districts could literally lose their seats over it. Another day in the life of a centrist in Congress.

The Filter Bubble

AFTER FOX NEWS FIRST HIT THE AIRWAVES IN 1996, IT rolled out in stages across various parts of the United States. Unsurprisingly, both Democratic and Republican members of

Congress accumulated an increasingly more conservative voting record once Fox News arrived on the channel menus of their local cable companies. The impact was shown to be particularly acute in the months immediately preceding a general election. The rightward tilt in congressional voting patterns in Fox News districts was no doubt a response to Fox viewers making their voices heard in their congressman's office.[27]

In 2005, MSNBC switched its format in an attempt to become a liberal alternative to Fox. It has grown in popularity and has provided liberals a venue to quench their thirst for progressive viewpoints. Recent studies have shown partisan media helps galvanize activists in both the Republican and Democratic parties, "giving extreme candidates a boost in congressional primaries and, ultimately, pushing moderate candidates out of the way."[28]

Social media sites like Facebook and Twitter also contribute to political polarization. Although they are effective ways to stay in touch with friends, convey thoughts, and keep up with the latest news, social media sites have also become echo chambers of partisanship, allowing users to choose both their friends and their news sources. A growing number of users admit to formulating their positions on public policy issues largely because of information they saw on social media.[29] Unfortunately, that information is often presented with a strong partisan bias, and even worse, sometimes it is a complete fabrication.

In the aftermath of the bitterly contested 2016 presidential election, pundits and researchers dissected every aspect of the campaign in an attempt to explain the unexpected result. No issue was more widely discussed than the role played by social media.

As Hillary Clinton led in the polls leading up to election day, social media trends told a different story. During the home stretch of the campaign, more than three hundred million tweets were posted on Twitter mentioning the two candidates. The majority of tweets referencing Donald Trump were positive, while the majority of tweets referencing Hillary Clinton were negative.[30] In a trend that should have been even more alarming to the Clinton campaign, the political website *BuzzFeed* found that over the last three months of the campaign, "fake election stories generated more total engagement on Facebook than top election stories from nineteen major news outlets combined."[31] Trump supporters angered by the overwhelmingly negative coverage he received from mainstream news outlets turned instead to social media to find news that was more to their liking. The problem was, much of that news was created by enterprising website designers—most notoriously a group of tech-savvy teenagers in Macedonia—who made money based upon the number of clicks their hoax news stories received.[32] The more outrageous the story, the more money they made.

In the final weeks of the 2016 campaign, these fake news stories were engaged by Facebook users more than eight million times. The overwhelming majority of the fraudulent websites contained fictitious news articles, including hoaxes about the Pope endorsing Trump, and Clinton saying she supported candidates like Trump who were "honest and can't be bought."[33] Both Facebook and Google have taken steps to prevent such websites from proliferating and taking advantage of pay-per-click advertising,[34] but such trends are likely to continue, especially now that liberal activists have proven to be just as susceptible to fake news fabrications as their conservative counterparts.[35] The fake news industry has become so lucrative that some of the most ridiculously hyperpartisan liberal and conservative websites are actually owned by the same people.[36]

Facebook has become a major source of traffic to online news sites, whether they be real or fake.[37] Facebook has by far the most users of any social media site and draws twice as many political news consumers as news aggregation sites like Google and Yahoo.[38] Facebook counts two billion users every month and has become, in the words of the *New York Times*, "the largest and most influential entity in the news business, commanding an audience greater than that of any American or European television network, any newspaper or magazine in the Western world and any online news outlet." Put more succinctly: "If it's an exaggeration to say that [Facebook's] News Feed has become the most influential source of information in the history of civilization, it is only slightly so."[39]

There are some positives to Facebook as it relates to political polarization. Users who log on to the site may be exposed to political news even if they are not specifically seeking it. For example, Facebook's news aggregation feature exposes politically disinterested users to information they might otherwise have missed. Also, non-ideological Facebook users may have friends in their networks who are politically interested, thereby providing another avenue for exposure to political information.[40]

These factors can be a positive influence on ideological moderates who might otherwise not be interested enough to go to the polls on Election Day. As was the case with network evening news programs in the days before cable television, the politically disinterested are more likely to vote when they are exposed to political information. Stimulating interest among moderates is critical to moving the political discourse more towards the center, so these are positive developments. Unfortunately, these features of Facebook are more than offset by the way the site can unintentionally stimulate extreme partisanship.

Each Facebook user sees a different mix of content based upon factors such as the type of friends with whom they engage, the news they prefer and the types of posts to which they respond. The more liberal leaning information the user seeks out, the higher priority that type of information is given in the news feed. The more often a user "likes" or comments on conservative or liberal political commentary, the more often that type of commentary will appear. Over time, users lose exposure to alternative points of view. Even the advertisements they see will conform to their existing beliefs and direct them to partisan sites that reaffirm their biases.[41]

This infamous "filter bubble" applies to Internet search engines as well as social media. The search algorithm tracks computer users' preferences so it can give them more of what they like and less of what they don't like. The combined impact is to filter out dissenting evidence and opinion, locking users into silos of like-minded conformity.[42] The problem is particularly acute on YouTube, which personalizes playlists based upon the past viewing preferences of the user, regardless of the accuracy of the information being conveyed. Watch one video about a 9/11, moon landing, or Elvis Presley conspiracy theory, and you can expect to see countless others appear in your recommended playlist. The impact on polarization is exacerbated by the fact that YouTube's daily viewership now equals the 1.25 billion hours of television that Americans watch every day.[43]

The problem of the filter bubble is well-known but not easy to solve. Research shows that even when provided opposing views in their social media news feed, users tend to ignore those stories and direct their attention to those that conform to their political preferences.[44] As a result, social media sites like Facebook, Twitter, and YouTube, which pride themselves on giving users more of what they want and less of what they don't, are unintentionally contributing to the nation's political polarization.

The polarized sorting of Internet content is not always accidental, as users can easily block news sources and individuals with whom they disagree. Journalist Caitlin Dewey, an expert on social media and the Internet, writes: "In the era of News Feeds and content-blockers . . . avoiding discourse and dissent has never been so easy," adding that "thanks to the proliferation of partisan media and the rise of intermediaries like Facebook and Google News, it's now also possible to tailor the information you get to your preexisting politics."[45]

Daschle and Lott agree that this "makes for a less informed yet more confident and outraged electorate." They comment that use of the Internet for political discourse "gives a platform to too many outlets for venomous comment," allowing partisans to believe they are in a public debate, when actually they are merely interacting with only "their own kind."[46]

Compared to non-ideological users, partisans are much more likely to group their Facebook friends into an echo chamber dominated by those who think just like they do. According to Pew Research Center, "those with stronger ideological tendencies are more likely to surround themselves with like-minded opinions."[47]

Author Frank Bruni accurately says this promotes a heightened level of toxicity to our political discourse, turning "conviction into zeal, passion into fury, disagreements with the other side into demonization of it."[48] Bruni believes this only increases the level of distrust that exists in politics, creating a "groupthink of micro-communities, many of which we've formed online." The combined impact of all of this has been dubbed by some as "the Facebook effect," but it also pertains to most other social media sites.[49] Unfortunately, the behavior of many social media users has become decidedly unsocial.

According to Pew surveys, 44% of self-identified liberals have reported that they have blocked or unfriended someone because they disagreed with that person's political views. This compares with 31% of conservatives.[50] Facebook's own research has confirmed that liberals are less open to alternative points of view and are more likely to drop a friend with whom they disagree. Even worse, 24% of liberals have said they have stopped talking to someone altogether because of politics, compared to 16% of conservatives.[51]

Today, isolating yourself from differing opinions has become a business opportunity. During the 2016 presidential election, a slew of websites and iPhone apps were created to help users block from their news feeds references to opposing political candidates and unfriend people who support them.[52]

Some of the most interesting research on the different behaviors of liberals and conservatives on social media relates to Twitter users. It is not surprising that partisans follow Twitter accounts consistent with their own political affiliations. People who tweet about politics direct their messages to, and receive messages from, primarily those who already agree with them. In a study of the postings of more than ten thousand Twitter users, researchers studied the words partisans use in their tweets. Using complex linguistic software, investigators were able to determine a clear pattern of language use differentiating liberals and conservatives.[53]

The results went far beyond the obvious issue distinctions, such as conservatives being more likely to talk about Benghazi and use the term Obamacare. The study found that liberals consistently used more expressive language, with liberals' use of swear words being one of their most notable differentiations with conservatives. Liberals were more likely than conservatives to use language associated with anxiety and feelings, and were more likely to use individually expressive first-person references, such as "I" and "me." Conservatives more frequently used terms like "we" and "our."[54] These results are consistent with other psychological research that has shown liberals to be more prone to expressions of uniqueness, while conservatives express a more group-oriented viewpoint.[55]

Republicans in the study focused more on religion, national identity, government, and law. They also tweeted more frequently about in-group identity, including the use of the popular hashtag #tcot—top conservative on Twitter. In addition to the socially expressive words, liberals were more likely to discuss entertainment and culture as a diversion from politics. As it relates to the negativity associated with political polarization, there was one overriding similarity—both groups pointed fingers often, criticizing the other party's leaders and followers more often than they praised their own.[56]

Every day, millions of articles and news clips are shared through social media. Presumably, many people do this to illustrate how well informed they are and to show off their newfound intel. Unfortunately, most of them have never read beyond the headline. We all know people who are guilty of the phenomenon known as "blind sharing," when social media users don't read the material they circulate. In a mockingly funny gag, a satirical news site called *Science Post* posted an article with the headline: "Study: 70% of Facebook users only read the headline of science stories before commenting." The underlying article was written in an incomprehensible filter text equating to nothing more than gibberish. The post went viral, being shared by nearly forty-six thousand people, most of whom we can safely assume were unaware of the joke.[57]

A 2016 international study led by Columbia University showed that 59% of the news links shared on social media were never clicked, meaning the news was shared without being read.[58] Unfortunately, this study was not satire.

Because of the way mainstream news organizations cover the news, moderate voters who want to learn more about political candidates sometimes find it difficult to distinguish between centrist and more extreme candidates. Mainstream news strives to preserve the appearance of political neutrality,[59] so news reporters are often unwilling to describe the actions of a party or a candidate as more extreme than the other, even when there is a clear distinction. Reporters seeking to write a story about polarization will highlight the actions of those on each extreme, as though no middle existed.

In January 2016, only days before the crucial Iowa Caucus, the *Los Angeles Times* printed a story called "From West to East, Iowa Voters Have Starkly Different Realities." The article purported to show how Iowa voters, and by implication all Americans, were deeply divided and polarized. To prove their point, the reporters visited the liberal college town of Iowa City and its religious conservative polar opposite, Orange City. No effort was made to talk to moderate voters as the reporters instead found the incendiary quotes they were looking for in what they described as "the most lopsidedly partisan counties in the state," whose voters "reflect the vast political chasm here and across the country, a divide that President Obama was unable to heal and which may prove insurmountable for whomever takes his place."[60] The reporters conveyed a compelling storyline for those interested in advancing the notion that we are a nation of hopelessly divided partisans—a common theme in the media these days.

CHAPTER 9

TURNOUT THE LIGHTS

—— ·◆· ——

Portraying the Unrepresentative as Representative

POLITICAL SCIENTIST MORRIS FIORINA HAS WRITTEN EX-
tensively about the impact of media on political polarization.
He hits the nail on the head when he writes that "journalists
tend to be greatly overexposed to a slice of America that is not
at all representative. The political class that journalists talk to
and observe is polarized, but the people who comprise it are not
typical. Biased exposure naturally leads journalists to portray
the unrepresentative as representative."[1] The people who are
most likely to discuss politics on Facebook and Twitter, and to
talk politics in the media, are also the most ideological.[2] They
may be the most willing to talk, but that does not mean they are
the most well-informed.

Cable news programming is often presented in a purposely
uncivil manner that inflames passions and deepens partisan
resentment.[3] Talk show hosts routinely give platforms to the
most extreme partisans, even those who provide ridiculously
inaccurate information and delve into debunked conspiracy
theories. Occasionally, the partisan news channels will give
airtime to some of the opposing party's most absurd characters in the hope that their lunacy discredits their entire party.
During the height of the "birther" movement in 2011, when it

was not uncommon to find guests on cable news and talk radio programs making the case that President Obama was born in Kenya, Bill O'Reilly complained (with some justification) that Democrats were purposely giving an audience to birthers in order to embarrass Republicans "by painting them as nuts."[4]

At about the same time, Fairleigh Dickenson University was conducting a poll that showed viewers of both Fox News and MSNBC were embarrassingly misinformed about current events, sometimes even more so than those who didn't pay any attention to the news at all. Fox and MSNBC viewers were found to be much less knowledgeable than those who received their political news primarily from the Sunday news programs, which most would agree are usually presented in a straightforward, unbiased way. Although viewers of both Fox and MSNBC performed poorly on the current events survey, you won't be surprised to learn that they were misinformed about different subjects along the predictable partisan lines.[5]

Perhaps the most amusing of the misinformed talk show guests are the celebrity activists, some of whom are well educated and passionate about their cause while others are, well, not. There are endless examples from both the left and the right of sports and entertainment celebrities going on television to give their opinion about subjects with which they are in no way familiar.

One of my favorite such interviews that occurred during my time in office was an appearance by actor Craig T. Nelson on Glenn Beck's television program in the summer of 2009, just as the Tea Party movement was kicking into high gear. Nelson was explaining to Beck why he was considering no longer paying his taxes. He felt his tax dollars were spent helping people who don't deserve it. "They're not going to bail me out," Nelson complained, "I've been on food stamps and welfare. Anybody help me out? No."[6] Beck failed to correct Nelson about the obvious absurdity of his statement.

Legions of Cosponsors

AFTER THE DEBT LIMIT DEBACLE, WITH TENSIONS RUNning high and public support for Congress near an all-time low, I wanted to find a way to prove that there are still some things about which all members of Congress could agree. As I had done by holding joint town hall meetings with my Republican colleague and in organizing the bipartisan Special Orders debate about gas prices, I considered ways to help restore public faith in the possibility of Congress working together in a bipartisan way. I wanted to prove, even if only in a symbolic way, that our system wasn't completely broken and that members of Congress could still come together.

Because of my strong record on veterans' issues, I was contacted by the American Legion about the need to modernize their congressionally mandated charter. Although the American Legion would have been the first to agree that the issue was certainly not the most pressing matter facing the country, an update of the charter was needed and only Congress was authorized to do it. I agreed to introduce the legislation, which made changes in the Legion's financial and organizational structure to account for modern technology and other advancements.

In the aftermath of the credit downgrade, relations between members of the two parties were particularly frosty. As I talked to other members about the bill, many commented that it was nice to finally be talking about something upon which everyone could agree.

Throughout the fall, as more cosponsors signed onto the bill, I realized that this presented an opportunity for a symbolic gesture that true bipartisanship was still possible. During the times when members were on the House floor together while votes were being cast, I went around to talk to my colleagues about the bill and the message it would send if we all cosponsored it together.

By the time the modernization of the charter was passed and signed into law in December, my bill had accumulated 432 cosponsors, nearly the entire House of Representatives and the most cosponsors of any bill ever introduced in Congress. I took to the floor to speak about the bill, telling my colleagues that I hoped we could use this small example as proof that bipartisanship is possible and that, hopefully, we could apply this lesson to other more pressing matters before Congress. Although that proved to be overly optimistic, I hope that somewhere in the experience this episode provides a lesson in the fact that during one of the most contentious times in modern congressional history, members were still able to join together in support of a cause that superseded partisan loyalties.

Tracking Income Inequality

A GRAPH MEASURING POLITICAL POLARIZATION OVER TIME tracks closely with any one of a variety of factors, such as the rise of cable media and Internet technology, and the increase in money in politics. But no issue tracks more closely with political polarization than income inequality.[7] Polarization is measured as the difference between the median political positions for the two parties in Congress, while income inequality is measured using the *Gini coefficient*, defined as the range of inequality based upon the overall distribution of a nation's wealth among all its citizens.[8]

Charted over the past fifty years, the two indicators have risen together in almost perfect synchronicity. Both measures also chart almost perfectly over the first half of the twentieth century, when economic inequality fell dramatically and political polarization declined right along with it.[9] A similar correlation exists when measured at the state level.[10] Political scientists debate the relative impact of economic inequality in *causing* the rise in polarization, or vice versa, but there is little doubt that the two are intrinsically linked.

The anxiety caused by income inequality cuts across both parties. From the redistributive policies generally favored by Democrats to the pro-business and tax reduction policies put forth by the Republicans, the two parties have traditionally held distinctly different views on the proper response to economic inequality. As we have increasingly seen in recent years, the issues driving the anxiety—particularly immigration, globalization, and trade—have changed the political outlook of those most concerned about income inequality.

Political scientists who have studied the impact of income inequality on the electorate have found that "during periods of increasing inequality when the fortunes of different economic groups are diverging, the policies preferred by each will diverge as well."[11] Social class is no longer a reliable predictor of ideology.[12] Today, wealthy and poor voters populate both ends of the political spectrum, and the traditional partisan boundaries have been blurred.[13] The Democrats' inability to appeal to working-class white voters cost them the Rust Belt region and gave Donald Trump the opening he needed to win the presidency.

As the 2016 elections demonstrated, anxiety among working-class voters has reached a fever pitch. Heightened concerns about issues such as immigration and foreign trade have allowed populist candidates like Trump and Bernie Sanders to attract huge followings and advance further in the electoral process than anyone would previously have thought possible. Their messages were conveyed as a response to the resentment felt by those most impacted by rising income inequality. That resentment has grown to the highest level in recent memory.

In a June 2016 survey, 54% of Americans said illegal immigrants hurt the economy by driving down wages, and 52% believed "trade agreements with other countries are mostly harmful because they send U.S. jobs overseas and drive down wages." The concern about income inequality was bipartisan, as even a majority (54%) of Republicans supported increasing the tax rate for the wealthy, an 18-point increase from 2012. A full 80% of Americans who reported themselves to be in uncertain financial condition said they were at least somewhat concerned about the prospect of unemployment.[14]

No wonder populist candidates of both parties are able to appeal to working-class Americans who feel that they have been left behind by America's economic policies. "There's a fundamental issue that all developed economies have to confront, which is that globalization and technology changes have meant millions of people have seen their jobs marginalized and wages decline," David Axelrod told the *New York Times*.[15] These concerns have stoked the fears of voters, moved political activists more toward the extremes, and given rise to candidates willing to portray themselves as opposed to the policies that have been blamed for the inequality working-class Americans see all around them. Unfortunately for those who want to restore centrism and moderation to American politics, the levels of income inequality—and the fears associated with it—aren't likely to diminish anytime soon.

Choose Your Poison

WHEN PEW RESEARCH CENTER COMPLETED ITS COMPRE-hensive 2014 public opinion survey on political polarization, one of the key findings was the difference between ideologues and centrists in participation in the political process. The survey found that extreme partisans are "far more likely to participate in the political process than the rest of the nation." Those in the center take less interest in politics and choose to remain on the sidelines.[16] Candidates and incumbents therefore tailor their campaign messages and voting records to please the extreme wings of their respective parties. When moderates don't vote, candidates are incentivized to focus on driving turnout of the most ideological voters rather than appealing to centrists, who subsequently become even more disenchanted. This downward spiral makes it even more likely moderates will stay home on Election Day.[17]

At the congressional level, this results in Republican and Democratic members being driven further apart. In their book *Partisan Divide*, former US House campaign committee leaders Tom Davis, a Republican, and Martin Frost, a Democrat, lament a process that leaves "the partisan nomination process to those who are the most ideologically inclined, the most activist-minded, and the least likely to compromise."[18] Quite simply, polarization in Congress reflects the increasing polarization among partisan activists.[19] Americans with less extreme views are therefore increasingly unrepresented in the halls of Congress.

The fate of candidates who aspire to public office is in the hands of partisan ideologues. Unlike in the past, when politicians were encouraged to appeal to the "median voter," politicians today must appeal to a much narrower base within their own party.[20]

The clout of party activists has risen dramatically as social media and technology has made it easier to organize, gain visibility and raise money. In both Congress and the state legislatures, this drives those who hold public office even further to the extremes.[21] "Career-minded legislators who typically want to go along to get along may resist moves to the center to avoid attracting a strong challenger in the primary."[22] Because "the electorate is made up primarily of impassioned partisans, political leaders will have even fewer incentives to pursue the compromises that are the antidote to political gridlock," according to political scientists Danny Hayes and Jennifer Lawless.[23]

The majority of public opinion in a congressional district does not necessarily coincide with the opinions of the activists, leaving the elected representative to choose between the majority opinion or the views of those most likely to vote in primaries. This complicates the way members of Congress who represent swing districts choose their positions on key issues. According to political scientists James Druckman and Lawrence Jacobs, elected officials today are less responsive to majority opinion because "the polarization of elites and voters has motivated politicians to advance their careers by abiding by the policy goals favored by party activists, contributors, and others. Compromising these goals can be costly, generating primary challengers and a decline in campaign contributions."[24]

Centrist legislators can have considerable leverage because they are often the pivotal votes necessary to pass major legislation in a divided Congress. But that leverage quickly evaporates for any centrist who is thinking beyond the two-year election cycle.[25] The most politicized elements of the party stand ready to punish compromisers, making moderation a dangerous proposition.[26] This presents an unenviable no-win situation for centrist members who represent swing districts: Either go along with party leadership in support of an overreaching agenda likely to be viewed unfavorably by the district's general election voters, or take a more moderate position guaranteed to be unpopular with the party activists who determine the winner of primaries. Choose your poison indeed.

The Genius of Gerrymandering

EVERY TEN YEARS, FOLLOWING EACH DECENNIAL CENSUS, the nation's 435 congressional districts are reapportioned among states to more accurately reflect the population variances throughout the country. Over the past seventy years, this has caused a regional realignment in Congress, as evidenced by the steady increase in seats in the growing Sun Belt and Western states, at the expense of seats formerly located in the stagnant Northeast and post-industrial Midwest. The number of congressional seats for each state is determined by the census, with every district in the country having about the same population, currently approximately 750,000 people.

State legislatures control the process for determining how the lines will be drawn. That's where the mischief begins. This system allows political leaders to choose their voters, rather than the other way around. Ever since the 1962 Supreme Court ruling in *Baker v. Carr*—the landmark "One Man, One Vote" case—the court has kept close watch on redistricting decisions in the states and has intervened several times in an attempt to preserve fairness in the process.[27] Nevertheless, nearly everyone agrees the excesses of the redistricting process have exacerbated the problem of polarization in Congress.

Abuses of the power of legislators to draw the boundaries of districts are not new. The commonly used name of the process—*gerrymandering*—harkens back to the founding of the Republic. Elbridge Gerry, a signer of the Declaration of Independence and member of the early Continental Congress, rose to become governor of Massachusetts. He was widely ridiculed by political opponents for his role in drawing creatively shaped electoral districts to benefit his own party in upcoming elections. The term gerrymandering stuck and today is used to describe the process of redrawing district lines, especially as it relates to using that process to benefit the party in power.

In the decades since the *Baker v. Carr* decision and enactment of the Voting Rights Act of 1965, state legislatures have prioritized the creation of majority-minority districts to promote the election of racial and ethnic minorities to Congress. Although this has increased the number of minorities serving in the House of Representatives, it has also provided a convenient way for Republican-held legislatures—often working in tandem with leaders from the minority communities—to remove reliably Democratic-leaning minority populations from districts, a process known as "bleaching."[28] The resulting congressional districts are largely homogenous and all but guaranteed to elect an ideologically partisan representative.

Contrary to conventional wisdom, a successful partisan redistricting plan does not necessarily mean maximizing the number of majority party voters who live in the newly drawn districts. Instead, successfully maximizing the number of seats for the majority party means packing as many of the opposing party's voters into a limited number of districts, while spreading smaller majorities of the dominant party's voters across a larger number of districts that are not quite as lopsided.[29] This process has worked with ruthless efficiency.

In 2012, the first national election after the most recent round of redistricting, Republicans won a 234-201 seat majority in the US House of Representatives despite the fact that Democrats won 1.4 million more votes than Republicans nationwide. In Pennsylvania, Republicans won a 13-5 majority in the congressional delegation even though Democrats won more votes statewide. Similar results were seen in states all across the country. In North Carolina, Democratic House candidates won 51% of the vote but only four of the state's thirteen congressional seats.[30] In Michigan, Democrats won 250,000 more votes than Republicans but only five of the state's fourteen districts.[31] Similarly disproportionate results benefited Democrats in Illinois and Maryland, proving the pendulum swings both ways based upon which party happens to control the process. Because district boundaries are locked in for ten years, these results will continue through the end of the decade, when the lines will again be redrawn.

Democrats have unintentionally made it easy for Republican legislatures to marginalize Democratic voters.[32] Because of the geographic sorting that has occurred across America, Democrats in particular have isolated themselves into geographic clusters that make it "awfully difficult to construct a [national] map that wasn't leaning Republican," according to University of Michigan political scientist Jowei Chen.[33] As a result, one-third of congressional seats currently held by Democrats come from three states: California, New York, and Massachusetts.[34]

The combination of micro-targeting computer software and the natural sorting of Americans into predictable partisan enclaves has made it easy to segregate groups of voters based upon past electoral performance. The results have made districts increasingly less competitive.

In the 2012 congressional races held in the newly gerrymandered districts, 168 members of Congress were elected with at least 67% of the vote, while only 62 members were elected with 54% or less of the vote. Those 62 seats were evenly divided, 31 Democrats and 31 Republicans. Among those in the safest seats, Democrats had the advantage, winning 101 of the 168 least-competitive seats.[35] This means a sizable majority of the Democratic Caucus was elected from seats that offer no realistic risk of competitiveness in a general election. My experience has been that members from these districts are the people most likely to speak in the Democratic Caucus meetings, pontificating about the need for centrists to show a backbone and act more like "real Democrats."

The problem got worse in 2016, when only 32 of 435 House races were decided by less than 10%. Members on both sides have become more safely ensconced in their seats with each passing election cycle. According to the nonpartisan *Cook Political Report,* 195 of the current congressional seats are safely Republican, while 168 are safely Democratic.[35] Those 363 members of Congress never have to give a second thought to their general election. Perhaps Chris Cillizza says it best: "In our current political environment, there is not only no reward for working across the aisle, but there is also a known penalty: The possibility of losing a primary to a challenger who claims you are insufficiently loyal to the conservative or liberal cause."[36]

Although less than eighty such districts remain, no two swing districts are alike. A mistake many observers make is to assume that a swing district consists primarily of moderate voters who shift back and forth depending on their shared electoral mood at the time. A district that votes approximately 50/50 in elections does not necessarily contain a large block of centrists. In fact, many swing districts combine highly Democratic areas with highly Republican areas, leaving few voters truly "up for grabs." In that case, candidates must cater to the voters in their own party rather than try to appeal to the other half of the district's voters. As primary electorates are pulled further to the extremes, representatives with moderate voting records are increasingly vulnerable to a primary challenge from the most partisan wing of their party.

Because the vast majority of congressional districts are not swing districts but instead are solidly partisan, members representing those districts feel no pressure to accommodate alternative points of view, appealing instead to the district's most partisan interests.[37] Rather than encouraging their representative to chart a more cooperative course, political activists in these districts demand greater levels of ideological adherence.[38] Additionally, members of Congress from solidly partisan districts are usually more philosophically partisan themselves, which in many cases is why they ran for office in the first place. This makes it even more unlikely members from those districts will be interested in working to find middle ground with those on the other side of the aisle.[39]

In identifying the negative impact safely partisan seats have on the potential for compromise, Cillizza accurately describes the problem: "Given the data, it shouldn't be surprising to anyone that the incentive to cooperate with the other side and find bipartisan compromise is nil."[40] The result: "Politicians, ever concerned with survival, typically take the path of least resistance – voting with their party almost all the time."[41]

Ron Brownstein agrees:

> THIS DECLINE IN competition has increased the electoral security for most House members but reduced their motivation to cooperate across party lines. Members in highly competitive districts . . . gravitate toward compromises attractive to the swing voters who typically decide their fates. But . . . in districts that lean so heavily to one side, ardent ideologues that excite the party base almost always have an advantage over moderates in winning party nominations.[42]

Writing about those occupying the safest seats, Brownstein says, "Appealing to swing voters, much less partisans on the other side, by pursuing centrist policies or compromises across party lines is rarely a priority for them . . . In districts designed that way, the greater risk for House members is that compromising with the other party will expose them to uncomfortable complaints from supporters or donors" who could promote a "primary challenge fueled by the charge that they are collaborating too often with the enemy. For these legislators, flexibility and bipartisan cooperation is often more politically dangerous than absolutism."[43]

As one who lost my seat in Congress due in large part to redistricting, I don't subscribe to the theory that gerrymandering is the main source of congressional polarization. But it surely plays a part.

Studies that examine the "ideology of members elected from congressional districts that changed substantially following redistricting" have shown that "members elected from these districts also tend to be more ideologically extreme."[44] Worse yet, congressional centrists are often replaced by more extreme members even if the district has not been redrawn.[45] However, the steep increase in polarization in the Senate has tracked that of the House, even though Senate lines never change.[46] Even in House districts that are drawn to be competitive, the candidates who emerge from the primary will often be those favored by the ideological wings of their parties, giving moderate voters a choice only among the extremes. As a result, members representing swing districts have been found to be only slightly less polarized than the overall House.[47]

There are more direct causes of congressional polarization than gerrymandering, namely closed-party primaries, the proliferation of partisan media, and the political and geographic sorting of Americans. But one thing is indisputable: The best way to reduce partisanship in Congress is to elect more centrists, and there are hundreds of districts in the country where centrist candidates have almost no chance to win, simply because of the way the lines are drawn. Today, the most moderate members of Congress are usually elected from districts that slightly favor the other party[48]—Republican members representing Democratic-leaning districts and Democratic members representing Republican-leaning districts—as was the case for my seat when I was in Congress. Holding this type of seat is not a long-term proposition for centrist members who find themselves vulnerable both in primaries and the general election. When they lose, they are often replaced by someone from the extreme wing of the opposing party.[49] This is what happened in my final election and in the case of most of my centrist colleagues.

The Price of Moderation

BEING IN THE POLITICAL CENTER PROVIDES OPPORTUNITY for bipartisan compromise but it also guarantees you will encounter political fire from both sides. This was the case for me when the Pennsylvania Legislature finalized the new congressional district maps for 2012.

As has been the case for decades, the census showed the population growth across the Rust Belt continues to lag well behind that of the Sun Belt and West. As a result, states like New York, Michigan, and Illinois lost congressional seats, while states experiencing rapid population growth, like Florida, Texas, and Arizona, all gained seats. This process has hit Pennsylvania especially hard due to its low rate of in-migration combined with the continuing exodus of its residents to other states. The problem has become so bad that Pennsylvania loses a resident every twelve minutes.[50] For the eighth consecutive redistricting cycle, Pennsylvania came out on the short end of congressional reapportionment, losing yet another seat after the 2010 census.[51] Unfortunately for me, the seat that was lost was the one I represented.

The 4th District, which I represented, was eliminated and merged with the neighboring 12th District, formerly home of the legendary John Murtha, who had died in 2010. His successor, Mark Critz, had been Murtha's district director and was now serving his first full term in Congress.

Critz and I would be forced to run against each other for the right to face Keith Rothfus, the opponent I defeated in 2010 who was now seeking a rematch. It was a game of musical chairs that the Republicans who controlled the state legislature hoped would result in Rothfus claiming the seat when the music stopped. But Republicans knew that was only likely to happen if Critz beat me first. I had already beaten Rothfus in the more Republican-leaning 4th District seat, despite the fact that 2010 proved to be a disastrous year for Democrats. The chances of the Tea Party-backed Rothfus beating me now, during a presidential election year—when more Democrats vote—was remote.

The newly drawn district in which Critz and I would compete had sixty thousand more registered Democrats than Republicans. This was nearly double the Democratic advantage from the district that I had represented when I defeated Rothfus two years earlier. The newly drawn 12th District tilted towards Republicans in voter performance, meaning Republican candidates would often win despite the Democratic registration advantage. This is because the district contained many conservative Democrats who would flip to vote for the Republican candidate if the Democrat moved too far to the left. That is what happened in my 4th District seat in 2010, as evidenced by the blowout losses suffered in my district by the Democratic nominees for governor and US Senate, as well as in the down-ballot races. I was able to survive that year because conservative Democratic voters viewed me differently than the other Democrats on the ballot.

The majority of the conservative Democrats who lived in the newly merged 12th District were the same voters who had supported me in past elections. Critz, on the other hand, came from a district that was evenly balanced in partisan performance, meaning he was not as prepared to run a race in which simply appealing to organized labor and traditional Democrats was not enough to win. To prevail in the general election in the new 12th District, Critz would have to win the support of the large swaths of conservative Democrats and moderate Republicans who had previously voted for me while supporting Republicans in every other race.

The new district contained substantially more of my former territory than Critz's, but the state legislature had carved out of the district New Castle and the surrounding region—the areas where I had received my strongest base of voter support in recent elections. In its place, the legislature added Critz's home turf of Johnstown, where Murtha had served for nearly forty years and labor unions had as strong an influence as anywhere in the country.

Because the new district had more Democrats than my current district, I knew I would have a strong advantage if I got to the general election. I also understood that it was likely to be a low turnout primary, which would favor the liberal and union activists who had for years been plotting to defeat me. They couldn't have beaten me in my own district, but the new map gave them the opportunity for which they had been waiting, and they took full advantage.

In the immediate aftermath of the Tea Party tidal wave of 2010, national liberal activists and bloggers lamented the fact that I had won reelection while sixty-three of my Democratic colleagues had lost their seats in the toxic political climate.[52] My left-wing critics resented the fact that my vote against the health care bill had likely saved me, and they especially detested the fact that I campaigned on a record of bipartisanship, often speaking in opposition to those in my own party whose views were outside the mainstream of my district.

In most areas of the country, the political influence of labor unions has dwindled to near irrelevance. But organized labor still holds considerable sway in Democratic primaries in the stagnant Rust Belt. Led by John DeFazio's steelworkers, organized labor flocked to support Critz when we were put in the same district together. Although rank-and-file union members in my former district often went against the wishes of their leadership, I knew that in this case the union endorsements would make a big difference in Johnstown, where I was not well-known and the unions would have a chance to define me on their terms.

In the months leading up to our April 24th primary, I was considered the heavy favorite. I was polling well ahead of Critz and substantially outraising him in campaign contributions. I was always leery of the polls in this race, because they assumed turnout would be the same across the district, which I knew was not likely to be the case. Critz's home base of Johnstown historically had higher-than-average turnout because of Murtha's well-oiled campaign machine, which I knew would be operating full throttle in this race.

Knowing the ultimate goal was to win the general election in November, I tried throughout the primary campaign to maintain my moderate message while focusing on the issues upon which Critz and I disagreed. He and his supporters chose a different path. They chose to focus on a left-of-center message and go all out to win the Democratic primary, despite the negative impact that strategy would have in the general election. The Democratic activists supporting his campaign denigrated my centrist record and criticized the times I had voted against the party's agenda. In contrast, I was always careful not to say anything that might alienate general election voters. I frequently highlighted the fact that I was the only Democrat in the race who could beat Rothfus in this type of conservative-leaning district. In fact, I already had.

Less than two weeks before the primary election, I was driving back from a community event when I received some bad news—Bill Clinton was going to endorse Critz that afternoon. The move didn't surprise me. The former president had intervened in other contested Democratic primaries, especially those in which one of the candidates had failed to support Hillary Clinton's 2008 campaign against Barack Obama. My unwillingness to endorse Hillary was particularly irritating to the Clintons given how hard they tried to win my support. I knew it was only a matter of time before Bill Clinton entered the fray.

His endorsement made a difference, but in the end, the election simply came down to turnout. Despite the relentless campaigning Critz and his liberal supporters had done in the parts of the district that I had previously represented, I still won nearly 70% of the vote there. Those centrist voters knew my moderate record and supported me. The problem was, only 18% of them bothered to show up on Election Day.

By contrast, 35% of Democrats showed up to vote in Johnstown and 91% of them voted for Critz. That was all she wrote. By doubling the turnout in his home area and successfully painting himself as the more loyal Democrat, Critz was able to overcome his geographical disadvantage and win the hard-fought primary by 1,500 votes. The problem for Critz, however, was that he and his supporters did too good a job of showing off his Democratic credentials. In hitching his wagon to the left-wing activists whose views were out of step in the district, Critz had put himself at a distinct disadvantage with the more conservative general election voters. He tried to move towards the center after the primary, but the damage had been done.

In November, Rothfus beat Critz and won a congressional seat that he still holds today. In a nationally watched battle of extremes, the Tea Party overpowered organized labor, even in union-heavy Western Pennsylvania. Predictably, Critz was never able to appeal to the centrist voters he needed to win in the parts of the district I had represented. In Republican-leaning northern Allegheny County, the population center of the district, Critz lost by a staggering 12% in an area where I had broken even with Rothfus two years earlier. Similar results occurred throughout the district, as Critz underperformed in all the areas where blue collar Democrats will vote Republican if they don't like the choice on their own side of the ballot. As was the case when I won reelection by twelve points in 2008, President Obama lost the district by double digits. This time, however, those crossover voters who had supported me four years earlier were less willing to shift back over to support Critz, which is why Rothfus was able to win.

Although the final outcome in this case was heavily influenced by redistricting, the race followed a familiar script. Motivated ideologues were able to defeat a centrist incumbent in the primary, but then lost the seat when partisans from the other side won the general election. Yet another swing district had lost its centrist representative in Congress.

CHAPTER 10

SOLUTIONS

——·•·——

Congressional Reforms

IT IS A COMMON MISCONCEPTION THAT THE RIGHT TO FILI-
buster is in the Constitution. To the contrary, the Constitution
leaves to the House and Senate the right to make their own
rules. In a few instances, the Constitution specifically requires
supermajorities, such as veto overrides and ratification of trea-
ties. It is clear, however, that filibuster-type procedures for or-
dinary legislation were discouraged by the framers.

Both Madison and Hamilton wrote about the dangers of requiring supermajorities, which had been a continuing source
of frustration under the complicated and painfully unworkable
Articles of Confederation. Channeling what today's critics might
say about the filibuster, Madison wrote: "In all cases where justice or the general good might require new laws to be passed,
or active measures to be pursued, the fundamental principle of
free government would be reversed. It would be no longer the
majority that would rule; the power would be transferred to the
minority."[1]

Since the early days of the Republic, the Senate has had the
same rules for passage of legislation as the House—a simple
majority. As time went by, senators discovered a quirk in Senate
rules that allowed for unlimited debate prior to a vote, although
the loophole was rarely abused. During the run-up to World
War I, a small group of anti-war senators held a filibuster that
delayed action in the Senate, leading to a rules change allowing "cloture" to be invoked—and debate to be stopped—with a

two-thirds vote (later reduced to the three-fifths required today).
For the next several decades, the filibuster was generally used
only in the case of issues the minority party considered to be of
monumental significance.[2]

The cloture rule took effect in 1917, and from that moment
to 1970, the most cloture motions filed during any two-year
session of Congress was seven. After that, the number rose as
the use of the filibuster became more common, generally peaking at between sixty and eighty cloture motions filed per session throughout the 1990s and early 2000s. Then, following the
2006 elections, the number of filibusters skyrocketed, peaking
at an astonishing 253 cloture motions filed during the 113th
session of Congress (2013-14).[3]

Minorities in both parties now use the filibuster as a routine procedural tactic, leading to stalemate in the Senate and
discussion about ending the filibuster once and for all. In 2013,
the Democratic majority took the first step by invoking the so-
called "nuclear option," changing the rules to allow a simple
majority vote to stop debate on executive branch and judicial
nominations except for the Supreme Court. Four years later,
Republicans further chipped away at the rule by voting to deny
the minority the right to filibuster Supreme Court nominees.
The right to filibuster remains in effect for legislative debate,
although many believe that in today's polarized environment, it
is only a matter of time before the filibuster is eviscerated.

Cornell University law professor Josh Chafetz, an expert on
the subject, fears that "there will come a point . . . when the
legislative filibuster consistently frustrates lawmaking in which
the party that controls Washington is deeply invested. When
that day comes, the history of legislative obstruction would suggest that the filibuster won't be long for this world."[4]

In practice, senators today are rarely called upon to literally
stand on the Senate floor and carry out an actual filibuster.
Even so, groups of senators could easily take turns and obstruct action for hours. As a result, cloture motions are filed on
even the threat of a filibuster.[5]

The obstructionism has ground Senate business to a halt.
As Madison feared, the supermajority vote needed to end a
filibuster has given the minority disproportionate power. That's
why abolishing the filibuster is such a hot topic among advocates of congressional reform. But there is reason to believe that

eliminating the filibuster might actually *increase* polarization and party-line voting.

In order to win a cloture vote on a legislative issue, the majority must win at least a few votes from the other side (except in the rare instances when the majority holds at least sixty seats). One could argue that the filibuster actually forces bipartisan cooperation—or at least some level of communication among the parties. Moving to a House-style system of majority rule could reduce the Senate minority to little more than a powerless nuisance. It might make it easier to pass legislation favored by the majority, but it's hard to see how this would lead to less partisanship. The problem is the abuse of the filibuster, not the fact that the filibuster exists. Nevertheless, we must find a way to restore the ability of government to function, and the filibuster as it is used today has become an impediment.

Mann and Ornstein recommend several commonsense reforms to modify but not eliminate the filibuster.[6] I offer here my two favorites.

First, limit the use of filibusters to one per bill. Currently, senators may threaten filibusters at every stage of the legislative process, providing multiple opportunities to obstruct. Sometimes even bills that end up passing unanimously are held up by hours of debate on multiple filibuster threats imposed for no reason other than to slow the process. Limiting the filibuster to one per bill would provide the minority the opportunity to make its point, but still allow legislation to proceed to a vote once it is clear there are enough votes for cloture.

Second, the burden should be on the minority to prove they have the votes to sustain the filibuster. Rather than the current requirement for a three-fifths vote of the entire Senate to invoke cloture, the rules should require forty-one votes from the minority to continue the debate. This would require the minority to keep at least forty-one senators near the chamber, making sustaining the filibuster a much more inconvenient task than it is today.

A number of other reforms have been proposed to improve the workings of Congress and ease the gridlock that has disrupted the legislative process. Not all of them would impact polarization or guarantee a complete return to bipartisan lawmaking, but some take a step in the right direction and are worthy of consideration.

For example, Congress should move to a full five-day work week in Washington. Both chambers should coordinate schedules to ensure both are in and out of session at the same time, and both should consider rules of attendance with actual consequences for absenteeism.[7]

Additionally, bipartisan House-Senate conference committees should be restored to their rightful status as an integral step in the legislative process, giving members on both sides of the aisle a chance to meet face to face to discuss the merits of pending policy issues and to iron out differences in specific bills.[8]

One thirty-year veteran of Capitol Hill described how conference committees have lost their significance, reminiscing about how House and Senate members "came together in an effort to produce a compromise measure" that could be signed into law. Conference committees were well attended and "points of difference were debated and motions that might satisfy both sides were offered." Today, to the contrary, "rare conference committee meetings have all the substance of a North Korean party congress . . . The real issues are resolved informally between the committee chairs . . . and those chairs themselves" are mere conduits for their party's leadership.[9] Movement to restore the legitimacy of conference committees would improve the quality of legislation produced by Congress, help ease tensions within both chambers, and lower the temperature of partisanship by a few degrees.

Several states have adopted formal mechanisms to promote the use of conflict mediation techniques, whereby a neutral mediator works with legislators to find common ground. According to congressional scholar Sarah Binder, the mediator is simply "a facilitator—a neutral third-party who does not express substantive views on the subject and cannot impose a solution."[10] Legislators can accept, reject, or modify the subsequent agreement. The use of the mediator, by definition, is indication that the legislative body is interested in finding a compromise that can move the legislation forward.

The problem with recommending this process for Congress is that, in many cases, participants in the debate are not interested in coming to agreement. They are interested in scoring political points and leveraging the legislative process to put members of the other party in a bad political position. The use of a facilitator would be viewed by the partisan activists as a sign of weakness—a willingness to work with the other side. Given the current absence of centrists on Capitol Hill, such mediation techniques—however well intentioned—would be viewed as an unwelcome intrusion into the process.

There are some recommendations for congressional reform that seem counterintuitive but which could help revive the spirit of negotiation and compromise. In the aftermath of Watergate, the public justifiably demanded greater public transparency. This meant more open deliberations, which led to a proliferation of "sunshine laws," particularly at the state level. While generally a good thing, sunshine laws can go too far, negatively impacting negotiators' ability to speak candidly and offer alternatives.

In an era where working with the other side can result in a primary challenge, televised legislative negotiations have become nothing more than a venue for grandstanding legislators to publicly demonstrate their unwillingness to compromise. As a result, writes political scientist Nathan Persily, "the entire give-and-take of negotiation is likely to disintegrate into a game of chicken, as opponents view the process more as a way to win political points than to solve problems."[11]

Sunshine laws should remain in place for formal deliberations, but bipartisan negotiators should be able to meet privately, out of public view, to offer compromises and share alternative proposals without being marked as a traitor by their own party's activists. This small change would make a big difference in rebuilding trust among members and insulating those problem solvers who are willing to cross the aisle in an attempt to hammer out a bipartisan agreement.[12]

Some congressional reforms sound good to the outside observer but are simply unrealistic given the fact that the majority party controls the rules in each chamber. No party can be expected to pass a rules change that would dramatically shift the balance of power or greatly diminish the political strength of its members. Nevertheless, I offer here two common reform recommendations that, if enacted, would change for the better the way business gets done on Capitol Hill.

House rules should require winning a supermajority of 60% for election as Speaker of the House. Madisonian concerns about supermajorities notwithstanding, this rules change would have a positive impact on polarization in the House. Congressional scholar Elaine Kamarck accurately points out that this idea would "test the ability of aspiring leaders to construct the bipartisan coalitions that are so integral to effective governance."[13] In almost every new session of Congress, successful candidates for speaker would have to win the support of at least a handful of members from the other party.

Candidates for speaker would have to assemble their coalition from the center out, rather than from the extreme in. A highly partisan figure would almost never be able to win election as speaker under such circumstances. For example, when the 104th Congress convened in January 1995, Newt Gingrich would have needed to win the support of at least thirty-one Democrats to win the gavel. Similarly, Nancy Pelosi would have needed at least twenty-eight Republicans to vote for her at the beginning of the 110th Congress. In both cases, the House would likely have had to compromise on a more centrist candidate, which would have helped alleviate some of the bitter partisanship that ensued during the tenures of those Speakers.

Kamarck also advocates for similar rules changes in the Senate. I would agree except for the fact that, under the Constitution, the vice president is actually the presiding officer of the Senate. The Senate majority leader is the head of the majority party, so forcing a bipartisan vote for that office doesn't seem justifiable. Nevertheless, such a change in the House would make a world of difference in calming partisan tensions and creating a more collegial working environment.

Another reform option is to ban lobbyists from contributing to or raising money for members of Congress whom they lobby.[14] The ethical considerations associated with this practice are obvious. Members' votes would be determined to a greater extent by the merits of the issue and views of their constituents. Any step toward limiting the influence of money in congressional decisions would be a positive development.

As is always the case with attempts to reign in money, loopholes would likely present themselves. For example, what about contributions to Super PACS supporting the candidate? Or contributions from the lobbyist's family or coworkers? What about constitutional considerations related to free speech as defined by the Supreme Court? Still, it's fun to think about, even though members of Congress are unlikely to voluntarily vote to limit such a key source of fundraising.

Congressman David Jolly of Florida introduced legislation in 2016 that would have banned members of Congress from directly asking for campaign contributions. He appeared on the television news program *60 Minutes* discussing his plan and lamenting the amount of time members spend fundraising. He was ostracized by his colleagues and the bill went nowhere.[15]

Florida has implemented a restriction on state legislators accepting campaign contributions during their two-month legislative session. A similar ban on members of Congress raising money while in Washington would give members greater incentive to spend their time doing their jobs rather than dialing for dollars and attending political fundraisers.

Any proposal to change congressional rules to restrict members' ability to raise campaign cash—however worthy the idea may be—is almost certainly dead on arrival. But no discussion of meaningful congressional reform should exclude the subject. It is simply too important to ignore. I raise the issue in the hope that greater public awareness may someday lead to a much louder public outcry.

Civics Education

IT IS AN UNDERSTATEMENT TO SAY AMERICANS ARE WOEfully uninformed when it comes to understanding how their government works and even the most basic facts about history. Young adults remain highly underrepresented at the voting booth, and people with moderate political views have disengaged from the process. This leaves the choice of our nation's leaders to partisan activists representing the extremes. Unless we find a way to engage more Americans in the political process and raise the level of civics education in the country, the cycle is bound to continue.

Civics education is disappearing from the curriculum of our public schools. Because civics is generally not a subject for which schools are held accountable under federal and state performance standards, it has been deemphasized. Without such a requirement or an alternative way to hold schools accountable for student aptitude, civics will continue to be an afterthought in our schools. If the federal government is unwilling to consider this type of mandate, the states should pick up the slack—as some have already done. North Dakota and Arizona have led the way by requiring students to pass a citizenship test in order to qualify for graduation.[16] In the absence of federal action, more states should do the same.

This is a common recommendation among pundits concerned about the state of politics in America, but now the business community has become involved, recognizing that America "cannot retain its economic edge without a well-educated electorate that is ready to meet the relentless challenges of democratic governance." In his *Harvard Business Review* article titled, "Fixing What's Wrong with U.S. Politics," David Moss recommends that business leaders "urge public officials—and the public at large—to restore civics to its rightful place in the classroom."[17]

I agree that business leaders have a stake in ensuring students understand the lessons of history and know how to apply those lessons to the challenges facing America today. Business leaders should invest in history education initiatives nationwide. This would "promote a deeper understanding of how American democracy functioned in the past" and could help lessen the extreme polarization that exists today—in part driven by a lack of understanding of the philosophical underpinnings of the American two-party system. "Americans need to remind themselves," Moss wrote in closing his article, "that the nation's progress has been rooted in two great philosophies of government, not one. Putting the health of democracy first is the surest way to get the best of both."[18]

Rick Shenkman, publisher and editor of the *History News Network*, takes it a step further by suggesting an innovative approach that I believe is worth considering. As a way to incentivize college students to keep up with current affairs, Shenkman would have them take voluntary current events tests. Those who pass would be eligible for modest federal tuition subsidies. Additionally, schools should make graduation contingent on achieving a passing grade on such a test.[19] Obviously, some in Washington would find this idea controversial. Funding would be an issue, and partisans on both sides would argue over the content of the test, undoubtedly claiming it to be biased one way or the other. Nevertheless, the idea has merit and is one way to improve the current events knowledge of the young voters who will determine America's future leaders.

In its 2014 recommendations to address political polarization in America, the Bipartisan Policy Center (BPC) dedicates an entire section to "engaging more people in civic life."[20] Recognizing the correlation between civics education and an individual's

interest in community service, BPC offers several practical recommendations designed to get more young people involved in
civic engagement, ranging from state-driven civics education
to year-long community service matching programs for young
people to expansion of government-funded programs like the
Peace Corps. Reasonable people can disagree about the specific
merits of each recommendation, but the overall premise—encouraging greater civic engagement among young people—is a
worthwhile endeavor.

Retired Supreme Court Justice Sandra Day O'Connor is
one of the leading voices about the need to improve Americans'
basic understanding of civics, government and the Constitution. Upon her retirement from the court, she founded iCivics,
an organization dedicated to "restoring civic education in our
public schools."[21] To achieve this goal, iCivics provides to public
schools free resources, such as interactive games, educational
videos, and printed materials. It also helps teachers gain a better understanding and appreciation for civics education. Today,
iCivics is active in all 50 states and is used by over 110,000
teachers across America. More than four million students,
many of them in low-income school districts, benefit from iCivics resources every school year. Supported by some of the most
prestigious philanthropic foundations in the country, iCivics
has received solid reviews and the results are encouraging.[22]

In 2006, the University of Florida opened the Bob Graham
Center for Public Service with the goal of "creating a community
of students, scholars and citizens who share a commitment to
revitalize the civic culture of Florida and the nation." Founded
by former Governor and US Senator Bob Graham, the first-of-
its-kind center has become "a place where students have the
opportunity to acquire the skills and knowledge to become
citizen leaders."[23] This is accomplished through a variety of
coursework, scholarships, and service opportunities available
to students, in addition to an innovative "Civil Debate Wall,"
which provides an electronic forum for students to engage in
civil discourse on current issues. In addition to its University of
Florida programming, the center also provides civics education
materials to public schools throughout Florida. After graduation, former students continue to have access to materials and
programming produced by the center, which keeps a database
of the professional growth of its graduates.[24]

Initiatives like iCivics and the Bob Graham Center are making a difference, but more are needed. The embarrassing lack of civic awareness and historical understanding that currently exists in America is a contributing factor to the dysfunction that has crippled our political process. It is not a solution unto itself, but by educating the next generation of citizens about civics and American history—as well as the importance of informed social engagement—we can help stem the tide of relentless partisanship that has gripped our political system.

Campaign Finance Reform

TO STATE THE OBVIOUS, OUR CAMPAIGN FINANCE SYSTEM is completely out of control. Any corporation, union or individual that wants to spend unlimited amounts of money to influence American elections can find a way to do so with minimal restrictions or disclosure requirements. Every attempt to limit the influence of money in elections has failed, particularly the 2002 McCain-Feingold legislation, which outlawed soft money contributions to parties, thereby spurring the formation of the outside groups that now dominate the process. Well-meaning reforms are subverted and billionaire activists exploit loopholes others didn't know existed. Like water, money will always find a way to seep through the cracks, no matter how hard one tries to stop it.

Members of Congress in competitive seats spend hours every day raising money, which distorts their policy priorities and provides an unwelcome distraction from the jobs they were elected to do. Even successful House candidates and incumbents who are able to raise millions of dollars often lose control of their message as outside groups enter the fray, effectively drowning out the candidate's own resources. The threat of a well-funded primary challenge moves members of Congress toward the extremes, exacerbating the already toxic level of polarization on Capitol Hill.

I have always supported strong spending limits for campaigns, but in today's world of Super PACs and unaccountable political non-profit organizations, the idea has become an anachronism. Until the Supreme Court takes a different view on the potential to restrict outside money, limiting the amount that candidates can raise and spend only further empowers the outside groups. For that reason, many have advocated restoring the ability of donors of all types to make unlimited contributions to political parties,[25] a practice that was outlawed under McCain-Feingold. This might not make much of a dent in the activities of outside groups, but at least it would give political parties the resources to fight back against the tsunami of money funded by groups trending much further to the extreme than the parties themselves.

As journalist Jonathan Rauch succinctly puts it: "Limits on donations to the parties drive money to unaccountable outsiders, so lift them."[26] Through an attempt to garner broad electoral appeal, parties have an incentive to win elections for their side, not just to push single-issue or extreme ideologies as is the case with many outside groups. Redirecting at least some of the resources that would otherwise go to outside groups would allow each party to help protect incumbents against insurgency primaries from the extremes.

New York University law professor Richard Pildes has written extensively about this option, believing it to be the best way to address polarization if one accepts as fact that larger, more impactful reforms are impossible in the current environment. The leverage this increased financial relevancy would give party leaders, Pildes argues, would help prevent polarization *within* each party, which could improve the odds of each side reaching a reasonable compromise with each other in congressional negotiations.[27]

Opening up a current restriction and allowing donors to make unlimited contributions to yet another entity—political parties—might seem counterintuitive to supporters of campaign finance reform. I am not entirely sold on this option, but until we find a way to restrict outside spending and limit the role of money in campaigns, it makes sense as a way to provide at least some ability for parties to fight back against attempts by outside groups to hijack the process and promote extreme candidates. In addition, this type of donation would be subject to greater disclosure requirements than are currently applied to nonprofit advocacy groups.

All political contributions should be disclosed, period. The public has a right to know who is funding the political ads they see. With universal disclosure, contributions would flow less readily to nonprofit 501(c)(4) organizations like Karl Rove's

Crossroads GPS, which was created specifically to give donors an option to contribute anonymously.[28] These types of so-called "social welfare groups" are exempt from disclosure laws, meaning they can run ads for or against political candidates without public awareness of whose money paid for the ad.

Comparatively little corporate money has gone to traditional Super PACs, presumably because those contributions are subject to public disclosure. This makes the nonprofit social welfare groups a particularly appealing option for corporations.[29]

There is a regulatory role in this issue involving both the Internal Revenue Service and the Securities and Exchange Commission, but Congress could make things easy by passing legislation to require disclosure of all contributions to election activities. Truthfully, given the astronomical sums of money spent on campaigns—and the willingness of billionaire individual contributors to publicly involve themselves in elections—this change would have less of an impact on campaign spending and subsequent polarization than some advocates of disclosure admit. But it is the right thing to do and would make a positive difference, especially in limiting corporate investment in campaigns.

Gerrymandering

REDISTRICTING REFORM IS THE MOST COMMONLY CITED method of reducing polarization. The number of competitive congressional seats is reduced after every census, as state legislators across the country draw district lines favoring their party's congressional candidates. Today only a few dozen of the 435 seats in the House are even remotely competitive. Making districts more competitive would increase turnover, bring more moderate legislators to the House, and increase the number of members who hear alternative viewpoints when they return home to the district.

The federal role in redistricting reform is limited.[30] In Congress, I cosponsored legislation introduced by my colleague John Tanner of Tennessee that would have required every state to establish independent five-member commissions with oversight over the redistricting process. If enacted, the law would surely face a legal challenge, but most scholars believe a strong case can be made that Article I, Section 4 of the Constitution provides Congress the necessary authority to set the rules governing the election of its members.[31] Unfortunately, we'll never know how the courts would rule because there is little appetite among members of Congress to enact laws that would make their own elections more competitive. Tanner's bill never saw the light of day, and the issue is unlikely to receive attention in Congress for the foreseeable future. For advocates of restricting reform, the real action is in the states.

At least a dozen states now use some form of commission to draw district lines.[32] Arizona and California are among the models, putting the power to draw districts in the hands of an independent citizen commission. According to the Brennan Center for Justice at the New York University School of Law, citizen "commissions appear to have increased partisan competition, while improving the fit between legislative outcomes and the desires of voters."[33]

Arizona's system has been successful, but the results have been most evident in California, where the commission was first put into effect for the 2012 elections. Of the state's fifty-three congressional districts, the commission produced twelve that were legitimately competitive, which might not sound like a lot until one considers the fact that exactly zero of California's congressional districts were viewed as competitive under the map that had been in place for the previous decade.[34]

For years, California incumbent legislators were virtually assured reelection at both the federal and state level. In the first election after the commission-drawn map took effect, "there was a big increase in turnover in the state's congressional delegation," according to the Brennan Center.[35] I would argue the high turnover was equally a result of the state's new primary system, but certainly the independent commission helped make at least some districts more competitive.

Redistricting reform is not the panacea that it's advocates claim. In fact, congressional election experts David Wasserman and Ally Flinn have estimated that only sixteen of the House swing seats that have been lost over the past two decades became uncompetitive as a result of gerrymandering. The others evolved into safe seats due to other factors, such as the political and geographic sorting of Americans.[37] Nevertheless, reform of the redistricting process would help reduce some of the polarization in Congress. More states should adopt independent commissions to draw political boundaries. It works, but it is much more impactful when combined with changes to the primary election system designed to limit the influence of the political extremes. The combination of the two reforms would increase the likelihood of more centrists being elected to Congress.

Elections

THE FIRST THING TO UNDERSTAND ABOUT PROPOSALS TO reform the congressional election process is that, for most members of Congress, the current system works pretty well. These members occupy safe seats, and if they play the game right they are able to go about their business without fear of a viable electoral challenge. "The game," unfortunately, is the unending cycle of relentless partisanship that results in the finger pointing and scapegoating so pervasive in Washington today.

Because they are insulated from the effects, many members of Congress are unconcerned about the polarization and gridlock that the rest of America finds so distasteful. Sure, they will talk about it, lamenting the damage the other side is doing to the country by preventing their own party from carrying out its priorities unimpeded. That kind of talk plays well back home. But admitting it is time to reform the system to make elections more competitive, limit an incumbent's financial advantage, marginalize the extremes, and bring more moderation and compromise into the process? Not so much.

There are arguments to be made against allowing registered voters of one party to participate in the primaries of the other, but opening up all primaries to independents and No Party Affiliation voters makes sense. It would add to the mix more centrist-minded voters, meaning candidates in those races would have to moderate their tone to appeal to a more thoughtfully diverse electorate.

Open primaries would also weaken the extremes in both parties who threaten their incumbent legislators with primary challenges for not adhering closely enough to party orthodoxy.[38] This would give incumbent elected officials greater freedom and an incentive to consider the entire district in their decision making, rather than only the most extreme factions that currently vote in primaries.

Solving the problem of low turnout will also help reduce polarization. There is a direct correlation between partisanship and voter participation. Partisans are enthusiastic voters, while nonvoters are mostly indifferent toward politics. "Extreme interest goes with extreme partisanship," is how one journalist has aptly described it.[39] This has led some to argue that the country is better off if those with little interest in politics stay home, in order to ensure that the most interested voters determine the outcome. There are several problems with this theory, not the least of which is the cognitive bias and misinformation that partisans bring with them to the polls. Those elected to Congress are supposed to represent the entire district, not just the partisan ideologues who vote in primaries. It is simply not consistent with the ideals of representative democracy to promote a system where a sizable majority of the adult population plays no part in determining who their candidates will be in the general election.

There are several ways to increase voter turnout:

The overall number of elections should be reduced by placing elections for all offices and pending issues (propositions, bond issues, etc.) on the same day.[40] Wherever possible, states and municipalities should coordinate their election schedules by including local and state elections on the same calendar with national races. States should also ensure that their presidential primary is held on the same date as the state's other primaries that year.

We must make voting easier. There is no magic to the American tradition of Tuesday voting, or even November voting for that matter. The first Tuesday in November became standard in national elections in 1845, when Congress tried to accommodate a still-mostly agrarian society that considered Saturday a work day.[41] Today, Tuesday voting is inconvenient for many voters and the workday schedule guarantees that the polls will be most crowded at exactly the time when the majority of voters are able to stop at the precinct. Moving Election Day to Saturday—or making it a national holiday—would make it easier for most Americans to vote, as would an expansion of the process of early voting that already exists in thirty-seven states. This would remove some of the burdens that today prevent less enthusiastic and less partisan voters from finding their way to the polls.

Some states have successfully implemented vote-by-mail procedures that have resulted in increased voter turnout,[42] and many people believe it is inevitable that the country will one day move to electronic voting. Although the concern about potential election fraud is real, Americans already do their banking and shopping online, as well as access their personal health information. The prevalence of high-profile data breaches in business and government websites has justifiably given pause to even the strongest supporters of electronic voting, but the potential for fraud also exists in our current voting system. More work needs to be done to secure the system and ensure the integrity of the process, but hopefully we will one day move to a system where all Americans can vote from home.

Similarly, we should make it as easy as possible for people to register to vote. It is unconscionable that nearly one-quarter of our fellow voting-age citizens are still not registered. States should allow voters to register online and be automatically registered when completing standard government functions, such as renewing a driver's license. Citizens should also be allowed to register to vote at any time of year, including Election Day. Studies have shown states with Election Day registration experience much higher rates of turnout than states that don't.[43] Again, these additional voters would help add a moderating influence to our elections.

I agree with Mann and Ornstein, who believe these changes would "moderate politics by expanding the electorate." They summarize the need to expand the vote as follows:

A POLITICAL SYSTEM that restrains its citizens' voting is vulnerable to two corrosive phenomena: turnout in which the most motivated voters, usually ideological activists, have much greater leverage than their numbers would indicate, and a temptation by partisan political operatives to manipulate turnout to their own advantage, often by suppressing votes of those favoring the other side.

Because minorities and young adults typically lean Democrat, Republicans in many states have attempted to enact policies designed to make it harder for them to vote.[45] In his book *The Party is Over*, Mike Lofgren, a thirty-year Republican congressional staffer, laments state legislative attempts "to make it more difficult to vote, with . . . narrower registration periods; residency requirements that may disenfranchise university students; shut-downs of early voting; and the repeal of same-day registration." He cites as one example passage of a Wisconsin law requiring voters to have photo IDs, such as driver's licenses, in conjunction with the closing of DMV locations in predominantly Democratic locations.[46]

In a 2016 editorial, the *New York Times* correctly observed that "Republican electoral prospects go up as the number of voters goes down."[47] This is why congressional Republicans have done so much better in recent midterm elections than in presidential elections when much higher percentages of people go to the polls. Certainly, not every Republican supports overt voter suppression techniques, but most believe that expansion of the vote would add proportionately more Democrats to the voting rolls. This is why mandatory voting for all citizens is politically unrealistic. Still, it is a good idea that would do wonders in reducing polarization in Congress.

As Stanford University professor Jonathan Rodden has written about mandatory voting: "Presumably this would have little impact in safe urban and rural districts, but in the heterogeneous districts . . . it is likely that candidates would discover a new fondness for the median voter in the district." He adds, "The primary constituency would likely become more moderate, and in the general election—even in highly polarized districts— the strategy of ignoring the moderates and mobilizing the base would be counterproductive." He concludes his argument by writing that he knows of no other potential reform "that would do more to incentivize representatives in centrist districts to behave as centrists."[48] Amen to that.

Some argue that people who are not interested enough to vote should stay home. In other words: "Why shouldn't political decisions be made by the citizens who care most about them?" Brookings scholar Bill Galston, one of the leading proponents of mandatory voting in the United States, addresses this criticism by pointing out that: "Although passionate partisanship infuses the system with energy, it has built-in disadvantages, one being that it erects roadblocks against problem solving." He hits the nail on the head when he observes that "committed partisans prefer gridlock to compromise, which is not a formula for effective governance." Mandatory voting, according to Galston, would "broaden the political participation of less partisan citizens."[49]

Approximately three dozen countries have some form of mandatory voting.[50] The Australian system is the one to which most advocates point when suggesting a similar system in the

United States. Australian citizens are required to vote, but are given "none of the above" as a ballot option. Those who don't show up are issued a small fine. Turnout in Australia hovers around 95%. Mann and Ornstein write that "Australian politicians across the political spectrum have told us that it changes the way they campaign because they know that all their fellow citizens, including their own partisans, adversaries' partisans, and nonpartisans will be at the polls. The way to gain votes does not come from working the base to fever pitch, but from persuading the centrists—the same kind of voters who are increasingly left out of the American political process." In countries where all citizens vote, candidates appealing to the extremes are "doomed to failure."[51]

It is true that mandatory voting in the United States would generate legal challenges, with claims that it is unconstitutional. Suggested ways around this include conducting the reforms at the state level or providing a federal incentive—instead of a penalty—for people to vote. Mann and Ornstein suggest a national lottery where every voter is entered into the drawing.[52] Regardless, enactment of mandatory voting is unrealistic given the fact that Republicans believe it would heavily favor Democrats. But this fear may be unfounded, especially in the long term.

Without question, if there was mandatory voting, Republicans would be forced to adjust their message to better appeal to moderate voters. But many in the Republican Party have for years been arguing the need to do just that. Under a system of mandatory voting, I believe Republican candidates could succeed by taking issue positions better aligned with centrist voters, while still maintaining their conservative principles. The success of Republican candidates across the traditionally Democratic Rust Belt in 2016 proves this idea is not far-fetched.

This tactic could actually make Republicans more competitive at the national level than they might otherwise be given the rapidly changing demographics of the country. Nevertheless, mandatory voting is an interesting idea that has no realistic chance of being enacted at the federal level. The most we could hope for in the near future is for states to experiment with the idea, thereby testing its merit.

Some other promising primary election reforms are already taking place in the states. A group called "Open Primaries" is working to increase the number of states that use the top-two open primary system, sometimes called "jungle primaries." The unique system is currently used in a handful of states, most notably California. Under the top-two format, a single primary election is held including all candidates regardless of party. All voters are eligible to vote in that single primary, with the two candidates receiving the most votes moving on to the general election. This has resulted in races where two candidates from the same party have faced each other in the general election, as occurred in California's 2016 US Senate race. Because all voters vote in the single primary, candidates must position themselves to better appeal to the entire spectrum of eligible voters, not just among their party's activists.[53]

In a *Los Angeles Times* column titled: "California Legislature is Looking More Moderate Due to Voting Reforms," George Skelton wrote about the impact the top-two system and redistricting reforms have had in reducing polarization. Both Republican and Democratic insiders agree that the California Legislature is more moderate as a result of the increased turnover created by the dual reforms. At both the congressional and state level, more extreme candidates who in the past would have easily won their party's nomination in closed primaries have now been forced to moderate their message in order to appeal to the wider voting block necessary to compete in the top-two system. For the first time in decades, California has seen numerous incumbents lose their re-elections because they could no longer compete in the broader primary electorate. "For many years, it was exceedingly rare for a legislative or congressional seat to change parties at all, let alone if held by the incumbent. That is now happening more and more," according to Skelton.[54]

The top-two reform holds promise for marginalizing extremist candidates and favoring those espousing more centrist views with broader appeal. Expansion of the system to other states should be a priority for those interested in decreasing congressional polarization.

Another alternative is ranked-choice voting, where voters rank their preferred candidates top-to-bottom. Also known as the "instant runoff," the candidates with the lowest vote totals are eliminated, with their votes redistributed to the other candidates until a majority is achieved. Like the jungle primary, the instant runoff is designed to limit the influence of the extremes. A few large cities have experimented with ranked-choice voting,[55] and Maine is moving toward ranked-choice for its

statewide and congressional elections.[56] Like the top-two system, ranked-choice has shown promise and is worthy of further
consideration.

Finally, term limits—the gold standard for advocates of electoral reform. Supporters of term limits—and there are many—
echo George Will's view that "the sensible reason for enacting
term limits is . . . to nurture deliberation, meaning a disposition
to reason about policies on their merits rather than their utility
in serving the careerism of legislatures."[57] Term limits were all
the rage in the 1990s, but in the face of poor results in the states
and legal impediments in the courts, the movement has fizzled.

Congressional term limits, which would apply to members
of the US House and Senate, have been ruled unconstitutional
by the US Supreme Court.[58] It is still theoretically possible that
a constitutional amendment could be passed imposing congressional term limits, but the possibility is remote.

In my view, term limits are bad for all kinds of reasons, not
the least of which is they don't work as intended. More than
a dozen states have had term limits for their state legislators
for a long enough period of time to study the results. Far from
ushering in fresh vision and new ideas, term limits incentivize
legislators to pay more attention to special interests than their
own constituents.

Because new legislators are often inexperienced and lack
depth on issues and the legislative process, they turn to others
for advice. Those others are career staff and professional lobbyists. Legislators also tend to position themselves early on for the
next step in their political career, either by running for higher
office or becoming a lobbyist themselves. As Mann and Ornstein
have observed, this incentivizes term-limited legislators "to go
for a big, short-term splash and leave the long-term mess to the
next wave of their successors." Term-limited legislatures have
also been found to be less productive and less innovative than
legislatures in states without term limits.[59]

As it relates to congressional polarization, term limits are
also unlikely to have a positive impact. In fact, it would probably make the things even worse.

Georgetown University professor Boris Shor is an expert on
congressional polarization. He has found that "polarization is
largely driven by replacement rather than adaption," meaning
the evidence suggests that "polarization is for the most part
driven by moderates leaving Congress and being replaced by

ideological extremists."[60] For confirmation, look no further than the recent Congresses, which have experienced unusually high turnover due to redistricting, primary challenges, and a high number of retirements. It would be hard to argue that the high turnover has had a positive impact on congressional performance, or that the turnover resulted in less polarization. Term limits are not part of the solution.

Conclusion

HAVING SERVED THREE TERMS AS ONE OF THE FEW CEN-trists in Congress, I believe many of these ideas have merit and would help ease tensions and bring more moderation to congressional deliberations. Most important, they would help make Congress more representative of the nation as a whole, rather than just the highly partisan activists who dominate the election process. Lowering the level of polarization won't be easy, and a combination of multiple reforms would have to be implemented to truly change the way Washington operates. Well-meaning people may differ on some of the ideas offered here, and there can be disagreement on the details and specifics. I offer these proposals to stimulate the conversation. They are designed to help make the single change that would guarantee a more representative and effective Congress—a Congress that would look more like America and provide for a better working relationship among members. That change is to elect more centrists. A lot more.

As long as we have a system designed to elect and protect partisans, polarization in Washington will continue. The extremes of both parties will dictate the outcomes of elections and the men and women elected to Congress will continue to respond to the desires of those extremes—pushing the two sides further apart. Members in gerrymandered districts often see only the most extreme partisans America has to offer, not the politically diverse majority of our citizens who want a functioning government and a Congress that can work together to get things done.

The partisanship has become so pervasive that many Americans take it for granted, unable to even consider the possibility that moderation is possible. This perception, combined with the geographic, social and demographic changes occurring in the country, have resulted in an America that is growing further apart, making reconciliation more unlikely by the day. Electing more centrists will not only change the way Congress views itself, but it will also change the way America views Congress. The reforms recommended here are designed to remove some of the institutional barriers to entry that prevent moderates from both parties from being elected to Congress and surviving as pragmatic lawmakers once they get there.

This is not to imply that there is no role in the legislative process for party loyalists and those at the ideological extremes. To the contrary, all voices should be heard and every point of view considered. The magic of our system is that, in theory, everybody's voice is equally represented. The problem is that today only those with the loudest voices are heard. The rules are skewed to advantage the extremes and freeze out those in the middle who would bring a much-needed sense of moderation.

One thing is for certain—the causes of polarization are not going to change by themselves. The role of partisan media will only continue to grow. The psychological biases that drive partisans to the extreme and prevent meaningful exchange of ideas are not going to suddenly disappear. Money will become even more of a factor in campaigns with each passing election cycle. The cultural divisions within America will grow deeper and solidify even further as geographic sorting segregates people into like-minded groups, preventing them from interacting regularly with people of opposing views. Americans will remain woefully ignorant of their country's history and the most basic responsibilities of civic engagement. Politicians will continue to take advantage of a system that allows them to write the rules in their favor, insulating themselves against challenge from the center. Without action, nothing will change. Polarization will only get worse.

It doesn't have to be that way.

To reduce polarization in Washington and state capitals, the two most important reforms are to increase voter turnout and to make it more difficult for ideologues to dominate the electoral system. Addressing the other most commonly cited causes of polarization—campaign finance, gerrymandering, partisan media, etc.—won't make nearly as much of a difference unless more moderates vote and states move away from closed partisan primaries. These changes would incentivize candidates to appeal to a wider range of voters. It doesn't guarantee a centrist will win or even be competitive, but it helps level the playing field. All the issues discussed in this chapter are important, but these two must be the nucleus for successful reform.

As a long-term measure to cultivate a more thoughtful and informed future generation of Americans, there should be a requirement for schools to promote and strengthen history and civics education. This would stimulate in many students a better foundational understanding of government and politics, and perhaps even an interest in community and public service. At minimum, it would give students a better historical understanding of the a functioning two-party system.

My time in the House showed me how difficult it is to be a centrist in Congress. At home, you win the respect of thoughtful moderates more interested in making progress than scoring political points. In Washington, you draw the ire of partisans on both sides. In primaries, you find yourself fighting for survival against activists who are outside of the mainstream and don't understand the first thing about how to win a swing district in the general election. You spend hours every day raising money—making hundreds of phone calls per week and attending countless fundraisers. You watch every word you say to avoid ending up the centerpiece of a campaign ad or viral social media post that could be targeted to voters of *either* party. At any time, you are in danger of being targeted by a Super PAC or other outside group that can come into the district and airdrop millions of dollars' worth of negative ads based upon a skewed interpretation of one of the thousands of votes you cast. You are pressured by party leaders to take votes you know are not representative of the district you were elected to serve.

Through it all, you work hard to build friendships with colleagues on both sides of the aisle, trying to solidify working coalitions in order to achieve the bipartisan compromise so elusive in Congress today. You meet with constituents to learn their issues and generate new ideas, some of which you turn into legislation. Regardless of their party affiliation, you help constituents with their casework concerns, ranging from VA benefits to adopting foreign babies to student loans to Social Security to emergency passport renewals, just to name a few. In casting votes, you do the best you can to strike the balance between representing the district and following your own compass.

One thing you don't do much of as a centrist is polarize. There is no time for that. You also don't spend much time thinking about how to make the other side look bad, because if you want to be successful, you have to work with members of both parties. Unlike those representing safely gerrymandered seats, members from swing districts hear both sides of an issue and have to consider multiple levels of information before deciding how to vote. Most partisans in Congress have the luxury of just voting the way their leadership wants them to. Not so for centrists.

Without a large and viable contingent of congressional centrists, millions of Americans are without representation. Insurgent candidates with populist messages have proliferated at every level of government, fanning the flames of resentment among partisans and further turning off moderates who are unenthusiastic about politics to begin with. Polarization seemingly gets worse by the day.

But there is hope. By enacting reforms consistent with the principles upon which our nation was founded, we can break the cycle. Let's find a way to get more people to vote and make elections less skewed toward the extremes. Let's enact some combination of reforms to create a more informed electorate and draw district boundaries in a nonpartisan way. Hopefully, the Supreme Court will one day restrict the ridiculously outsized importance of money in politics, but until then, let's take the necessary steps to provide the public with information about who is funding campaign advertisements. Congress has it within its power to modify its rules in ways that can better encourage bipartisan cooperation. There are lots of good ideas.

Expecting politicians to vote against their own self-interest is an unlikely path, but the truth is, it *is* in their interest to improve the way Washington works. Most members of Congress are smart, hard-working men and women who want to do a good job and make a difference for their district and their country. Yes, some are fiercely partisan by nature, but many are forced to be more partisan than they would like to be because the system necessitates it. Moderation is discouraged and compromise is punished. Nowadays, the only way most members of Congress can keep their seats is to play to the extremes. That's what has to change. If you ask them privately, most members of Congress will tell you they also want it to change. So maybe some of these ideas aren't so unrealistic after all.

In the end, the burden falls upon us. America gets the Congress that we the people elect.

BIBLIOGRAPHY

113th Congress House Floor Procedures Manual. *Congressional Institute,* 2013.

Abramowitz, Alan. *The Disappearing Center.* New Haven: Yale University Press, 2010.

Agiesta, Jennifer. "CNN/ORC Poll: Most Want Compromise in DC." *CNN. com.* March 9, 2017.

AIPAC website http://www.aipac.org/about/how-we-work. (Accessed August 15, 2016).

Alicke, Mark and Olesya Govorun. "The Better-Than-Average-Effect, The Self in Social Judgment." *Psychology Press,* 2005.

Allegheny County Council biography. At-Large Council Representative. http://apps.alleghenycounty.us/website/CouncilAtLg.asp. (Accessed April 24, 2016).

"Allegheny County Sheriff's Records Show Donations From Deputies," *Youngstown Vindicator,* February 15, 2005.

Allen, Jonathan and John Bresnahan. "Sources: Biden Likened Tea Partiers to Terrorists." *Politico,* August 1, 2011.

Allen, Jonathan and Amie Parnes. *HRC: State Secrets and the Rebirth of Hillary Clinton.* New York: Crown Publishers, 2014.

Allen, Mike. "Men Who Put Foes in Headlocks Now Try to Get a Grip on Politics." *New York Times,* May 17, 1999.

America's Best Racing. http://www.americasbestracing.net/en/the-latest/blogs/2013/02/19/horseplayers-benter-rarely-backs-a-bad-bet/ (Accessed April 17, 2016).

Amish America. http://amishamerica.com/pennsylvania-amish.

Anderson, Monica. "Social Media Causes Some Users to Rethink Their Views on an Issue." Washington, DC: *Pew Research Center,* November 7, 2016.

Andrews, Wilson and Larry Buchanan. "Mass Shooting or Terrorist Attack? Depends on Your Party." *New York Times,* June 13, 2016.

"Annual Estimates of the Resident Population of Incorporated Places: April 1, 2010 to July 1, 2014." US Census Bureau, 2015.

Arceneaux, Johnson and Vander Wielen Lindstadt. "Democratic Representation and the Emergence of Partisan News Media: Investigating Dynamic Partisanship in Congress." *American Journal of Political Science.* 2015. Doi:10.1111/ajps.12171.

Ariely, Dan. "Our Buggy Moral Code," TED Talk. Long Beach, California, February, 2009. https://www.ted.com/talks/dan_ariely_on_our_buggy_moral_code (Accessed May 15, 2016).

Arrold, Tony. "Gambler More Than Broke Even." *The Australian*. February 2, 2008. http://www.theaustralian.com.au/archive/news/gambler-more-than-broke-even (Accessed April 17, 2016).

Bailey, Holly. "Joe Wilson Raised (And Spent) Big Money after "You Lie!" *Newsweek*, October 20, 2009.

"Barack Obama's Health Care Plans Turn Nasty as Angry Crowds Protest Outside Town Hall Meetings," *London Telegraph*, August 12, 2009.

Barnes, Fred. "The Rise of the House Republican Class of 2006." *The Weekly Standard*. January 5, 2011.

Bartels, Larry and Wendy Rahn. "Political Attitudes in the Post-Network Era." Annual meeting of the American Political Science Association, 2000.

Benen, Steve. "Waxman, Blue Dogs Strike A Deal." *Washington Monthly*. July 29, 2009.

Berfield, Susan. "Zambelli and Pyrotecnico, Super-Producers of Fireworks Shows." *Bloomberg*. June 27, 2013.

Berinsky, Adam. "Rumors and Health Care Reform: Experiments in Political Misinformation." *Cambridge University Press*, 2015. doi: 10.1017/S0007123415000186.

Berman, Russell. "What if the Parties Didn't Run Primaries?" *The Atlantic*. October 19, 2015.

———. "What's the Answer to Political Polarization in the U.S.?," *The Atlantic*, March 8, 2016.

Binder, Sarah, *Stalemate: Causes and Consequences of Legislative Gridlock*. Washington, DC: Brookings Institution Press, 2003.

Biography.com: http://www.biography.com/people/newt-gingrich-9311 1969

Bishop, Bill. *The Big Sort: Why the Clustering of Like-Minded America is Tearing Us Apart*. New York: First Mariner Books, 2008.

Blake, Aaron. "Why You Should Stop Blaming Gerrymandering So Much. Really." *Washington Post*, April 8, 2017. https://www.washingtonpost.com/news/the-fix/wp/2017/04/08/why-you-should-stop-blaming-gerrymandering-so-much-really. (Accessed April 8, 2017).

Blankenhorn, David. "State of the Union: Why Polarization Matters." *The American Interest*, December 22, 2015.

Bob Graham Center website. University of Florida. www.bobgrahamcenter.ufl.edu

Bomboy, Scott. "Surveys: Many Americans Know Little About the Supreme Court." *Constitution Daily*. blog.constitutioncenter.org, February 17, 2016.

Botkin-Kowacki, Eva. "In a Time of Division, Could Science Find a Way to Unite." *Christian Science Monitor*, February 22, 2017.

Brady, David, Hahrie Han and Jeremy Pope. "Primary Elections and Candidate Ideology: Out of Step with the Primary Electorate?" *Legislative Studies Quarterly* 32(1), 2007.

Bresnahan, John. "Blue Dogs Refuse to Pony Up for DCCC." *Politico*, October 24, 2007.

Brock, David, Ari Rabin-Havt and *Media Matters for America*. "The Fox Effect: How Roger Ailes Turned a Network into a Propaganda Machine." New York: *Anchor Books*, 2012.

Broder, John. "Democrats Oust Longtime Leader of House Panel." *New York Times*, November 20, 2008.

Brownstein, Ronald. *The Second Civil War: How Extreme Partisanship has Paralyzed Washington and Polarized America*. New York: Penguin Books, 2007.

Bruni, Frank. "How Facebook Warps Our Worlds." *New York Times*, May 22, 2016.

Bruzgulis, Anna. "In Florida, No-Party Voters Are Growing – Question is Why." *PunditFact*, July 8, 2015.

Bump, Phillip. "The Psychology of Political Beliefs: or Why Hard Data Isn't Always Convincing." *Washington Post*, November 27, 2015.

"Cable News Ratings: CNN on the Rise in 2015; Fox News Channel Remains Dominant," *Variety*, December 30, 2015. http://variety.com/2015/tv/news/cable-news-ratings-cnn-top-gainer-fox-news-channel-domi nant-1201666151/ (Accessed June 1, 2016).

Carroll, Louise. "Black Hand, Iron Fist: Mafia-Type Society Operated with Impunity in Lawrence County." *Ellwood City Ledger*, March 17, 2015.

Caygle, Heather. "How the GOP Abandoned One of its Own." *Politico*, August 17, 2016.

Chafetz, Josh. "The Filibuster Was Already Doomed Before the Nuclear Option Vote." *Washington Post*, April 6, 2017.

Chung, Yulanda. "The Winning Edge." *Asia Week with CNN*, Volume 26, No. 43. November 3, 2000.

Cillizza, Chris. "This is the Most Amazing Chart on Congress You'll See Today." *CNN Politics*, April 7, 2017. http://www.cnn.com/2017/04/07/politics/house-swing-seats-congress/index.html. (Accessed April 8, 2017).

———. "Want to Know Why the Government is Shut Down? This Chart Explains it." *Washington Post*, October 7, 2013. http://www.washing tonpost.com/news/the-fix/wp/2013/10/07/want-to-know-why-the-government-is-shut-down-this-chart-explains-it. (Accessed June 10, 2016).

Clabough, Raven. "Tea Partier Confronts Obama Over Remark Made by Biden." *The New American*, August 2011.

CNN/ORC International public opinion survey, March 9, 2017.

Coglianese, Vince. "Media Matters for America Funder Bill Benter Emerges as Financial Sponsor of Pro-Hagel Ads." *Daily Caller*, January 8, 2013.

"Compromise is in the Eye of the Beholder," Washington, DC: *Pew Research Center*, January 26, 2016.

Concha, Joe. "Only 43 Percent Can Name a Supreme Court Justice." *The Hill*, March 20, 2017.

Connolly, Ceci and staff from the Washington Post. *Landmark: The Inside Story of America's New Health Care Law, And What it Means for All of Us*. New York: Public Affairs, 2010.

Cook, Flinn and Wasserman. "Introducing the 2017 Cook Political Report Partisan Voter Index." *The Cook Political Report*, April 7, 2017.

Cook Political Report, December 16, 2016 and April 7, 2017.

Cooper, Anderson interview with Florida Attorney General Pam Bondi, *CNN*, June 14, 2016.

Corasaniti, Nick and Matt Flegenheimer. "As TV Ad Rates Soar, 'Super PACs' Pivot to Core Campaign Work." *New York Times*, December 22, 2015."

Coulson, Crocker. "Jumping Johnny DeFazio No Longer Jumping As High." *Pittsburgh Post-Gazette*, June 13, 1985.

C-SPAN/Penn Schoen Berland Survey on Americans' knowledge of Supreme Court, March 7-9, 2017.

Davis, Tom, Martin Frost and Richard Cohen. *The Partisan Divide: Congress in Crisis*. Campbell, California: Premiere, 2014.

"Democracy Agenda: Redistricting." Brennan Center for Justice. New York University School of Law, February 4, 2016. https://www.brennan center.org/analysis/democracy-agenda-redistricting. (Accessed June 26, 2016).

Dennis, Steven. "House Health Deal Reached; No Floor Vote Until September." *Roll Call*, July 29, 2009.

DeSilver, Drew. "Turnout Was High in the 2016 Primary Season, But Just Short of 2008 Record." Washington, DC: *Pew Research Center*, June 10 2016.

Dewey, Caitlin. "'Unfriending' Trump Supporters is Just Another Example of How We Isolate Ourselves Online." *Washington Post*, December 16.

———. "6 in 10 of You Will Share This Link Without Reading It, a New, Depressing Study Says." *Washington Post*, June 16, 2016.

———. "The Truth Behind Your Orlando Shooting Hoaxes, Theories and Conspiracies." *Washington Post*, June 19, 2016.

"Difficult-to-Read Font Reduces Political Polarity, Study Finds." *ScienceDaily*, November 2012. www.sciencedaily.com/releases/2012 /11/121102151946.htm. (Accessed May 15, 2016).

Dionne, E.J. "Democrats Won with Votes on Loan." *Real Clear Politics*, November 9, 2006.

Ditto, Liu, Clark, Wojcik, Chen, Grady and Zinger. "At Least Bias is Bipartisan: A Meta-Analytic Comparison of Partisan Bias in Liberals and Conservatives." April 13, 2017. SSRN: https://ssrn.com/ abstract=2952510.

Dollinger, S.J. "Creativity and Conservatism, Personal Individual Differences." *Science Direct*, April 11, 2007. https://www.psychologytoday. com/files/u81/Dollinger_2007_.pdf (Accessed July 16, 2017).

Down With Tyranny blog. November 6, 2010, http://downwithtyranny. blogspot.com/2010/11/different-surviving-house-members-will. html?m=1. (Accessed July 30, 2016).

———. June 28, 2015, http://downwithtyranny.blogspot.com/2015/06 /31-of-34-democrats-who-voted-against-.html?m=1. (Accessed August 16, 2016).

Druckman, J. and L. Jacobs. "Who Governs?: Presidents, Public Opinion and Manipulation." Chicago: *The University of Chicago Press*, 2015.

Druckman, Peterson and Sothuus. "How Elite Partisan Polarization Affects Public Opinion Formation." *American Political Science Review*. Vol. 107, No. 1, February 2013. doi: 1017/S0003055412000500.

Dunning, David, et al. "Ambiguity and Self-Evaluation: The Role of Idiosyncratic Trait Definitions in Self-Serving Assessments of Ability."

Journal of Personality and Social Psychology. Vol 57(6) 1082-1090, 1989.

Ellwood City Ledger. Obituaries, March 1, 2007.

"Exclusive Interview with Bill Benter." YouTube, 7:38. Posted by Southampton Business School. University of Southampton, March 25, 2014. https://m.youtube.com/watch?v=YOVrZrJ-wtc

Explore PA History website, www.explorepahistory.com

Fair Vote website: www.fairvote.org

Farhi, Paul. "How Mainstream Media Missed the March that Social Media Turned into a Phenomenon." *Washington Post,* January 22, 2017.

The Federalist Papers, Essay 58

Fiorina, Abrams and Pope. *Culture War?* New York: Pearson Education, 2011.

Fletcher, Richard and Rasmus Kleis Nielsen. "Using Social Media Appears to Diversify Your News Diet, Not Narrow It." *NeimanLab,* June 21, 2017. http://www.niemanlab.org/2017/06/using-social-media-appears-to-diversify-your-news-diet-not-narrow-it/. (Accessed June 22, 2017).

Flynn, Nyhan and Reifler. "The Nature and Origins of Misperceptions: Understanding False and Unsupported Beliefs about Politics." *Dartmouth University* and the *European Research Council,* 2017.

"Fox and MSNBC Viewers Largely Misinformed: Fairleigh Dickenson University Poll." *International Business Times,* November 22, 2011. http://www.ibtimes.com/fox-msnbc-viewers-largely-misinformed-fairleigh-dickenson-university-poll-373546. (Retrieved June 1, 2016).

French, David. "The Orlando Debate is Beyond Partisan – It's Dangerously Polarizing." *National Review,* June 14, 2016.

Galston, William. "Reforming Institutions: The Next President Should Not Miss This Moment to Make Government Work." Washington, DC: *Brookings Institution,* July 24, 2012.

Garand, James. "Partisan Change and Shifting Expenditure Priorities in the American States, 1945-1978." *American Politics Quarterly* 13.

Gemperlein, Joyce. "Party Chief Pleads Guilty in Coal Case." *Pittsburgh Post-Gazette,* August 11, 1979.

Gerber, Elisabeth and Rebecca Morton. "Primary Election Systems and Representation." *Journal of Law, Economics and Organization,* 1998.

Gersema, Emily. "Which Brain Newtorks Respond When Someone Sticks to a Belief?" *USC News,* December 23, 2016.

Gilbert, Craig. "Donald Trump's Election Flips Both Parties' Views of the Economy." *Milwaukee Journal Sentinel,* April 14, 2017.

Gillin, Joshua. "Fact-Checking Fake News Reveals How Hard it is to Kill Pervasive 'Nasty Weed' Online." *PolitiFact* and *Tampa Bay Times,* March 14, 2017. www.tampabay.com/news/perspective/fact-checking-fake-news-reveals-how-hard-it-is-to-kill-pervasive-nasty. (Accessed March 14, 2017).

Goldfarb, Michael. "J Street Exposed." *The Weekly Standard,* September 24, 2010.

Good, Chris. "J Street's Half-Truths and Non-Truths About Its Funding." *The Atlantic,* September 24, 2010.

———. "Raising More Money, J Street Discloses Big Donors." *The Atlantic,* September 24, 2010.

Gottfried, Barthel and Mitchell. "Trump, Clinton Voters Divided in their Main Source for Election News." Washington, DC: *Pew Research Center,* January 18, 2017.

"Governing in a Polarized America: A Bipartisan Blueprint to Strengthen our Democracy." Washington, DC: Bipartisan Policy Center, 2014.

Guo, David. "Widow Settles Hotel Fire Suit." *Pittsburgh Post-Gazette,* March 18, 1982.

Guttman, Nathan. "J Street, Newly Combative, Takes on the Jewish Establishment." *The Forward,* March 25, 2015.

Hackett, Conrad. (Twitter @conradhackett). February 26, 2017.

Haidt, Jonathan. "Top 10 Reasons American Politics are so Broken." *Washington Post,* January 7, 2015. https://www.washingtonpost.com/news/wonk/wp/2015/01/07/the-top-10-reasons-american-politics-are-worse-than-ever. (Accessed January 1, 2016).

———. *The Righteous Mind: Why Good People are Divided by Politics and Religion.* New York: Random House LLC, 2013.

Hamilton, Jessica. "Texas Lt. Gov. Dan Patrick Deletes 'Reap What You Sow' Tweet After Mass Shooting at LGBT Club." *Houston Chronicle,* June 12, 2016.

Hanna, Richard. "The Centre Cannot Hold." *The Economist,* January 16, 2016.

Harvard Institute of Politics website. http://iop.harvard.edu.

Hasen, Richard. "Karl Rove's Crossroads GPS Manages to Make it Even Harder to Find the Dark Money in U.S. Politics." *Los Angeles Times*; February 11, 2016.

Hendren, John. "Obama's Health Care Foe: GOP or Dems?" *ABC News,* July 25, 2009.

Hernandez, Ivan and Jesse Lee Preston. "Disfluency Disrupts the Confirmation Bias." *Journal of Experimental Social Psychology,* 2013.

Hetherington and Rudolph. *Why Washington Won't Work.* Chicago: University of Chicago Press, 2015.

Hiatt, Fred. "Where is McConnell's Sense of Leadership?" *Washington Post,* February 1, 2010.

Hohmann, James. "The Legislative Filibuster Will Be At Risk As Soon As the Senate Goes Nuclear." *The Daily 202 Washington Post* blog, April 6, 2017.

———. "How Nancy Pelosi Kept Democrats United Behind Obamacare." *The Daily 202 Washington Post* blog, May 3, 2017.

Homans, Charles. "The New Party of No: How a President and a Protest Movement Transformed the Democrats." *New York Times Magazine,* March 13, 2017.

Hopkins, Daniel and John Sides, eds. *Political Polarization in American Politics.* New York: Bloomsbury, 2015.

Hopper, Joseph. "The Rhetoric of Motives in Divorce." *Journal of Marriage and the Family,* November 1999.

House, Billy. "In Age of Trump, Some Democrats and Republicans Explore Alliance." *Bloomberg Politics,* February 2, 2017. https://www.

bloomberg.com/politics/articles/2017-02-02/in-age-of-trump-some-democrats-and-republicans-explore-alliance. (Accessed February 21, 2017).

"How Immigration and Concerns about Cultural Change Are Shaping the 2016 Election." *Public Religion Research Institute* and *Brookings Institution,* June 23, 2016.

"How to Burst the 'Filter Bubble' That Protects Us from Opposing Views." *MIT Technology Review,* November 29, 2013. http://www.technolo gyreview.com/view/522111/how-to-burst-the-filter-bubble-that-protects-us-from-opposing-views. (Accessed July 17, 2016).

Huysman, Fritz. "Dem Official Admitted Coal Fraud, Jury Told." *Pittsburgh Post-Gazette,* August 7, 1979.

Huysman, Fritz. "Man Pleads Guilty in Coal Fraud." *Pittsburgh Post-Gazette,* August 10, 1979.

iCivics website; www.icivics.org

Isenstadt, Alex. "Town Halls Gone Wild." *Politico,* July 31, 2009.

J Street website. Myths and Facts. http://jstreet.org/page/mythsand facts/our-donors (Accessed June 30, 2016).

"John DeFazio Announces Candidacy for New Allegheny County Council At-Large Seat." DeFazio for Allegheny County Council, press release, January 22, 1999. http://www.prnewswire.com/news-releases/ john-defazio-annnounces-candidacy-for-new-allegheny-county-coun cil-at-large-seat-pledges-to-fight-for-the-interests-of-all-county-resi dents-73489332.html (Accessed April 24, 2016).

"John McCain says Obama Directly Responsible for Orlando Shooting." *CNN,* June 16, 2016. http://www.cnn.com/2016/06/16/politics/ john-mccain-obama-directly-responsible-orlando-shooting. (Accessed June 20, 2016).

Kahan, Peters, Dawson, Cantrell and Slovic. "Motivated Numeracy and Enlightened Self-Government." *Yale Law School.* Public Law Working Paper No. 307, September 3, 2013.

Kane, Paul. "A New Dynamic May Be Emerging in the House: A Right and Left Flank Within the GOP Willing to Buck Leadership." *Washington Post,* March 25, 2017.

Kaplan, Gimbel and Harris. "Neural Correlates of Maintaining One's Political Beliefs in the Face of Counterevidence." *Scientific Reports.* Article 39589, 2016. doi:10.1038/srep39589.

Kaplan, Michael. "The High Tech Trifecta." *Wired,* March 1, 2002.

———. "The Hundred and Fifty Million Dollar Man." *Cigar Aficionado,* Nov/Dec 2003.

Kaufman, Gimpel and Hoffman. "A Promise Fulfilled? Open Primaries and Representation." *Journal of Politics,* 65(2).

"Keep Experimenting With Ranked-Choice Voting." *Minneapolis Star Tribune,* December 6, 2016.

Keillor, Garrison. BrainyQuote.com. Xplore, Inc, 2017.

Keohane, Joe. "How Facts Backfire." *Boston Globe,* July 11, 2010.

Kinder, D.E. "Opinion and Action in the Realm of Politics." *Handbook of Social Psychology.* 4th ed., Gilbert, Fiske and Lindzey, eds. New York: McGraw-Hill, 1998.

King, David. "Congress, Polarization, and Fidelity to the Median Voter." Kennedy School of Government Working Paper, *Harvard University*, 2003.

Klosowski, Thorin. "Why You Think You're Great at Everything, Even When You Suck." *Lifehacker* blog, January 2, 2014. http://life hacker.com/why-you-think-you-rc-great-at-everything-even-when-you-1492423875" (Accessed May 15, 2016).

Kondracke, Mort. "Democrats, GOP Should Heed Voters' Call for Moderation." *Real Clear Politics*, January 4, 2007.

"Labor History Sites to Visit while in Pittsburgh." Pennsylvania AFL-CIO website. http://www.paaflcio.org. (Accessed July 15, 2016).

Lake, Eli. "Soros Revealed as Founder of Liberal Jewish-American Lobby." *Washington Times*, September 24, 2010.

Lawless, Jennifer and Sean Theriault. "Off the Softball Field, Congresswomen are Plenty Partisan." Washington, DC: *Brookings Institution*, June 15, 2016.

Lawrence County Historical Society, www.lawrencechs.com/new_castle. html.

Lawrence County Tourist Promotion Agency, www.visitlawrencecounty. com.

Layton, Lyndsey. "House GOP Uses Procedural Tactic To Frustrate Democratic Majority." *Washington Post*, May 19, 2007.

Lee, Chris. "Revisiting Why Incompetents Think They're Awesome." *Ars Technica*, May 25, 2012.

Lee, Stacy. "Homestead Bost Building Exhibit Celebrates Western Pennsylvania Steel Icon." *Pittsburgh Tribune-Review*, February, 20, 2013.

Leherr, Dave. "4 Killed, 9 Injured in New Castle Holiday Inn Blaze." *Pittsburgh Post-Gazette*, November 4, 1977.

Lejeune, Tristan. "Florida Prosecutor Suspended for anti-Orlando Post." *The Hill*, June 18, 2016..

Lelkes, Sood and Iyengar. "The Hostile Audence: The Effect of Access to Broadband Internet on Partisan Affect." *American Journal of Political Science*, 2015. doi:10.1111/ajps.12237.

Lepore, Jill. "Long Division: Measuring the Polarization of American Politics," *The New Yorker*, December 2, 2013.

Levendusky, Matthew. "How Partisan Media Polarize America." Chicago: *University of Chicago Press*, 2013.

Levin, Sam. "Fake News for Liberals: Misinformation Starts to Lean Left Under Trump." *The Guardian*, February 6, 2017. https://www.the guardian.com/media/2017/feb/06/liberal-fake-news-shift-trump-standing-rock (Accessed February 20, 2017).

Levinovitz, Alan. "Trump Supporters Refuse to Believe Their Own Eyes." *Slate.com*, January 27, 2017.

Lofgren, Mike. *The Party is Over: How Republicans Went Crazy, Democrats Became Useless, and the Middle Class got Shafted.* New York: Penguin Books, 2012.

Lott, Trent and Tom Daschle. *Crisis Point: Why We Must – and How We Can – Overcome Our Broken Politics in Washington and Across America.* New York: Bloomsbury Press, 2016.

Lubell, Jennifer. "Blue Dogs, Wasman Trade Proposals." *Modern Healthcare*, July 28, 2009.

MacGillis, Alec. "The Democrats' Bad Map." *ProPublica* and *New York Times*, October 22, 2016.

"Magistrate Dismisses Fatal Motel Fire Case." *Pittsburgh Press*, November 5, 1977.

Manjoo, Farhad. "Can Facebook Fix Its Own Worst Bug." *New York Times Magazine*, April 25, 2017.

Mann, Thomas and Norman Ornstein. *It's Even Worse Than It Was.* New York: Basic Books, 2016. New and expanded version of 2012 *It's Even Worse Than It Looks.*

Martin, Jonathan and Alexander Burns. "Is 'Brexit' the Precursor to a Donald Trump Presidency? Not so Fast." *New York Times*, June 24, 2016.

Mayer, Gerald. "Union Membership Trends in the United States." *Congressional Research Service*, August 31, 2004.

McCormick, Lain, et al. "Comparative Perceptions of Driver Ability – a Confirmation and Expansion." *Accident Analysis and Prevention.* Volume 18, Issue 3, June 1986.

McGrath, Patrick. "One Republican To Show Up at Conference for U.S. House Frosh." *The Harvard Crimson*, November 28, 2006.

McHugh, Roy. "Ex-Wrestler Tries to Get Hold on Concessions." *Pittsburgh Press*, April 27, 1983.

McIntosh, Steve. "Overcoming Polarization by Evolving Both the Right and Left." *The Institute for Cultural Evolution*, February 2016.

McKinley, James and Sam Dillon. "Some Parents Oppose Obama School Speech." *New York Times*, September 3, 2009.

McMorris, Bill. "Bill Benter: The Horse Lord." *Washington Free Beacon*, August 31, 2012. http://freebeacon.com/democracy-alliance/bill-benter-the-horse-lord. (Accessed July 9, 2016).

McNulty, Tim. "Pence Hits Pelosi For Rothfus." *Pittsburgh Post-Gazette*, September 7, 2010.

Megerian, Chris and Mark Barabak. "From West to East, Iowa Voters Have Starkly Different Realities and Fears." *Los Angeles Times*; January 31, 2016.

Mercier and Sperber. "Why do Humans Reason? Arguments for an Argumentative Theory." *Behavioral and Brain Sciences*, 2011.

Micek, John. "PA Lost a Resident Once Every 11.5 Minutes Last Year, Study Finds." *PennLive/Patriot-News of Harrisburg*, December 22, 2016.

Milbank, Dana. "The Blue Dogs' Pitiful Last Whimper." *Washington Post*, November 3, 2015.

Miller, Steve. "Biden: Tea Stands for 'Terrorist.'" *New York Post*, August 2, 2011.

"Minority's Motion to Recommit Should Not Be Curtailed." Washington, DC: he Wilson Center, July 7, 2011. https://www.wilsoncenter.org/publications/minoritys-motion-to-recommit-should-not-be-curtailed. (Retrieved June 18, 2016).

Mooney, Chris. "Science Confirms: Politics Wrecks Your Ability to Do Math." *Grist*, September 8, 2013.

———. "The Science of Why We Don't' Believe Science: How Our Brains Fool Us on Climate, Creationism and the End of the World." *Mother Jones*, April 18, 2011. http://www.motherjones.com/print/106166. (Accessed April 30, 2016).

Moss, David. "Fixing What's Wrong with U.S. Politics." *Harvard Business Review*; March 2012.

Mt. Lebanon Democratic Committee website. http://www.mtlebanon democrats.com/candidates/john-defazio. (Accessed April 24, 2016).

Nasaw, David. *Andrew Carnegie*, New York: Penguin Press, 2006.

National Council on State Legislatures website. http://www.ncsl.org /research/elections-and-campaigns/primary-types.aspx.

National Journal, February 28, 2009

New Castle News. Obituaries, March 1, 2007.

"Newly Elected Members of Congress to Attend Harvard Congressional Issues Conference." Harvard Kennedy School press release, November 27, 2006.

Nyhan, Brendan and Jason Reifler. "The Roles of Information Deficits and Identity Threat in the Prevalence of Misperceptions," *Dartmouth College Press*, February 11, 2016.

Olson, Laura. "Pennsylvania Poised to Lose Another Seat in Congress in 2020." *The Morning Call*, January 1, 2016.

OpenSecrets.org

Ornstein, Norman. "The Motion to Recommit, Hijacked by Politics." *American Enterprise Institute*, May 19, 2010.

Parton, Heather Digby. "Bye-Bye, Blue Dog 'Democrats': What The End of Conservative Dems Means for America." *Salon*, November 12, 2014. http://www.salon.com/2014/11/12/bye_bye_blue_dog_democrats_ what_the_end_of_conservative_dems_means_for_america (Accessed July 16, 2016).

"Pennsylvania: Population and Housing Counts Unit," *US Census Bureau.* CPH-2-40, 1990.

Persily, Nathaniel, ed. *Solutions to Polarization in America*. New York: Cambridge University Press, 2015.

Peters, Jeremy. "One Area in Which Congress Excels: Naming Post Offices." *New York Times*, May 28, 2013.

Pfister, Bonnie. "Trib Poll: Altmire, Hart Close in 4th District Race." *Pittsburgh Tribune-Review*, October 25, 2006.

Phillips, Kate. "The Caucus" blog. *New York Times*, March 11, 2009. http://thecaucus.blogs.nytimes.com/2009/03/11/public-lands-bill-defeated-in-house (Accessed July 16, 2016).

Pildes, Richard. "How to Fix our Polarized Politics? Strengthen Political Parties." *Washington Post*, February 2014.

Pinker, Steven. *How the Mind Works*. New York: W.W. Norton, 1997.

Pittsburgh Post-Gazette, County Council member biographies, January 8, 2000, http://old.post-gazette.com/regionstate/20000108DeFazio9 .asp. (Accessed April 24, 2016).

"Political Polarization and Media Habits: From Fox News to Facebook, How Liberals and Conservatives Keep Up with Politics." Washington, DC: *Pew Research Center*, 2014.

"Political Polarization in the American Public: How Increasing Ideological Uniformity and Partisan Antipathy Affect Politics, Compromise and Everyday Life." Washington, DC: *Pew Research Center*, 2014.

"Politics in America 2008." *Congressional Quarterly*, 2007.

Poole, Keith and Howard Rosenthal. "Polarized America: The Dance of Ideology and Unequal Riches." Cambridge: *The MIT Press*; 2008.

"Portrait of an American City: 200 Years of New Castle History." YouTube. Posted by Lawrence County Historical Society, December 31, 2010.

Powell, Albrecht. "Old Order Amish in Western Pennsylvania." *About Travel*, November 25, 2014.

Powers, Scott. "Bill Nelson Says Hate Calls Are Pouring In." *FloridaPolitics .com*, June 13, 2016.

Presnell, Max. "Playing Percentages All the Way to a Billion." *Sydney Morning Herald*, August 14, 2009.

Prior, Markus. *Post-Broadcast Democracy: How Media Choice Increases Inequality in Political Involvement and Polarizes Elections*. New York: Cambridge University Press; 2007.

Purdum, Todd. "Blue is the New Red." *Vanity Fair*, February 2007.

Rauch, Jonathan. "How American Politics Went Insane." *The Atlantic*, July/August 2016.

Read, Max. "Donald Trump Won Because of Facebook." *New York Magazine*, November 9, 2016.

Reed, Paula. "Ex-Sheriff Pleads Guilty to Macing." *Pittsburgh Post-Gazette*, November 22, 2006.

Reiss, Jaclyn. "Trump Calls for President Obama to Resign After Orlando Shooting." *Boston Globe*, June 12, 2016.

Reppetto, Thomas A. *American Mafia: A History of its Rise to Power*. New York: Henry Holt & Co., 2004.

"Republicans and Voter Suppression." *New York Times*, April 4, 2016.

Resistance Near Me website. https://resistancenearme.org

Resnick, Brian. "Motivated Ignorance is Ruining Our Political Discourse." *Vox.com*, May 15, 2017.

Richardson, Valerie. "Some Republicans Embrace Chaos, Stand Firm in Face of Hostile Town Hall Crowds." *Washington Times*, April 13, 2017.

Roarty, Alex. "Democrats Blast GOP for Refusing to Call Orlando Shooting a Hate Crime." *Roll Call*, June 13, 2016.

Roche, Walter. "Wealthy Pittsburgh Donor's Mideast Role Eyed." *Pittsburgh Tribune Review*, October 3, 2010.

Rogin, Josh. "Horse-Racing Gambler Funding Pro-Hagel Campaign." *The Cable*, January 7, 2013.

Romano, Andrew. "How Ignorant Are Americans?" *Newsweek*, March 20, 2011.

Romano, John. "The Odd Quality that Separates Tampa Bay from most of America." *Tampa Bay Times*, March 18, 2017.

Ryan, David. "History of Shenango China." *USA Today*.

Ryan, T.J. "No Compromise: Political Consequences of Moralized Attitudes" *American Journal of Political Science*, 2016. doi: 10.1111/ajps.12248.

Ryssdal, Kai. *Wall Street Journal* Marketplace interview. January 5, 2009. http://www.marketplace.org/2009/01/05life/when-people-cheat -wall-street. (Accessed June 23, 2016).

Sands, David. "House Rule Changes Squander Good Will." *Washington Times*, January 7, 2009.

Santangelo, Denise. "George R. Zambelli Known as Mr. Fireworks." *St. Louis Post Dispatch*, December 30, 2003.

Santich, Kate. "Pulse Families, Survivors to Get Second OneOrlando Payout." *Orlando Sentinel*, March 3, 2017.

Saul, Michael. "Rage Boils Over at Town Hall Meetings Over Health Care." *New York Daily News*, August 11, 2009.

Schaffner, Brian and Samantha Luks. "This is What Trump Voters Said When Asked to Compare His Inaugural Crowd With Obama's." *Washington Post*, January 25, 2017.

Schmitz, Jon. Based on reporting by Mackenzie Carpenter and Dennis Roddy. "Inside the Haiti Rescue Mission." *Pittsburgh Post-Gazette*, January 24, 2010.

Seelye, Katherine. "Maine Adopts Ranked-Choice Voting. What is it, and How Will it Work?" *New York Times*, December 3, 2016.

Seitz-Wald, Alex. "New Liberal PAC Targets Democrats for Primaries." *NBC News*, February 15, 2017.

Sheehy, Gail. "Hillaryland at War." *Vanity Fair*, June 30, 2008. http://www.vanityfair.com/news/2008/08/clinton200808. (Accessed September 5, 2016).

Shenkman, Rick. *Ignorant America: Just How Stupid Are We?* New York: Basic Books, 2008.

Shenkman, Rick. *Political Animals: How our Stone-Age Brain Gets in the Way of Smart Politics*. New York: Basic Books; 2016.

Shermer, Michael. "How to Convince Someone When Facts Fail." *Scientific American*, January 1, 2017.

Sides, Jonathan. "Not Gerrymandering, but Districting: More Evidence on How Democrats Won the Popular Vote but Lost the Congress." Monkey Cage blog. *Washington Post*, November 15, 2012. http://themonkeycage.org/2012/11/not-gerrymandering-but-districting-more-evidence-on-how-democrats-won-the-popular-vote-but-lost-the-congress. (Accessed June 10, 2016).

Silverman, Craig. "Fake Election News Stories Outperformed Real News on Facebook." *BuzzFeed News*, November 16, 2016.

Silverman, Craig. "This is How Your Hyperpartisan Political News Gets Made." *BuzzFeed News*, February 27, 2017.

Silverman, Craig and Lawrence Alexander. "How Teens in the Balkans are Duping Trump Supporters with Fake News." *BuzzFeed News*, November 3, 2016.

Simon, Scott. "How YouTube is Changing Our Viewing Habits." *NPR Weekend Edition Saturday*, March 4, 2017.

Simonich, Milan. "Ring of Legends: Killer Kowalski and Other Big Names Come to Town to Wrestle up Support for Charity." *Pittsburgh Post-Gazette*, November 12, 1998.

Skelton, George. "California Legislature is Looking More Moderate Due to Voting Reforms." *Los Angeles Times*, November 12, 2014.

Slajda, Rachel. "GOP Kills Science Jobs Bill by Forcing Dems to Vote for Porn." *Talking Points Memo*, May 14, 2010. www.talkingpointsmemo.com/dc/gop-kills-science-jobs-bill-by-forcing-dems-to-vote-for-porn

(Accessed June 18, 2016).

Smith, Bradley. "If Citizens United Falls, Will Progressives Notice?" *The Atlantic*, May 23, 2016.

Sports Betting Australia: http://www.sportsbettingaust.com/billbenter.html (Accessed April 17, 2016).

Stern, West and Schmitt. "The Liberal Illusion of Uniqueness," *Psychological Science*, 2014, pp.

Stier, Marc. *Grassroots Advocacy and Health Care Reform: The HCAN Campaign in Pennsylvania*. New York: Palgrave MacMillan, 2013.

Stoller, Matt. "And Now to the Bickering." *MyDD*, November 8, 2006.

Stone, Andrea. "Most Americans Think Founders Wanted Christian USA." *USA Today*, September 11, 2007.

Sultan, Niv. "Election 2016: Trump's Free Media Helped Keep Cost Down, But Fewer Donors Provided More of the Case." *OpenSecrets.org*, April 13, 2017. https://www.opensecrets.org/news/2017/04/election-2016-trump-fewer-donors-provided-more-of-the-cash/

Swan, Jonathan. "Inside the Resistance." Axios, February 19, 2017. https://www.axios.com/inside-the-resistance-2272850728.html (Accessed February 21, 2017).

Sylwester, K. and M. Purver. "Twitter Language Use Reflects Psychological Differences Between Democrats and Republicans." PLoS ONE 10(9): e0137422. doi: 10.1371/journal.pone.0137422. (2015).

Tady, Scott. "Warner Bros. First Theater to Reopen in New Castle." *Ellwood City Ledger*, April 4, 2013.

Taintor, David. "Poll: Majority of Americans Don't Know What GOP Stands For." *Talking Points Memo*, October 4, 2011. http://talkingpointsmemo.com/dc/poll-majority-of-americans-dont-know-what-gop-stands-for (Accessed June 19, 2016).

"The Motion to Recommit in the House of Representatives: Effects, Recent Trends and Options for Change." *Congressional Research Service*, November 20, 2008.

"Memories of Studio Wrestling WIIC TV Channel 11." *TV of Your Life*. http://www.tvovyourlife.com/swlocal.htm (Accessed April 24, 2016).

"The Political Typology: Beyond Red vs. Blue." Washington, DC: *Pew Research Center*, June 26, 2014.

"The Superiority Illusion: Where Everyone is Above Average." *Scientific American*, April 1, 2013. http://blogs.scientificamerican.com/scicurious-brain/the-superiority-illusion-where-everyone-is-above-average. (Accessed May 15, 2016).

Thomas, Bob. "The Clown Prince of Hollywood: The Antic Life and Times of Jack L. Warner." New York: McGraw-Hill, 1990.

Thurber, James and Antoine Yoshinaka, *American Gridlock: The Sources, Character and Impact of Political Polarization*. New York: Cambridge University Press, 2015.

Time Magazine Special Report. The Midterms. November 30, 2006.

Tiouririne, Adam. "Hillary Clinton's Twitter Chart of Doom." *Bloomberg Politics*, November 16, 2016.

Todd, Chuck. "Congress Gets a Case of the Blues." *National Journal*, October 18, 2006.

Todd, Chuck and Carrie Dann. "How Big Data Broke American Politics." *NBC News.com*, March 14, 2017.

Todd, Chuck. *Meet the Press*, July 5, 2015.

Torsten, Ove. "Mafia Has Long History Here, Growing From Bootlegging Days." *Pittsburgh Post-Gazette,* November 6, 2000.

Town Hall Project. https://townhallproject.com/

Treiman, Daniel. "AIPAC and J Street, the Emotional Disconnect." *The Telegraph*, March 27, 2012.

"Twitter Language Use Reflects Psychological Differences Between Democrats and Republicans." Queen Mary University of London press release. September 16, 2015. http://www.qmul.ac.uk/media/news/items/se/163133.html. (Accessed May 26, 2016).

"Union Members 2015." Bureau of Labor Statistics. U.S. Department of Labor. News Release USDL-16-0158, January 28, 2016.

University of Pittsburgh Office of Admissions. 2016 freshman class profile.

U.S. Senate website. http://www.senate.gov/pagelayout/reference/clo ture_motions/clotureCounts.htm. (Accessed June 23, 2006).

U.S. Term Limits, Inc. v. Thornton, 514 U.S. 779, 1995.

"United Steelworkers' John DeFazio Honored at 'Images of Homestead' at Restored Pump House," United Steelworkers of America press release, May 19, 1999. http://www.prnewswire.com/news-releases/united-steelworkers-john-defazio-honored-at-images-of-homestead-at-restored-pump-house-74595662.html. (Accessed April 24, 2016).

Urbina, Ian. "Beyond Beltway, Health Debate Turns Hostile." *New York Times*, August 7, 2009.

Vollmer, Judith. "2nd Admits Coal Fraud." *Pittsburgh Press*, August 9, 1979.

———. "Holiday Inn Owner Told to Pay in Fire." *Pittsburgh Press*, November 8, 1979.

Wall, Joseph Frazier. *Andrew Carnegie*. Pittsburgh: University of Pittsburgh Press, 1970.

Walsh, Lawrence. "Widow Settles for $500,000 In Route 422 Holiday Inn Fire." *Pittsburgh Press*, January 21, 1982.

Wang, Sam. "The Great Gerrymander of 2012." *New York Times*, February 2, 2013.

Warren, Louis S. "The Hunter's Game: Poachers and Conservationists in Twentieth-Century America." *Yale University Press* (1997). ISBN: 0-300-06206-0

Wasserman, David. "Purple America Has All But Disappeared." *fivethirtyeight.com*, March 8, 2017.

Wayne, Alex. "House Panel Chairman Promise to Move Similar Health Care Overhaul bills." *CQ*, March 11, 2009.

"Welcome to the Historic Pump House." Rivers of Steel National Heritage Area website. https://www.riversofsteel.com/preservation/heritage-sites/battle-of-homestead.

Weiner, Rachel and Scott Clement. "Why Obama Gets Less Blame than Bush for High Gas Prices." *Washington Post*, March 30, 2012.

Wereschagin, Mike and Justin Vellucci. "DeFazio making a relic of old style of Pennsylvania Corruption." *Pittsburgh Tribune-Review*, November

26, 2006.

Westley, Lindsay. "Escapes: A Tour of Western Pennsylvania Amish Country." *Washington Post*, October 25, 2012.

"What Are My Odds?" YouTube, 36:57. 2004 Bill Benter speech to Third Congress of Chinese Mathematicians. Posted by Betfair Pro Trader, April 1, 2015. https://m.youtube.com/watch?v=YOVrZrJ-wtc

"What is Illusory Superiority?" *Short Thoughts Psychology* blog, August 26, 2012.

"Where Political Lines Are, and Aren't, Being Drawn." *Washington Post Wonkblog*, May 16, 2014.

White, Lawrence. "Occupy Lake Wobegon." *Psychology Today*, May 14, 2012.

Wikipedia, The Free Encyclopedia. "Omnibus Public Lands Act of 2009." https://en.wikipedia.org/wiki/Omnibus_Public_Land_Management _Act_of_2009. (Accessed June 27, 2016).

————. "Ralph Wolf and Sam Sheepdog." https://en.wikipedia.org/wiki/ Ralph_Wolf_and_Sam_Sheepdog. (Accessed July 15, 2017).

Will, George. "Restoration," New York: *The Free Press*, 1992.

Wilson, Tony. "Mr. Huge." *The Monthy: Austrailian Politics, Society and Culture*, December 2005-January 2006.

Wingfield, Isaac and Benner. "Google and Facebook Take Aim at Fake News Sites." *New York Times*, November 14, 2016.

Working For Us website. http://www.sourcewatch.org/index.php/Work ing_For_Us_PAC. (Accessed April 24, 2016).

World's Greatest Gamblers website. www.worlds-greatest-gamblers.com/ gamblers/horse-racing/william-benter/ (Accessed April 17, 2016).

"Things That Are Still Here." PBS television documentary. *WQED* Public Television. Pittsburgh, 2004.

WrestlingData.com.

Yan, Holly. "Obama, Maybe It's Time for Mandatory Voting." *CNN.com*, March 9, 2015.

Yee, Allie. "The Great Southern Gerrymander Continues in 2016." *Facing South*, November 11, 2016.

Yeselson, Richard. "Not With a Bang, But a Whimper: The Long, Slow Death Spiral of America's Labor Movement." *The New Republic*, June 6, 2012.

Zernike, Kate. "In House, New Class Arrives for Lessons in Lawmaking." *New York Times*, November 15, 2006.

NOTES

Introduction

1. Andrews and Buchanan, "Mass Shooting or Terrorist Attack? Depends on Your Party."
2. French. "The Orlando Debate is Beyond Partisan – It's Dangerously Polarizing."
3. Anderson Cooper interview with Florida Attorney General Pam Bondi, *CNN*, June 14, 2016.
4. CNN report on McCain's comments, June 16, 2016.
5. Reiss, "Trump Calls for President Obama to Resign After Orlando Shooting."
6. Roarty, "Democrats Blast GOP for Refusing to Call Orlando Shooting a Hate Crime."
7. Hamilton. "Texas Lt. Gov. Dan Patrick Deletes 'Reap What You Sow' Tweet After Mass Shooting at LGBT Club."
    For more information about the partisan reaction to the Orlando shooting, see also:
    Lejeune, Tristan, "Florida Prosecutor Suspended for anti-Orlando post," *The Hill*, June 18, 2016.
    Dewey, Caitlin, "The Truth Behind Your Orlando Shooting Hoaxes, Theories and Conspiracies," *Washington Post*, June 19, 2016.
8. Powers, "Bill Nelson Says Hate Calls Are Pouring In."
9. Santich, "Pulse Families, Survivors to Get Second OneOrlando Payout."

Chapter 1

1. Agiesta, "CNN/ORC Poll: Most Want Compromise in DC," *CNN.com*, March 9, 2017.
2. Todd and Dann, "How Big Data Broke American Politics," *NBC News.com*, March 14, 2017.
3. Fiorina, Abrams and Pope, *Culture War?* p. 19.
4. Haidt, *The Righteous Mind: Why Good People are Divided by Politics and Religion.* p. 320.
5. Fiorina, Abrams and Pope, *Culture War?* p. 17.
    Abramowitz, Alan, *The Disappearing Center*, Prologue p. X.
6. Fiorina, Abrams and Pope, *Culture War?* pp. 198-200.
    Hopkins and Sides, *Political Polarization in American Politics.* p. 39.

7. *Political Polarization in the American Public: How Increasing Ideological Uniformity and Partisan Antipathy Affect Politics, Compromise and Everyday Life*, Pew Research Center.
8. Ibid.
9. *Compromise is in the Eye of the Beholder*, Pew Research Center.
10. *Political Polarization in the American Public: How Increasing Ideological Uniformity and Partisan Antipathy Affect Politics, Compromise and Everyday Life*, Pew Research Center.
11. *The Political Typology: Beyond Red vs. Blue*, Pew Research Center.
12. *Political Polarization and Media Habits: From Fox News to Facebook, How Liberals and Conservatives Keep Up with Politics*. Pew Research Center.
13. Poole and Rosenthal, *Polarized America: The Dance of Ideology and Unequal Riches*. p. 71.
    Haidt, *The Righteous Mind*, p. 322.
14. Hetherington and Rudolph, *Why Washington Won't Work*, pp. 1-3.
15. Brownstein, *The Second Civil War: How Extreme Partisanship has Paralyzed Washington and Polarized America*.
16. Prior, *Post-Broadcast Democracy: How Media Choice Increases Inequality in Political Involvement and Polarizes Elections*.
17. Fiorina, Abrams and Pope, *Culture War?* pp. 8-9, 29, 166.
18. Bonica, Adam, "Data Science for the People," in *Solutions to Political Polarization in America*.
19. Abramowitz, *The Disappearing Center*.
20. Mann and Ornstein, *It's Even Worse Than It Was*.
21. Brownstein, *The Second Civil War*, pp. 25, 183-84, 216.
22. Cain, Bruce, "Two Approaches to Lessening the Effects of Partisanship," in *Political Polarization in American Politics*.
23. Hare and Poole, "How Politically Moderate are Americans? Less Than it Seems." in *Political Polarization in American Politics*.
    Poole and Rosenthal, *Polarized America: The Dance of Ideology and Unequal Riches*. p. 32.
24. Barber and McCarty, "Causes and Consequences of Polarization," in *Political Polarization in American Politics*.
25. Bishop, *The Big Sort*, p. 26.
26. Hetherington and Rudolph, *Why Washington Won't Work*, p. 23.
27. Levendusky and Malhotra, "The Media Make Us Think We Are More Polarized Than We Really Are," *Political Polarization in American Politics*, pp. 109-111.
28. Cain, Bruce, "Two Approaches to Lessening the Effects of Partisanship," in *Solutions to Political Polarization in American Politics*, pp. 158, 2015.
29. Shor, Boris, "Polarization in American State Legislatures," in *American Gridlock: The Sources, Character and Impact of Political Polarization*.
30. Poole and Rosenthal, *Polarized America: The Dance of Ideology and Unequal Riches*.
31. Fiorina, Abrams and Pope, *Culture War?* pp. 68-69, 167.
32. Mayer, "Union Membership Trends in the United States," *CRS*.

Bureau of Labor Statistics, USDL-16-0158, January 28, 2016.

Yeselson, "Not With a Bang, But a Whimper: The Long, Slow Death Spiral of America's Labor Movement.".

33. Nasaw, *Andrew Carnegie*, pp. 411-455.

Wall, *Andrew Carnegie*, pp. 555-562.

Lee, "Homestead Bost Building Exhibit Celebrates Western Pennsylvania Steel Icon."

Pennsylvania AFL-CIO website. "Labor History Sites to Visit while in Pittsburgh."

34. Rivers of Steel National Heritage Area website, "The Bost Building," https://www.riversofsteel.com/preservation/heritage-sites/bost-building. (Accessed April 24, 2016).

Rivers of Steel National Heritage Area website, "Welcome to the Historic Pump House," https://www.riversofsteel.com/preservation/heritage-sites/battle-of-homestead. (Accessed April 24, 2016).

"United Steelworkers' John DeFazio Honored at 'Images of Homestead' at Restored Pump House."

35. Crocker, "Jumping Johnny DeFazio No Longer Jumping As High."

36. *Pittsburgh Post-Gazette*, John DeFazio new County Council member biography, January 8, 2000.

37. TV of Your Life, *Memories of Studio Wrestling WIIC TV Channel 11*, http://www.tvofyourlife.com/swlocal.htm (Accessed April 24, 2016).

38. Puroresu Wiki: Biography of Bruno Sammartino. http://www.puro-resu.wiki/Bruno_Sammartino (Accessed April 24, 2016).

39. Coulson, Crocker, "Jumping Johnny DeFazio No Longer Jumping As High."

40. Puroresu Wiki: Biography of Bruno Sammartino.

41. Coulson, Crocker, "Jumping Johnny DeFazio No Longer Jumping As High."

42. WrestlingData.com. http://wrestlingdata.com/index.php Retrieved April 24, 2016.

43. *Pittsburgh Post-Gazette*, John DeFazio new County Council member biograph.

44. McHugh, "Ex-Wrestler Tries to Get Hold on Concessions,"

45. Ibid.

John DeFazio for Allegheny County Council, press release, January 22, 1999.

For more on DeFazio's campaign, see also:

Mt. Lebanon Democratic Committee website.

Allegheny County Council biography, At-Large Council Representative.

Allen, "Men Who Put Foes in Headlocks Now Try to Get a Grip on Politics."

46. Reed, "Ex-Sheriff Pleads Guilty to Macing."

Wereschagin and Vellucci, "DeFazio making a relic of old style of Pennsylvania Corruption."

"Allegheny County Sheriff's Records Show Donations From Deputies," *Youngstown Vindicator*.

47. Bishop, *The Big Sort*, p. 14.

48. Brownstein, *The Second Civil War*, pp. 185-89.
49. Wasserman, "Purple America Has All But Disappeared."
50. Romano, "The Odd Quality that Separates Tampa Bay from Most of America."
51. Bishop, *The Big Sort*, p. 40.
52. Ibid.
53. Ibid, p. 68-69.
54. Ibid.
55. Ibid.
56. Ibid, p. 71.
57. Blankenhorn, "State of the Union: Why Polarization Matters."
58. Rauch, "How American Politics Went Insane."
59. Poole and Rosenthal, *Polarized America*, p. 68.
60. Ibid., see also: King, David, "Congress, Polarization, and Fidelity to the Median Voter."
61. National Conference of State Legislatures, http://www.ncsl.org/research/elections-and-campaigns/primary-types.aspx (Accessed June 17, 2016).
62. Todd, *Meet the Press*, July 5, 2015. Quoted in: Bruzgulis, Anna, "In Florida, No-Party Voters Are Growing – Question is Why."
63. Persily, *Solutions to Polarization in America*.
    Kaufman, Gimpel and Hoffman, "A Promise Fulfilled? Open Primaries and Representation," *Journal of Politics*, 65(2): 457-476.
    Gerber and Morton, "Primary Election Systems and Representation," *pp*. 304-324.
    Brady, Han and Pope, "Primary Elections and Candidate Ideology: Out of Step with the Primary Electorate?" pp. 79-105.
64. Hetherington and Rudolph, *Why Washington Won't Work*, p. 213.
65. Hackett, Conrad (@conradhackett) February 26, 2017 Twitter post, referencing data accumulated by Dan Hirschman.
66. Yan, "Obama, Maybe It's Time for Mandatory Voting," Referenced in: Lott and Daschle, *Crisis Point*, p. 31.
67. DeSilver, "Turnout Was High in the 2016 Primary Season, But Just Short of 2008 Record."

Chapter 2

1. U.S. Census Bureau, "Pennsylvania: Population and Housing Counts Unit," 1990 CPH-2-40; and "Annual Estimates of the Resident Population of Incorporated Places: April 1, 2010 to July 1, 2014." Lawrence County Tourist Promotion Agency.
2. *Lawrence County Historical Society* – History of New Castle.
   Carroll, "Black Hand, Iron Fist: Mafia-Type Society Operated with Impunity in Lawrence County."
3. *Explore PA History*. Warner Brothers' First Theater Historical Marker.
4. Lawrence County Historical Society. "The Show Must Go On."
5. Tady, "Warner Bros. First Theater to Reopen in New Castle."
6. *Explore PA History*. Warner Brothers' First Theater Historical Marker.

7. *Cinema Treasures*. Cascade Picture Palace. www.cinematreasures. org/theaters/33428

8. *Lawrence County Historical Society* – History of New Castle. Lawrence County Historical Society – YouTube video: "Portrait of an American City: 200 Years of New Castle History." Posted December 31, 2010.

9. Ryan, "History of Shenango China," *USA Today*.

10. U.S. Census Bureau, "Pennsylvania: Population and Housing Counts Unit," CPH-2-40.

11. *Amish America*. Lawrence County Tourist Promotion Agency, "Tourism Today: Amish Countryside."

12. Powell, "Old Order Amish in Western Pennsylvania," *About Travel*, November 25, 2014.

13. Westley, "Escapes: A Tour of Western Pennsylvania Amish Country."

14. Ryan, "History of Shenango China."

15. Berfield, "Zambelli and Pyrotecnico, Super-Producers of Fireworks Shows." Santangelo, "George R. Zambelli Known as Mr. Fireworks."

16. Lawrence County Tourist Promotion Agency, "Fireworks Capital of America."

17. Berfield, Susan, "Zambelli and Pyrotecnico, Super-Producers of Fireworks Shows."

18. Toresten, "Mafia Has Long History Here, Growing from Bootlegging Days." Carroll, "Black Hand, Iron Fist: Mafia-Type Society Operated with Impunity in Lawrence County". Reppetto, "American Mafia: A History of its Rise to Power."

19. *Ellwood City Ledger* Obituaries, March 1, 2007. *New Castle News* Obituaries, March 1, 2007.

20. Huysman, "Dem Official Admitted Coal Fraud, Jury Told." Vollmer, "2nd Admits Coal Fraud."

21. Gemperlein, "Party Chief Pleads Guilty in Coal Case." Huysman, "Man Pleads Guilty in Coal Fraud."

22. Leherr, "4 Killed, 9 Injured in New Castle Holiday Inn Blaze."

23. Vollmer, "Holiday Inn Owner Told to Pay in Fire."

24. "Magistrate Dismisses Fatal Motel Fire Case," *Pittsburgh Press*.

25. Ibid.

26. Guo, "Widow Settles Hotel Fire Suit." Walsh, "Widow Settles for $500,000 In Route 422 Holiday Inn Fire."

27. Hohmann, "How Nancy Pelosi Kept Democrats United Behind Obamacare."

28. Brownstein, *The Second Civil War*, pp. 342-43.

29. Ibid.

30. Ibid.

31. Berinsky, "Rumors and Health Care Reform: Experiments in Political Misinformation."

32. Flynn, Nyhan and Reifler, "The Nature and Origins of Misperceptions: Understanding False and Unsupported Beliefs about Politics."

33. Hetherington and Rudolph *Why Washington Won't Work.*
34. Bump, "The Psychology of Political Beliefs: or Why Hard Data Isn't Always Convincing."
35. Hetherington and Rudolph, *Why Washington Won't Work*, pp. 78, 87-94.
36. Ibid.
37. Flynn, Nyhan and Reifler, "The Nature and Origins of Misperceptions: Understanding False and Unsupported Beliefs about Politics," p. 5. Weiner and Clement, "Why Obama Gets Less Blame than Bush for High Gas Prices." (Interestingly, the problem was more acute among Democrats than Republicans).
38. Hetherington and Rudolph, *Why Washington Won't Work*, pp. 78, 87-94.
39. Gilbert, "Donald Trump's Election Flips Both Parties' Views of the Economy."
40. Blankenhorn, "State of the Union: Why Polarization Matters.".
41. Haidt, *The Righteous Mind,* pp. 92-94.
42. Ibid.
43. Mooney, "Science Confirms: Politics Wrecks Your Ability to Do Math."
44. Kahan, et. al, "Motivated Numeracy and Enlightened Self-Government."
45. Mooney, "The Science of Why We Don't' Believe Science: How Our Brains Fool Us on Climate, Creationism and the End of the World."
46. Bump, "The Psychology of Political Beliefs: or Why Hard Data Isn't Always Convincing."
47. Haidt, *The Righteous Mind,* p. 98.
48. Taber and Lodge, reported by Chris Mooney, *Mother Jones*, April 18, 2011.
49. Bishop, *The Big Sort.*
50. Nyhan and Reifler, *The Roles of Information Deficits and Identity Threat in the Prevalence of Misperceptions.*
51. Ibid.
52. Levinovitz, "Trump Supporters Refuse to Believe Their Own Eyes." Schaffner and Luks, "This is What Trump Voters Said When Asked to Compare His Inaugural Crowd With Obama's."
53. Keohane, "How Facts Backfire."
54. Resnick, "Motivated Ignorance is Ruining Our Political Discourse."
55. Bump, "The Psychology of Political Beliefs: or Why Hard Data Isn't Always Convincing."
56. Ditto, et. al., "At Least Bias is Bipartisan: A Meta-Analytic Comparison of Partisan Bias in Liberals and Conservatives."
57. Mooney, "The Science of Why We Don't' Believe Science: How Our Brains Fool Us on Climate, Creationism and the End of the World."
58. Ibid.
59. Ibid.
60. Hopper, "The Rhetoric of Motives in Divorce." Referenced and quoted by David Blankenhorn in "State of the Union: Why Polarization Matters."
61. Kaplan, "The High Tech Trifecta."

62. Benter interview with University of Southampton, posted on YouTube by Southampton Business School.
63. Benter speech to Third Congress of Chinese Mathematicians, 2004. Posted to YouTube.
64. Kaplan, "The Hundred and Fifty Million Dollar Man."
Kaplan, Michael, "The High Tech Trifecta."
Sports Betting Australia.
Wilson, "Mr. Huge."
World's Greatest Gamblers website.
65. Arrold, "Gambler More Than Broke Even," *The Australian*, February 2, 2008.
66. Wilson, "Mr. Huge."
67. Ibid.
Kaplan, Michael, "The High Tech Trifecta."
68. Benter interview with University of Southampton.
69. America's Best Racing.
Chung, "The Winning Edge."
Presnell, "Playing Percentages All The Way To A Billion."
70. Kaplan, "The High Tech Trifecta."
71. Ibid.
72. Kaplan, "The Hundred and Fifty Million Dollar Man."
Wilson, "Mr. Huge."
73. Ibid.
Kaplan, "The High Tech Trifecta.".
74. Wilson, "Mr. Huge."
75. Benter speech to Third Congress of Chinese Mathematicians, 2004.
76. Benter interview with University of Southampton.
77. Kaplan, "The High Tech Trifecta."
78. Ibid.
79. Wilson, "Mr. Huge."
80. Kaplan, "The High Tech Trifecta."

Chapter 3

1. Rauch, "How American Politics Went Insane."
2. Farhi, "How Mainstream Media Missed the March that Social Media Turned into a Phenomenon."
3. Ibid.
4. Resistance Near Me https://resistancenearme.org/ and the Town Hall Project, https://townhallproject.com/
5. Twitter postings for @PattonOswalt on May 4, 2017, @Alyssa_Milano on May 4, 2017 and @GeorgeTakei on May 5, 2017. (All accessed May 7, 2017).
6. Brownstein provides an excellent history in *The Second Civil War*. pp. 328-336, 358, 374.
7. Ibid.
8. Ibid.
9. Ibid, p. 7.

10. Pfister,"Trib Poll: Altmire, Hart Close in 4th District Race."
11. *Time* Special Report, November 30, 2006.
12. Dionne, "Democrats Won with Votes on Loan.".
13. Todd, "Congress Gets a Case of the Blues."
14. Kondracke, "Democrats, GOP Should Heed Voters' Call for Moderation."
15. Stoller, "And Now to the Bickering." Quoted in Brownstein, *The Second Civil War*. p. 7.
16. Brownstein, Ronald, *The Second Civil War*, p. 359.
17. Bishop, *The Big Sort*, p. 272.
18. Fiorina, Abrams and Pope, *Culture War?* pp. 248-249.
19. Brownstein, *The Second Civil War*, p. 359.
20. Ibid.
21. Zernike, "In House, New Class Arrives for Lessons in Lawmaking."
22. All biographies from CQ's "Politics in America 2008."
    Interesting information on rise of the Republicans in the class: Barnes, Fred, The Rise of the House Republican Class of 2006; *The Weekly Standard*, January 5, 2011.
23. Harvard Kennedy School press release, "Newly Elected Members of Congress to Attend Harvard Congressional Issues Conference."
24. Harvard Institute of Politics website.
25. McGrath, "One Republican To Show Up at Conference for U.S. House Frosh."
26. "Blue is the New Red," *Vanity Fair*, February 2007.
27. Prior, *Post-Broadcast Democracy*. p. 31.
28. Ibid. pp. 18, 31.
    Kevin Arceneaux and Martin Johnson, "Polarization and Partisan News Media in America," in: *American Gridlock: The Sources, Character and Impact of Political Polarization*, pp. 317-19.
29. Prior, *Post-Broadcast Democracy*, pp. 27, 46.
30. Ibid, p. 120.
31. Hayes and Lawless, "District Polarization and Media Coverage of U.S. House Campaigns," in *American Gridlock*, pp. 288-300.
32. Lelkes, Sood and Iyengar, "The Hostile Audence: The Effect of Access to Broadband Internet on Partisan Affect."
33. Prior, Markus, *Post-Broadcast Democracy*, pp. 155-156.
34. Ibid.
35. Ibid, pp. 134-135, 214-215
36. Bartels and Rahn, "Political Attitudes in the Post-Network Era," Annual meeting of the American Political Science Association, 2000.
37. Prior, *Post-Broadcast Democracy*, p. 238.
38. Ibid, p. 51.
39. Arceneaux, "Don't Blame Polarization on Partisan News," in *Political Polarization in American Politics*.
40. Jacobson, "Partisan Media and Electoral Polarization in 2012," in *American Gridlock*, p. 261.
41. Brownstein, *The Second Civil War*, p. 360.
42. Sourcewatch, http://www.sourcewatch.org/index.php/Working_For_Us_PAC. (Accessed July 5, 2016).

43. Ibid.
44. Seitz-Wald, "New Liberal PAC Targets Democrats for Primaries."
45. Rauch, "How American Politics Went Insane."
46. Ibid.
47. Ryan, "No Compromise: Political Consequences of Moralized Attitudes."
48. Ibid.
49. "Compromise is in the Eye of the Beholder," Pew Research Center.

Chapter 4

1. Biography.com, http://www.biography.com/people/newt-gin-grich-93111969 (Accessed June 22, 2016).
2. Mann and Ornstein, *It's Even Worse Than It Was*, pp. 34-37.
3. Ibid.
   Brownstein, *The Second Civil War*, pp. 140-141.
   Lofgren, *The Party is Over: How Republicans Went Crazy, Democrats Became Useless, and the Middle Class got Shafted*, pp. 34-35.
4. Brownstein, *The Second Civil War*, p. 141.
5. Ibid. pp. 140-141.
   Mann and Ornstein, *It's Even Worse Than It Was*, pp. 34-37
6. Persily, *Solutions to Polarization in America*, pp. 218-219.
7. Mann and Ornstein, *It's Even Worse Than It Was*, pp. 34-37.
8. CQs "Politics In America" 2008 – the 110th Congress." p. 295.
9. Lott and Daschle, *Crisis Point: Why We Must – and How We Can – Overcome Our Broken Politics in Washington and Across America.* p. 29.
10. Ibid.
11. Bradley Smith, "If Citizens United Falls, Will Progressives Notice?"
12. Poole and Rosenthal, *Polarized America*, pp. 142-145.
13. Hasen, Richard, "Karl Rove's Crossroads GPS Manages to Make it Even Harder to Find the Dark Money in U.S. Politics."
14. Rauch, Jonathan, "How American Politics Went Insane."
15. OpenSecrets.org, https://www.opensecrets.org (Accessed April 20, 2017).
16. Corasaniti and Flegenheimer, "As TV Ad Rates Soar, 'Super PACs' Pivot to Core Campaign Work."
17. OpenSecrets.org, https://www.opensecrets.org/pacs/superpacs
18. Thurber and Yoshinaka, *American Gridlock: The Sources, Character and Impact of Political Polarization*, p. 4.
19. Michael Barber and Nolan McCarty, "Causes and Consequences of Polarization," pp. 32-33 in *Solutions to Polarization in America*.
20. Ibid.
21. McCarty, Nolan, "Reducing Polarization by Making Parties Stronger," p. 139 in *Solutions to Polarization in America*.
22. Bonica, McCarty, Poole & Rosenthal, *Congressional Polarization and its Connection to Income Inequality*, pp. 371-72 in *American Gridlock*.
23. Cain, Bruce, "Two Approaches to Lessening the Effects of Partisanship," in: *Solutions to Polarization in America*.

24. Poole and Rosenthal, "Polarized America: The Dance of Ideology and Unequal Riches."

25. Ibid, p. 161.

26. Bonica, McCarty, Poole & Rosenthal, "Congressional Polarization and its Connection to Income Inequality," pp. 371-72, in *American Gridlock.*
    Niv Sultan, "Election 2016: Trump's Free Media Helped Keep Cost Down, But Fewer Donors Provided More of the Case," *OpenSecrets. org*, April 13, 2017.

27. Michael Barber and Nolan McCarty, "Causes and Consequences of Polarization," pp. 32-33 in Persily, Nathaniel, editor: *Solutions to Polarization in America.*

28. Gary Jacobson, "Eroding the Electoral Foundations of Partisan Polarization," in *Solutions to Polarization in America*, p. 87.

29. Hacker and Pierson, "Confronting Asymmetric Polarization," p. 62 in *Solutions to Polarization in America.*

30. Haidt, "Top 10 Reasons American Politics are so Broken."

31. Peters, "One Area in Which Congress Excels: Naming Post Offices."

32. Haidt, "Top 10 Reasons American Politics are so Broken."

33. Wikipedia, "Ralph Wolf and Sam Sheepdog."

34. Lawless and Theriault, "Off the Softball Field, Congresswomen are Plenty Partisan."

35. Ibid.

Chapter 5

1. AIPAC website.

2. Treiman, Daniel, "AIPAC and J Street, the Emotional Disconnect."

3. Guttman, Nathan, "J Street, Newly Combative, Takes on the Jewish Establishment."
   J Street website, www.jstreet.org (Accessed July 9, 2016).

4. Lake, Eli, "Soros Revealed as Founder of Liberal Jewish-American Lobby."

5. Goldfarb, Michael, "J Street Exposed."

6. Ibid.

7. Good, Chris, "J Street's Half-Truths and Non-Truths About Its Funding."
   Good, Chris, "Raising More Money, J Street Discloses Big Donors."

8. J Street website, Myths and Facts.

9. Roche, Walter, "Wealthy Pittsburgh Donor's Mideast Role Eyed."

10. Coglianese, Vince, "Media Matters for America Funder Bill Benter Emerges as Financial Sponsor of Pro-Hagel Ads."

11. McMorris, Bill, "Bill Benter: The Horse Lord."

12. Coglianese, Vince, "Media Matters for America Funder Bill Benter Emerges as Financial Sponsor of Pro-Hagel Ads."
    Rogin, Josh, "Horse-Racing Gambler Funding Pro-Hagel Campaign."

13. For detailed accounts of Altmire's role in the superdelegate fight during the 2008 presidential primary, see:

Allen and Parnes, *HRC: State Secrets and the Rebirth of Hillary Clinton*, pp. 16-23.

Sheehy, "Hillaryland at War."

14. Broder, "Democrats Oust Longtime Leader of House Panel."

15. Milbank, "The Blue Dogs' Pitiful Last Whimper."

16. Bresnahan, "Blue Dogs Refuse to Pony Up for DCCC."

17. *Down With Tyranny* blog.

18. Parton, "Bye-Bye, Blue Dog 'Democrats': What The End of Conservative Dems Means for America."

19. Ibid.

20. Poole and Rosenthal, *Polarized America: The Dance of Ideology and Unequal Riches.*

    San Francisco Chronicle, October 24, 2004.

21. Hanna, "The Centre Cannot Hold."

22. Hetherington and Rudolph, *Why Washington Won't Work.*

23. Ibid, p. 21.

24. Bishop, *The Big Sort,* p. 24.

    Hare, Poole and Rosenthal, "Polarization in Congress Has Risen Sharply. Where is it Going Next?," in *Political Polarization in American Politics.*

    See also: Abramowitz, Alan, *The Disappearing Center,* pp. 36, 141. "Centrists are 'extremely rare' in Congress."

25. Bishop, *The Big Sort,* pp. 246-247.

26. Rauch, "How American Politics Went Insane."

27. Ibid.

28. Binder, *Stalemate,* pp. 24-25.

29. Abramowitz, "The New American Electorate: Partisan, Sorted, and Polarized," in *American Gridlock,* p. 41.

30. Lepore, "Long Division: Measuring the Polarization of American Politics."

31. Brownstein, *The Second Civil War,* p. 214.

32. Binder, *Stalemate,* p. 87.

33. Lepore, "Long Division: Measuring the Polarization of American Politics."

34. Binder, *Stalemate,* p. 127.

35. Rauch, "How American Politics Went Insane."

36. Binder, *Stalemate,* p. 127.

37. Fiorina, "Gridlock is Bad. The Alternative is Worse," in *Political Polarization in American Politics.*

38. Lott and Daschle, *Crisis Point: Why We Must – and How We Can – Overcome Our Broken Politics in Washington and Across America.*

39. Prior, *Post-Broadcast Democracy,* p. 116.

40. Jacobson, "Partisan Media and Electoral Polarization in 2012," in *American Gridlock,* p. 264.

41. *Political Polarization and Media Habits: From Fox News to Facebook, How Liberals and Conservatives Keep Up with Politics,* Pew Research Center.

42. Hayes and Lawless, "District Polarization and Media Coverage of U.S. House Campaigns," in *American Gridlock,* p. 301.

43. *Political Polarization and Media Habits: From Fox News to Facebook, How Liberals and Conservatives Keep Up with Politics*, Pew Research Center.

44. Stroud and Alexander, "The Polarizing Effects of Partisan and Mainstream News," in *American Gridlock*, pp. 338-339
See also: Bishop, *The Big Sort*, pp. 74-75.

45. Hayes and Lawless, in *American Gridlock*, p. 290.

46. Haidt, J., "Top 10 Reasons American Politics are so Broken," *Washington Post*; January 7, 2015.

47. Hayes and Lawless, in *American Gridlock*, p. 291.

48. Stroud and Alexander, in *American Gridlock*, pp. 340-341.
Hayes and Lawless, in *American Gridlock*, pp. 300-301.
Levendusky, "Are Fox and MSNBC Polarizing America," in *Political Polarization in American Politics*. pp. 96-98.

49. "Cable News Ratings: CNN on the Rise in 2015; Fox News Channel Remains Dominant," *Variety*, December 30, 2015.

50. Fiorina, Abrams and Pope, *Culture War?* p. 20.
Hetherington and Rudolph, *Why Washington Won't Work*, p. 27.

51. Lelkes, Sood and Iyengar, "The Hostile Audence: The Effect of Access to Broadband Internet on Partisan Affect."

52. *Political Polarization and Media Habits: From Fox News to Facebook, How Liberals and Conservatives Keep Up with Politics*, Pew Research Center.
A similar disparity existed when Trump and Clinton voters were asked about their information sources during the 2016 presidential election. For more information, see: Gottfried, Barthel and Mitchell, "Trump, Clinton Voters Divided in their Main Source for Election News," *Pew Research Center*, January 18, 2017.

Chapter 6

1. McKinley and Dillon, "Some Parents Oppose Obama School Speech."

2. Ibid.

3. Ibid.

4. Ibid.

5. Hetherington and Rudolph, *Why Washington Won't Work*, p. 3.

6. Ibid, pp. 3-4.

7. Arceneaux, "Don't Blame Polarization on Partisan News," in *Political Polarization in American Politics*, pp. 102-103.

8. Ibid.

9. Stroud and Alexander, "The Polarizing Effects of Partisan and Mainstream News," in *American Gridlock*, pp. 342-348.
Levendusky and Malhotra, "The Media Makes Us Think We're Polarized," in *Political Polarization in American Politics*. pp. 106-111.

10. Berinsky, "Rumors and Health Care Reform: Experiments in Political Misinformation."

11. Flynn, Nyhan and Reifler, "The Nature and Origins of Misperceptions: Understanding False and Unsupported Beliefs about Politics," p. 29.

12. Lieber, "Politics Stops at the Water's Edge? Not Recently," in *Political Polarization in American Politics.* pp. 62-63.
13. Hetherington and Rudolph, *Why Washington Won't Work,* p. XX of Introduction.
14. Hiatt, "Where is McConnell's Sense of Leadership?"
15. Druckman, Peterson and Slothuus, "How Elite Partisan Polarization Affects Public Opinion Formation."
16. Ibid.
17. Homans, Charles, "The New Party of No: How a President and a Protest Movement Transformed the Democrats."
18. Swan, "Inside the Resistance."
19. Richardson, "Some Republicans Embrace Chaos, Stand Firm in Face of Hostile Town Hall Crowds."
20. Ibid.
21. Haidt, *The Righteous Mind,* p. 100.
    Kinder, *Opinion and Action in the Realm of Politics,* pp. 778-867.
22. Shenkman, *Political Animals.* p. 107, quoting Steven Pinker, *How the Mind Works.*
23. Bishop, *The Big Sort,* pp. 75-76.
    Haidt, *The Righteous Mind,* pp. 101-103.
    Shenkman, *Political Animals,* p. 156.
24. Haidt, *The Righteous Mind,* pp. 101-103.
25. Bishop, *The Big Sort,* pp. 75-76.
    Haidt, *The Righteous Mind,* pp. 101-103.
26. Haidt, *The Righteous Mind,* pp. 101-103.
27. Ibid.
28. Ibid.
29. Gersema, "Which Brain Newtorks Respond When Someone Sticks to a Belief?"
    Kaplan, Gimbel and Harris, "Neural Correlates of Maintaining One's Political Beliefs in the Face of Counterevidence."
30. Ibid.
31. Gersema, "Which Brain Newtorks Respond When Someone Sticks to a Belief?"
32. Blankenhorn, *Why Polarization Matters.*
33. Bishop, *The Big Sort,* pp. 63-64, 67-68.
34. Ibid, p. 63-64.
35. Ibid.
36. Shenkman, *Political Animals,* p. 180.
37. Bishop, *The Big Sort,* pp. 58-68.
38. Ibid, pp. 66-67.
39. Shenkman, *Political Animals,* p. 158.
40. University of Pittsburgh Office of Admissions, profile of 2016 freshman class.
41. Shenkman, *Political Animals:* p. 158.
42. Ryssdal, Kai, "When People Cheat on Wall Street," *Wall Street Journal's Marketplace,* January 5, 2009.
    Ariely, February 2009 TED Talk.
43. Shenkman, *Political Animals,* p. 158.

44. *Wall Street Journal* Marketplace interview by Kai Ryssdal.
45. Haidt, *The Righteous Mind*, p. 104.
    Mercier and Sperber, "Why do Humans Reason? Arguments for an Argumentative Theorgy," 34; 57-74.
46. Haidt, *The Righteous Mind*, p. 104.
47. Results of *Newsweek* survey. Article by Romano, "How Ignorant Are Americans?"
48. American Revolution survey. http://www.prnewswire.com/news-releases/83-percent-of-us-adults-fail-test-on-nations-founding-78325412.html (Accessed June 19, 2016).
49. Stone, "Most Americans Think Founders Wanted Christian USA."
50. Taintor, "Poll: Majority of Americans Don't Know What GOP Stands For."
51. Shenkman, "Ignorant America: Just How Stupid Are We?"
52. Romano, "How Ignorant Are Americans?"
53. Concha, "Only 43 Percent Can Name a Supreme Court Justice." C-SPAN/Penn Schoen Berland Survey, March 7-9, 2017.
54. Bomboy, "Surveys: Many Americans Know Little About the Supreme Court."
55. Shenkman, *Political Animals,* p. 110.
56. Ibid.
57. Ibid.
58. Ibid.
59. Shenkman, *Just How Stupid Are We?* pp. 37-38.
60. Lepore, Jill, "Long Division: Measuring the Polarization of American Politics."
61. Ibid.
62. White, "Occupy Lake Wobegon," Phycology Today, May 14, 2012.
63. Garrison Keillor, BrainyQuote.com, *Xplore, Inc,* 2017. https://www.brainyquote.com/quotes/quotes/g/garrisonke137097.html. (Accessed June 10, 2017).
64. Shenkman, *Political Animals,* p. 112.
65. Ibid.
66. Alicke and Govorun, "The Better-Than-Average-Effect, The Self in Social Judgment."
67. Dunning, et al., "Ambiguity and Self-Evaluation: The Role of Idiosyncratic Trait Definitions in Self-Serving Assessments of Ability." McCormick, et al., "Comparative Perceptions of Driver Ability – a Confirmation and Expansion."
68. Dunning, et al., "Ambiguity and Self-Evaluation: The Role of Idiosyncratic Trait Definitions in Self-Serving Assessments of Ability."
69. Alicke and Govorun, "The Better-Than-Average-Effect, The Self in Social Judgment."
70. "The Superiority Illusion: Where Everyone is Above Average,"
71. *Short Thoughts Psychology* blog, "What is Illusory Superiority?"
72. Lee, "Revisiting Why Incompetents Think They're Awesome."
73. Klosowski, "Why You Think You're Great at Eveything, Even When You Suck,"
74. Shenkman, *Political Animals:* p. 107.

75. Haidt, *The Righteous Mind,* pp. 58-60, 364.
76. McIntosh, "Overcoming Polarization by Evolving Both the Right and Left."
77. Shermer, "How to Convince Someone When Facts Fail,"
78. Mooney, "The Science of Why We Don't' Believe Science: How Our Brains Fool Us on Climate, Creationism and the End of the World."
79. Hernandez and Preston, "Disfluency Disrupts the Confirmation Bias."
80. "Difficult-to-Read Font Reduces Political Polarity, Study Finds."
81. Wikipedia, Omnibus Public Land Management Act of 2009.
82. Phillips, *New York Times* "The Caucus" blog, March 11, 2009.
83. *National Journal,* February 28, 2009, pp. 21-38.
84. McHugh, "Ex-Wrestler Tries to Get Hold of Concessions."

Chapter 7

1. Connolly, "Landmark," pp. 15-19.
2. Wayne, "House Panel Chairman Promise to Move Similar Health Care Overhaul bills."
3. Hendren, "Obama's Health Care Foe: GOP or Dems?"
4. Lubell, "Blue Dogs, Wasman Trade Proposals."
5. Dennis, "House Health Deal Reached; No Floor Vote Until September."
Benen, "Waxman, Blue Dogs Strike A Deal."
6. Shenkman, *Political Animals,* pp. 156-57.
7. Ibid.
8. Isenstadt, Alex, "Town Halls Gone Wild."
9. Urbina, "Beyond Beltway, Health Debate Turns Hostile."
10. Ibid.
11. "Barack Obama's Health Care Plans Turn Nasty as Angry Crowds Protest Outside Town Hall Meetings," *London Telegraph.*
12. Urbina, "Beyond Beltway, Health Debate Turns Hostile."
13. Saul, "Rage Boils Over at Town Hall Meetings Over Health Care."
14. Bailey, "Joe Wilson Raised (And Spent) Big Money After 'You Lie!'"
15. For more on the Haiti rescue mission, see: Schmitz, "Inside the Haiti Rescue Mission."

Chapter 8

1. Connelly, "Landmark," pp. 54-56.
2. Ibid.
3. McNulty, "Pence Hits Pelosi For Rothfus."
4. Mann and Ornstein, *It's Even Worse Than It Was,* p. 206.
5. Ibid.
6. Kane, "A New Dynamic May Be Emerging in the House: A Right and Left Flank Within the GOP Willing to Buck Leadership."
7. House, "In Age of Trump, Some Democrats and Republicans Explore Alliance."

8. Mann and Ornstein, *It's Even Worse Than It Was*, p. 9.
9. Ibid, p. 5-6.
10. Ibid, p. 15-25.
    Rauch, "How American Politics Went Insane."
11. Allen and Bresnahan, "Sources: Biden Likened Tea Partiers to Terrorists."
    Miller, "Biden: Tea Stands for 'Terrorist.'"
12. Clabough, "Tea Partier Confronts Obama Over Remark Made by Biden."
13. Moss, "Fixing What's Wrong with U.S. Politics."
    Lofgren, *The Party is Over: How Republicans Went Crazy, Democrats Became Useless, and the Middle Class got Shafted*."
14. Mann and Ornstein, *It's Even Worse Than It Was*, p. 5-9.
15. Persily, *Solutions to Polarization in America*, p. 254.
    Ryan, "No Compromise: Political Consequences of Moralized Attitudes."
    Thurber and Yoshinaka, *American Gridlock*, p. 5.
16. Hetherington and Rudolph, *Why Washington Won't Work*, p. 2.
17. Persily, *Solutions to Polarization in America*. p. 125-126.
18. Abramowitz, *The Disappearing Center*, p. 3.
19. Mann and Ornstein, *It's Even Worse Than It Was*.
20. 113th Congress House Floor Procedures Manual.
    "Minority's Motion to Recommit Should Not Be Curtailed," *The Wilson Center*.
    Ornstein, "The Motion to Recommit, Hijacked by Politics."
    Sands, "House Rule Changes Squander Good Will."
    "The Motion to Recommit in the House of Representatives: Effects, Recent Trends and Options for Change," *Congressional Research Service*.
21. Layton, "House GOP Uses Procedural Tactic To Frustrate Democratic Majority."
22. Ibid.
23. *Fox News* politics website, http://www.foxnews.com/politics/2009/09/17/congress-votes-strip-acorn-federal-funding.html, September 17, 2009. (Accessed June 10, 2017).
24. Slajda, "GOP Kills Science Jobs Bill by Forcing Dems to Vote for Porn."
25. Ornstein, "The Motion to Recommit, Hijacked by Politics."
26. Lott and Daschle, *Crisis Point*, pp. 39-40.
27. Arceneaux, "Why You Should Not Blame Polarization on Partisan News," in *Political Polarization in American Politics*.
    Arceneaux, Johnson, Lindstadt and Vander Wielen, "Democratic Representation and the Emergence of Partisan News Media: Investigating Dynamic Partisanship in Congress."
28. Arceneaux and Martin, "Polarization and Partisan News Media in America," in *American Gridlock*, p. 310.
    For more on how partisan media impacts partisans, see also:
    Brock, Rabin-Havt and Media Matters for America, *The Fox Effect: How Roger Ailes Turned a Network into a Propaganda Machine*.
    Levendusky, "How Partisan Media Polarize America."

Jacobson, "Partisan Media and electoral Polarization in 2012," in: *American Gridlock*.

29. Anderson, "Social Media Causes Some Users to Rethink Their Views on an Issue."
30. Tiouririne, "Hillary Clinton's Twitter Chart of Doom."
31. Silverman, "Fake Election News Stories Outperformed Real News on Facebook."
32. Silverman and Alexander, "How Teens in the Balkans are Duping Trump Supporters with Fake News."
33. Read, "Donald Trump Won Because of Facebook."
34. Wingfield, Isaac and Benner, "Google and Facebook Take Aim at Fake News Sites."
35. Levin, "Fake News for Liberals: Misinformation Starts to Lean Left Under Trump,"
36. Silverman, "This is How Your Hyperpartisan Political News Gets Made."
    For more on how fake news works, why it is so lucrative and so difficult to stop, see:
    Gillin, "Fact-Checking Fake News Reveals How Hard it is to Kill Pervasive 'Nasty Weed' Online."
37. Lelkes, Sood and Iyengar, "The Hostile Audence: The Effect of Access to Broadband Internet on Partisan Affect."
38. *Political Polarization and Media Habits: From Fox News to Facebook, How Liberals and Conservatives Keep Up with Politics*, Pew Research Center.
39. Manjoo, "Can Facebook Fix Its Own Worst Bug?"
40. *Political Polarization and Media Habits: From Fox News to Facebook, How Liberals and Conservatives Keep Up with Politics*, Pew Research Center.
    Fletcher and Nielsen, "Using Social Media Appears to Diversify Your News Diet, Not Narrow It."
41. Bruni, "How Facebook Warps Our Worlds."
42. Ibid.
43. Simon, "How YouTube is Changing Our Viewing Habits."
44. Manjoo, "Can Facebook Fix Its Own Worst Bug."
45. Dewey, Caitlin, "'Unfriending' Trump Supporters is Just Another Example of How We Isolate Ourselves Online."
46. Lott and Daschle, *Crisis Point*, pp. 57-58.
    "How to Burst the 'Filter Bubble' That Protects Us from Opposing Views."
47. *Political Polarization and Media Habits: From Fox News to Facebook, How Liberals and Conservatives Keep Up with Politics*, Pew Research Center.
48. Bruni, "How Facebook Warps Our Worlds."
49. Ibid.
50. Dewey, "'Unfriending' Trump Supporters is Just Another Example of How We Isolate Ourselves Online." *Washington Post*, December 16, 2015.

51. *Political Polarization and Media Habits: From Fox News to Facebook, How Liberals and Conservatives Keep Up with Politics,* Pew Research Center.

52. Dewey, "'Unfriending' Trump Supporters is Just Another Example of How We Isolate Ourselves Online."

53. "Twitter Language Use Reflects Psychological Differences Between Democrats and Republicans," Queen Mary University of London press release.
Sylwester and Purver, PLoS ONE 10(9): e0137422. doi: 10.1371/journal.pone.0137422.

54. Ibid.

55. Stern, West and Schmitt, "The Liberal Illusion of Uniqueness," pp. 137-144.
Dollinger, "Creativity and Conservatism, Personal Individual Differences," pp. 1025-1035.

56. "Twitter Language Use Reflects Psychological Differences Between Democrats and Republicans," Queen Mary University of London press release.
Sylwester and Purver, PLoS ONE 10(9): e0137422. doi: 10.1371/journal.pone.0137422.

57. Dewey, "6 in 10 of You Will Share This Link Without Reading It, a New, Depressing Study Says."

58. Ibid.

59. Hacker and Pierson, "*Confronting Asymmetric Polarization,*" in *Solutions to Polarization in America.*

60. Megerian and Barabak, "From West to East, Iowa Voters Have Starkly Different Realities and Fears."

Chapter 9

1. Fiorina, Abrams and Pope, *Culture War?* pp. 20-22.

2. Ibid, p. 66.

3. Hetherington and Rudolph, *Why Washington Won't Work,* p. 27.

4. Jacobson, "Partisan Media and Electoral Polarization in 2012," in *American Gridlock:* p. 282.

5. "Fox and MSNBC Viewers Largely Misinformed: Fairleigh Dickenson University Poll."

6. Hetherington and Weiler, "Authoritarianism and Polarization in American Politics, Still?" in *American Gridlock,* p. 97.

7. Bonica, McCarty, Poole and Rosenthal, "Congressional Polarization and its Connection to Income Inequality" in *American Gridlock,* p. 368-372.

8. Barber and McCarty, "Causes and Consequences of Polarization," in *Solutions to Polarization in America,* p. 31.
Rigley and Wright, "The Policy Consequences of Party Polarization," in: *American Gridlock,* p. 239.

9. Bonica, McCarty, Poole and Rosenthal, "Congressional Polarization and its Connection to Income Inequality" in *American Gridlock,* p. 368-372.

10. Garand, "Partisan Change and Shifting Expenditure Priorities in the American States, 1945-1978," *American Politics Quarterly* 13: 355-391.
11. Poole and Rosenthal, "Polarized America: The Dance of Ideology and Unequal Riches," p. 192.
12. Haidt, *The Righteous Mind,* p. 323.
13. Abramowitz, "How Race and Religion Have Polarized," in *Political Polarization in American Politics,* p. 84-87.
14. "How Immigration and Concerns about Cultural Change Are Shaping the 2016 Election."
15. Martin and Burns, "Is 'Brexit' the Precursor to a Donald Trump Presidency? Not so Fast."
16. *Political Polarization in the American Public: How Increasing Ideological Uniformity and Partisan Antipathy Affect Politics, Compromise and Everyday Life.* Pew Research Center.
    Thurber and Yoshinaka, *American Gridlock,* p. 4.
    Davis, Frost and Cohen, *The Partisan Divide,* p. 148.
17. Fiorina, Abrams and Pope, *Culture War?* p. 208.
    Barber and McCarty, "Causes and Consequences of Polarization," in *Solutions to Polarization in America,* p. 39.
18. Davis, Frost and Cohen, *The Partisan Divide,* p. 148.
19. Abramowitz, *The Disappearing Center,* p. 157.
20. Thurber and Yoshinaka, *American Gridlock,* p. xxii.
21. Shor, "Polarization in American State Legislatures," in *American Gridlock,* p. 204.
22. Arcencaux and Johnson, "Polarization and Partisan News Media in America," in: *American Gridlock,* p. 328-329.
23. Hayes and Lawless, "District Polarization and Media Coverage of U.S. House Campaigns," in *American Gridlock:* p. 301.
    See also – Abramowitz, *The Disappearing Center,* pp. 7, 43.
24. Druckman and Jacobs, *Who Governs?: Presidents, Public Opinion and Manipulation,* pp. 11-12.
25. Hacker and Pierson, "Confronting Asymmetric Polarization," in *Solutions to Polarization in America,* p. 64.
26. Druckman and Jacobs, *Who Governs?* pp. 10.
27. Davis, Frost and Cohen, *The Partisan Divide,* p. 43.
28. Poole and Rosenthal, *Polarized America,* p. 60.
29. Ibid, p. 61.
    Bishop, *The Big Sort,* p. 29.
    Davis, Frost and Cohen, *The Partisan Divide,* pp. 161-162.
    "Where Political Lines Are, and Aren't, Being Drawn," *Washington Post Wonkblog.*
30. Wang, "The Great Gerrymander of 2012."
31. Davis, Frost and Cohen, *The Partisan Divide,* p. 72.
    For more information about the impact of gerrymandering on the 2012 congressional elections, see:
    Sides, "Not Gerrymandering, but Districting: More Evidence on How Democrats Won the Popular Vote but Lost the Congress."
    Berman, "What's the Answer to Political Polarization in the U.S.?,"

32. Yee, "The Great Southern Gerrymander Continues in 2016."
33. MacGillis, "The Democrats' Bad Map."
34. Ibid.
35. *The Cook Political Report*, December 16, 2016.
36. Cillizza, "This is the Most Amazing Chart on Congress You'll See Today."
37. Hetherington and Rudolph, *Why Washington Won't Work*, p. 1.
38. Ibid, p. 214.
39. Ibid, p. 2.
40. Cillizza, "Want to Know Why the Government is Shut Down? This Chart Explains it."
41. Cillizza, "This is the Most Amazing Chart on Congress You'll See Today."
42. Brownstein, *The Second Civil War*, pp. 208-09.
43. Ibid.
44. Altman and McDonald, "Redistricting and Polarization," in *American Gridlock*, p. 55.
45. Abramowitz, *The Disappearing Center*, pp. 101, 142-143.
    Altman and McDonald, "Redistricting and Polarization," in *American Gridlock*, p. 51.
    Poole and Rosenthal, *Polarized America*, pp. 194, 200.
46. Lepore, "Long Division: Measuring the Polarization of American Politics."
47. Abramowitz, *The Disappearing Center*, p. 150.
48. Ibid, pp. 150-151.
49. Altman and McDonald, *American Gridlock*, pp. 52-53.
50. Micek, "PA Lost a Resident Once Every 11.5 Minutes Last Year, Study Finds."
51. Olson, "Pennsylvania Poised to Lose Another Seat in Congress in 2020."
52. *Down With Tyranny* blog, November 6, 2010.
    Stier, Marc, *Grassroots Advocacy and Health Care Reform: The HCAN Campaign in Pennsylvania.*

Chapter 10

1. *The Federalist Papers*, Essay 58
2. Mann and Ornstein, *It's Even Worse Than It Was*, pp. 86-88.
3. U.S. Senate website.
4. Chafetz, "The Filibuster Was Already Doomed Before the Nuclear Option Vote."
   For a discussion of the impact of elimination of the filibuster, see:
   Karol, "American Political Parties," in *Solutions to Polarization in America*. pp. 214-215.
   Binder, *Stalemate*, pp. 88-89.
   Hohmann, "The Legislative Filibuster Will Be At Risk As Soon As the Senate Goes Nuclear."
5. Thurber and Yoshinaka, "The Sources and Impact of Political Polarization," in *American Gridlock*, pp. 380-82.

6. Mann and Ornstein, *It's Even Worse Than It Was*, pp. 167-169.
7. *Governing in a Polarized America: A Bipartisan Blueprint to Strengthen our Democracy*, Bipartisan Policy Center.
8. Thurber and Yoshinaka, "The Sources and Impact of Political Polarization," in: *American Gridlock*, pp. 380-82.
9. Lofgren, *The Party is Over*, p. 29.
10. Binder, Sarah, *Stalemate*, p. 128.
11. Persily, "Stronger Parties as Solutions to Polarization," in *Solutions to Polarization in America*, p. 135.
12. Rauch, "How American Politics Went Insane."
13. Kamarck, "Solutions to Polarization," in *Solutions to Polarization in America*, p. 100-101.
14. Thurber and Yoshinaka, "The Sources and Impact of Political Polarization," in *American Gridlock*, pp. 380-82.
15. Caygle, "How the GOP Abandoned One of its Own."
16. Lott and Daschle, *Crisis Point*, p. 251.
17. Moss, "Fixing What's Wrong with U.S. Politics."
18. Ibid.
19. Shenkman, *Political Animals*, pp. 20-21.
20. *Governing in a Polarized America: A Bipartisan Blueprint to Strengthen our Democracy*, Bipartisan Policy Center.
21. iCivics website.
22. Ibid.
23. Bob Graham Center website
24. Ibid.
25. *Governing in a Polarized America: A Bipartisan Blueprint to Strengthen our Democracy*, Bipartisan Policy Center.
    Davis, Frost and Cohen, *The Partisan Divide*, pp. 272-273.
26. Rauch, "How American Politics Went Insane."
27. Pildes, "How to Fix our Polarized Politics? Strengthen Political Parties."
28. Hasen, "Karl Rove's Crossroads GPS Manages to Make it Even Harder to Find the Dark Money in U.S. Politics."
29. Ibid.
30. Galston, "Reforming Institutions: The Next President Should Not Miss This Moment to Make Government Work."
31. Brownstein, *The Second Civil War*, p. 380.
32. Berman, Russell, "What's the Answer to Political Polarization in the U.S.?"
33. "Democracy Agenda: Redistricting," Brennan Center for Justice at New York University School of Law.
34. Persily, *Solutions to Polarization in America*, p. 86-88
35. "Democracy Agenda: Redistricting," Brennan Center for Justice at New York University School of Law.
36. Rodden, "Geography and Gridlock in the United States," in, *Solutions to Polarization in America*, pp. 112-113.
37. Cook, Flinn and Wasserman, "Introducing the 2017 Cook Political Report Partisan Voter Index," *The Cook Political Report*, April 7, 2017.

See also: Blake, "Why You Should Stop Blaming Gerrymandering So Much. Really."

38. Brownstein, *The Second Civil War*, pp. 377-378.

39. Bishop, *The Big Sort*, p. 291, quoting Paul Lazarfeld.

40. Fiorina, Abrams, and Pope, *Culture War?* p. 221.

41. Lott and Daschle, *Crisis Point:* p. 221.
Mann and Ornstein, *It's Even Worse Than It Was*, p. 140.

42. Lott and Daschle, *Crisis Point*, p. 222.

43. Mann and Ornstein, *It's Even Worse Than It Was*, p. 133-136.

44. Ibid, pp. 132-133.

45. Berman, Russell, "What's the Answer to Political Polarization in the U.S.?"

46. Lofgren, *The Party is Over*.

47. "Republicans and Voter Suppression," *New York Times*, April 4, 2016.

48. Rodden, "Geography and Gridlock in the United States," in *Solutions to Polarization in America*, p. 115.

49. Galston, "Reforming Institutions: The Next President Should Not Miss This Moment to Make Government Work."

50. Mann and Ornstein, *It's Even Worse Than It Was*, p. 140-142.

51. Ibid.

52. Ibid.

53. Berman, Russell, "What if the Parties Didn't Run Primaries?"

54. Skelton, "California Legislature is Looking More Moderate Due to Voting Reforms."
See also: Lijphat, "Polarization and Democratization," in: Persily, *Solutions to Polarization in America*, pp. 74-75.
Masket, "The Costs of Party Reform," in, *American Gridlock*, p. 233.

55. Fair Vote website.
"Keep Experimenting With Ranked-Choice Voting," Minneapolis Star Tribune.

56. Seelye, "Maine Adopts Ranked-Choice Voting. What is it, and How Will it Work?"

57. Will, George, "Restoration."

58. *U.S. Term Limits, Inc. v. Thornton*, 514 U.S. 779, 1995.

59. Mann and Ornstein, *It's Even Worse Than It Was*, p. 124-125.

60. Shor, "Polarization in American State Legislatures," in *American Gridlock*, p. 213-14.

INDEX

ABOUT THE AUTHOR

—·◆·—

JASON ALTMIRE SERVED THREE TERMS IN THE UNITED States House of Representatives from 2007 to 2013. He was a bipartisan centrist known for working with both sides of the aisle, which led to an extraordinary record of success. He had 29 of his legislative initiatives signed into law, went five and a half years without missing a single vote, and introduced a bill that gained the most cosponsors of any congressional bill in American history. During his time in office, the nonpartisan *National Journal* calculated Altmire's voting record to be at the exact midpoint of the House—the Dead Center—giving him the most centrist voting record in Congress. He has been profiled by numerous national publications and has appeared on a wide variety of television news programs. During his career in business, he has served in senior executive positions in the healthcare industry. He earned a Master's degree in Health Administration from George Washington University, and a Bachelor of Science degree from Florida State University. He has also been an adjunct professor at George Washington University, focusing on politics and policy. He lives in Ponte Vedra Beach, Florida with his wife, Kelly. They have two daughters.

CPSIA information can be obtained
at www.ICGtesting.com
Printed in the USA
LVOW12*1137090418

572751LV00001BA/13/P